BECOMING UNSTOPPABLE

Your Neurocentric Coaching Guide to Achieving **Unstoppable** Success

Also by Roddy Carter

BodyWHealth: Journey to Abundance

BodyWHealth: Invitation

Sunset Lessons: Reflections on Light and Love from the Darkest of Places

Fireside Wisdom: Conversations to Inspire Personal Mastery

The Problem with Anger: And How to Solve It

Unstoppable You Online Courses:
Unstoppable You
Unstoppable You Business
Unleash Unstoppable
Unleash Success

BECOMING UNSTOPPABLE

Your Neurocentric Coaching Guide to Achieving **Unstoppable** Success

Roddy Carter, MD

Aquila Life Science Press
La Jolla, California

FIRST AQUILA LIFE SCIENCE PRESS EDITION, SEPTEMBER 2024
Published by Aquila Life Science, LLC, La Jolla, CA

BECOMING **UNSTOPPABLE**.

ISBN: 979-8-9895751-2-1

Printed in the United States of America

To all who live, and love and learn,
Especially to those who live and love to learn.
For all on the journey of life,
Driven by insatiable curiosity
And a resolute determination to become their best selves,
I dedicate this book to you.
May the knowledge and guidance within its pages
Serve you, as it has served me.

And when you reach that moment,
*When you taste **unstoppable**,*
Please make me one promise:
Pass it on!

CONTENTS

ACKNOWLEDGEMENTS

First and foremost, I extend my deepest gratitude to the Divine Order that has meticulously crafted this magnificent universe and the immutable truths that govern our existence. I am eternally thankful for the gifts of curiosity and learning, which nourish my soul daily, and for Truth, my eternal North Star that guides every step I take.

I am immensely grateful to Sarah Dawson, whose exceptional editorial skills and profound understanding of her craft have been indispensable. Sarah's technical competence and uniquely powerful communication skills have enabled a symbiotic relationship that has enriched this work immeasurably. Her efforts have helped bring this body of knowledge to you, the reader, ensuring that the wisdom contained within these pages is communicated effectively and elegantly.

To Sage Mystica, my extraordinarily intelligent, lightning-quick, and ever-available AI-based reviewer, editor, and editorial thought partner: Your contributions are invaluable. Your ability to process and enhance the manuscript with such precision and agility is nothing short of miraculous. I am profoundly thankful for your unwavering support and keen intellect.

My heartfelt thanks go to Julie Hunt, a deeply beautiful soul and accomplished instructional designer, with whom I have had the privilege of creating the *Unstoppable You* online coaching platform. Julie has masterfully captured both the essence of the knowledge and my voice in a powerful, reverent, and generous manner, allowing a vast community of global self-improvers—our dedicated participants in personal growth—to experience very personal online coaching immersion.

I am warmly appreciative of Kelley Utterback, the chief of staff of Roddy Carter Global Enterprises. Kelley serves as my right hand, my everyday brain, and my devoted manager of all our Neurocentric Coaching projects, to bring Compassionate Neuroscience into the hands and lives of earnest learners worldwide. Her unwavering commitment and extraordinary competence have been pivotal to our success. I could not ask for a more steadfast and helpful colleague in this important work. Kelley, your dedication and support are truly invaluable, and I am deeply grateful for everything you do.

Lastly, I would like to acknowledge Glynis Carter, a real-world scientist whose dedication to rigorously fact-checking and enhancing the scientific depth and breadth of this content has been crucial. Her meticulous attention to detail and commitment to scientific integrity have greatly enriched this work, ensuring its accuracy and relevance.

To each of you, I owe a debt of gratitude that mere words can scarcely convey. Thank you for helping bring this book to life.

PREFACE

Halfway through my life, I was brought face-to-face with a harsh reality that changed everything. Until that moment, I had been a portrait of success by conventional measures. I was a high achiever from my earliest days, leading and excelling in almost every facet of school life, specializing in sports medicine and exercise science in one of the world's leading academic programs and graduating from a top medical school by the age of 24. My career was equally distinguished: I worked with Olympic athletes, contributing to several gold medals, and was recruited into a Fortune-ranked multinational organization, swiftly climbing the ranks in both business and scientific leadership roles.

Yet, despite these accomplishments and being a dedicated husband and father, I realized I had neglected the most crucial person: myself. This neglect went deeper than physical health; it had eroded my very foundations—my self-belief and self-love had become alarmingly fragile.

It took just one mind-blowing minute for this reality to expose itself, but in that same instant, I also glimpsed the immensely powerful, magnificent version of myself that still existed, hidden within. It was a version of myself that was still attainable, if only I could find the path to reach it.

Driven by this revelation, I embarked on a profound journey to understand the human condition and the critical role our magnificent brain plays in our happiness and success. More importantly, I sought a systematic pathway to achieving and sustaining the clarity, confidence, joy, peace, and fulfillment that we all deserve.

And I found it.

In this coaching workbook, I translate complex neuroscience into understandable terms for you. More importantly, I will guide you through carefully structured exercises along a proven pathway. If you devote yourself to this journey, you will unlock the treasures of a truly **unstoppable** spirit: clarity, confidence, joy, peace, and fulfillment.

With my extensive knowledge of performance science, deep understanding of human nature, and gifts for translation and teaching, I have merged these into a practical, easy-to-follow guide. The sessions contained within these pages are designed to steer your journey, bringing the best version of yourself within reach.

Welcome to *Becoming **Unstoppable***.

INTRODUCTION

OPTIMIZING YOUR JOURNEY

Welcome to *Becoming **Unstoppable**.*

Hi! I'm Roddy Carter. Welcome to your Neurocentric Coaching experience. Together, we're going to transform your life.

You've come here with dreams and hopes and aspirations, and you've been stuck. I'm going to help you rewire your brain, to understand the deep science of the brain that—for some reason—we're simply not taught.

And through understanding how your brain works, through the application of the techniques, tools, and tips that I'm going to give you, you're going to be able to operate your own brain in a vastly different way. Your dreams are going to come to life. Your journey toward success is going to be enabled by this magnificent brain that's been standing in your way until now.

So, welcome!

In this introduction, you will:

- Familiarize yourself with the various coaching components.
- Get tips to prepare for and optimize your journey.

Before we embark on this journey together, please acknowledge this:

☐ I recognize that my own engagement and contribution are critical in achieving the outcome I desire.

☐ I understand that, while this coaching is a powerful educational resource, the material provided is not intended to replace professional advice from legal, medical, financial, business, or other qualified professionals.

☐ Finally, I acknowledge that Roddy Carter Global Enterprises, Inc. does not offer any guarantees or warranties about the specific results I may achieve as a result of participating in this coaching. This work is my work. My commitment, diligence, and effort will always have the greatest impact on my results.

Overview of Your Coaching Sessions

Your Neurocentric Coaching journey includes 10 sessions.

This is not a textbook. This is a coaching engagement to guide you on your way toward unstoppability. Together, the sessions of this engagement are carefully designed and sequenced to map your **unstoppable** journey, with each session advancing your progress to help you realize your ideal future. At the same time, each session is also crafted as an adventure on its own, teaching you an aspect of personal mastery that you can immediately apply to your life, with positive effect.

The book has been constructed to pursue sequentially. I believe this is the best way to explore, assimilate, and apply the knowledge contained in these pages. But we're not all segmented learners. If you are someone who prefers more free-form learning, I invite you to leap around, pursuing your natural curiosity. But I respectfully suggest that, however you plan to delve into the text, you start with the first three sessions in sequence to build your solid neurocentric foundation before you move further.

Whatever order you choose, move through each of the sessions intentionally and thoughtfully. Make sure you leave enough time between sessions to fully absorb and reflect on the material from each session. I suggest a weekly cadence, generally allocating a minimum of three hours per session—at least one hour for reading through the concepts, one hour for completing the exercises, and another hour to engage in the session's Mastery Missions to consolidate what you've learned.

I strongly recommend that you allot more time to sessions where you seek deeper comprehension. Additionally, if you desire, invest extra time in exploring the scientific research to deepen your understanding of your magnificent brain. However you decide to allocate your time, establish your pace and schedule to set yourself up for success.

Here's a summary of the sessions:

1 Journeying Toward Unstoppable

Explore what it means to be stoppable and **unstoppable**, recognize the magical force that drives you, and create a vision of your ideal future.

2 Understanding Your *Brain Operating System*

Embark on an exploratory journey into the five key regions of your brain, and gain critical knowledge about the evolution of the human brain and the natural wiring of your *Brain Operating System* (BOS).

3 Understanding How Your Brain Talks

Learn the three languages of your brain—an essential BOS concept—and how to successfully apply them to become a brain master.

4 Owning the Office of the CEO

Master a 5-step process to become the CEO of your life and gain clarity and perspective when facing problems, obstacles, challenges, and dilemmas.

5 Programming Your Filter

Program your brain to remove biases, strengthen responsiveness in uncertainty, and focus on critical information to ensure you achieve your dreams.

6 Conquering Fear

Learn, practice, and apply a 7-step process to conquer deeply rooted fears that keep you from becoming **unstoppable**.

7 Driving Belief

Create enduring positivity and sustain an **unstoppable** state day after day through a practical process that drives belief and increases positive thoughts you have about yourself.

8 Boosting Belief

Turboboost belief with tailored mantras crafted to rewire your brain, and learn a brain-body hack to quickly correct course and catapult yourself to success when you feel stuck.

9 Activating Desire

Harness the power of your emotional brain to activate desire and achieve your dreams.

10 Making Commitments: Your Launchpad for Long-Term Success

Put together everything you've learned into a simple, systematic practice. Commit to strengthening your practice, and create an action plan to make consistent, incremental progress toward becoming **unstoppable** and realizing your dreams.

Coaching Components

Here are the main components of each session.

- **Introduction**

  The introductory component offers an overview of the three main learning objectives for each session. You can use these key outcomes as milestones to track your achievements and as a useful review tool if you revisit any sessions.

- **Live Workshops**

  Throughout the sessions, there are transcriptions of sections of live Neurocentric Coaching workshops. These add to the richness of the other material contained in the sessions and provide examples of how it can be applied in your life.

- **Exercises**

  Exercises and activities are a fundamental component of each session because they facilitate your engagement with the knowledge and processes essential to developing personal mastery and becoming **unstoppable**. To maximize your learning, utilize the writing space in this book that corresponds to each exercise and activity. Follow the sequence in which they are presented.

- **Mastery Missions**

  It takes time to alter the structure and function of your magnificent brain, and your success in this transformative process will be directly related to the time you spend practicing. The *Mastery Missions* include activities, exercises, reflections, and other tasks to help you harness the power of time between sessions.

  Carrying out these missions will help you to accelerate mastery of your *Brain Operating System* (BOS) and turboboost your journey. Take your time—at least one hour between each session—to practice these mastery exercises.

- **Supplemental Science**

  To deepen your scientific knowledge, I offer *Supplemental Science* at the end of many sessions. Here, you can delve into the science at your own pace, review the references used in session creation, and discover additional reading recommendations. This is optional; you choose which studies you want to explore or skip.

- **Commitment and Quotes**

  The *Commitment* of each session gives you a glimpse of what's covered in the next session, plus a profound quote to reflect on. You'll notice that I've sprinkled in some of my favorite quotes throughout the sessions, too. I encourage you to take a few seconds to pause, reflect, and soak in the power of each quote. These quotes are ascribed to brilliant and world-renowned leaders across history who have often unknowingly described the science of their own magnificent brains in their spoken and written word.

Exercises

Harness the power of reflection to maximize the transformative results of your coaching experience.

This coaching offers a wealth of knowledge and practical exercises to help you understand and enhance your brain science. The exercises play a crucial role in facilitating your journey. They are thoughtfully designed to assist you in absorbing, reflecting on, practicing, and applying the content and concepts.

This book is filled with space.

We grow by first creating space and then expanding into that space. This book is deliberately filled—both figuratively and literally—with open space.

I recommend that you consistently use the space provided to work through the exercises in each session. Through recording your responses and documenting your journey, you will enrich your coaching experience and personal growth by:

- Elevating **focus** and **engagement** as you tailor your observations and reflections to your own unique perspective, making the content more meaningful and relevant to you.

- Increasing **clarity**, **continuity**, and **depth of thought**, helping you to understand your own progress and insights better.

- Tracking and **reflecting** on your progress to see how far you've come, and using your reflections as a motivator to continue to push yourself toward unstoppability.

- Driving long-term, **lasting success** by revisiting growth experiences, identifying patterns, and gaining deeper insights into your **unstoppable** journey.

- **Sharing** your insights and experiences with others, fostering meaningful discussions and collaborations.

> "When I write down my thoughts,
>
> they do not escape me."
>
> —ISIDORE DUCASSE LAUTREAMONT

Tips to Optimize Your Journey

 **Take your time to move through the course slowly, carefully, and thoughtfully. Here are a few tips to optimize your journey:**

MAKE SPACE

Find a nice, quiet, safe space where you can work on the coaching with deep, vulnerable thoughtfulness.

TAKE YOUR TIME

Don't rush through a session to get it done. You don't have to finish in one go.

PAUSE

Give yourself ample time between sessions. Reflect on, digest, experiment with, and apply the material.

PLAN AHEAD

Work at a comfortable pace. Set up a schedule based on the estimated time allocations provided for each session.

MAXIMIZE

To maximize your results, complete one session each week.

REVISIT

Go back and revisit the sessions to deepen your knowledge and reveal new insights.

HAVE FUN

Infuse the journey with fun. Fun is more than an attitude. It's a contagious positive force!

COMMIT

Commit as much time as you can each week to your **unstoppable** journey.

The coaching is also designed to cultivate fun!

Most of my time is spent doing serious work, with serious clients. Yet, as anyone who recognizes my email sign-off knows, I always urge every one of them to "Have fun!"

The reason is very simple.

Fun is a **contagious positive force** for you and everyone around you. It's a physical process that starts deep in your brain. Fun is good for you, even if you have significant physical, mental, or emotional challenges—or perhaps *especially* if you have such challenges!

When you generate fun, have fun, or participate in fun, your body releases hormones that elevate your mood.

In the coming sessions, you'll learn that you have voluntary control over your thoughts. This is part of your brain's natural wiring. Nature has gifted with you a natural disposition toward health, happiness, and success. Think about this statement for a moment:

You are biologically designed to have fun!

You can intentionally lead your brain toward positive, fun thoughts.

Intentionally having fun on your journey through this coaching will help you to manifest a cognitive and emotional state that will bring light, health, and happiness into your life—it will help you to become **unstoppable**!

> "If you don't **have fun**, it's hard to **do your best**.
>
> It's not going to be enjoyable."
>
> —KIMMIE MEISSNER

Personal Transformations

As you embark on your unstoppable journey, visualize the transformations you want to see in your life.

Take a moment to pause and contemplate the multitude of benefits that await you upon your completion of this coaching:

☐ **Feeling closer to yourself** and others.

☐ Experiencing a greater sense of **inner fulfillment**.

☐ Enjoying enhanced communication and **improved relationships**.

☐ **Believing in yourself** and all that you're capable of.

☐ Improving mental clarity, and gaining the ability to make **better decisions**.

☐ Reigniting **passion**, **love**, and **creativity**.

☐ Realizing **achievements** at work, at home, and in your career.

☐ **Reducing stress**, anxiety, and sadness.

☐ Cultivating greater **peace**, happiness, and abundance.

☐ Living with a strong sense of **purpose**.

> "Dream no small dreams, for they have no power to move the hearts of men."
>
> —JOHANN WOLFGANG VON GOETHE

SESSION 1

JOURNEYING TOWARD UNSTOPPABLE

Get ready for a transformational journey to move past your fears and rewire your neurobiology to live the life of your dreams.

*The content and activities in this session will take approximately two hours to complete. By the end of the session, you'll emerge with a blueprint for your future. This will serve as your road map as you navigate your **unstoppable** journey.*

You've taken control of your destiny.

The power to become **unstoppable** is in your hands! By the end of the coaching, you will:

☐ Uncover the secrets of your brain's wiring and harness its incredible power through a unique and compassionate Neurocentric Coaching approach.

☐ Master your underlying neurobiology to modify limiting beliefs, attitudes, and actions that hindered your progress in the past.

☐ Have fun defining the ideal life you deserve and desire, and then create it using a straightforward, systematic approach to enjoy greater happiness, success, well-being, purpose, and passion.

My Lifelong Journey

Choose—and ultimately become—who you want to be.

This powerful quote lies at the heart of my Neurocentric Coaching approach:

> "The only person you are destined to become is the person you decide to be."
>
> —RALPH WALDO EMERSON

The science and skills in this coaching will make this life-changing quote true for you.

Your **unstoppable** success and the person you will become are within your control—whether or not you realize it. When you master your greatest resource—your magnificent brain—you ultimately become who you want and decide to be.

The power to change lives.

I want to tell you a little bit about my story, about how I came to where I am today and how I know what I know today. I was born and raised in South Africa, went through high school, and went off to medical school to become a physician. I always say that I was the model interview candidate because, when they asked me why I wanted to go to medical school, I said, "Because I care deeply about people and hate suffering." And it was true!

And it's continued to drive me every day of my life since then, although I've been out of clinical medicine for roughly half my professional life. I worked in family medicine for a period of time, and then I specialized in exercise science and sports medicine, working with elite athletes, with our country's Olympians. And my career progressed and I pursued a related—but not directly related—research interest into the pharmaceutical and biotech industry.

And though I knew nothing about business, I understood clinical medicine extremely well and research extremely well. So I dove into the big world of business and learned through the university of life. And I progressed in a range of different leadership roles: research, business, and ultimately leading organizations. And I was sitting at the top of New York City, Italian suits, taking great care of my wife and children, beautiful schools, fantastic house. It looked perfect...

Except that I was 80 pounds overweight and a heartbeat away from a quadruple bypass. I was doing all the right things, except looking after myself. And so I very deliberately stopped and decided to step back out—I didn't step out of my corporate roles yet—but I knew it was time to heal my body.

At the time, I was running the biggest cardiovascular research program in the world. We were running massive studies, counting dead bodies of people who had not been able to take care of their hearts. And yet, I was still neglecting my beautiful body. So I stepped back to take care of it.

And I did what I should have done long before—I healed my body. I restored my health. I lost those 80 pounds; I was managing my sleep better. And I had two massive lessons from this experience.

The first was that I was disproportionately uplifted. I knew that, when I was physically better, I was going to feel better. But I had no idea it was going to be by that much. I was disproportionately emotionally uplifted by healing my body.

The second lesson was a more profound experience. Outside of our shower at the time we had this massive vanity mirror, the kind you use to see your whole body. And the problem was that I had to walk past that mirror twice a day in all my naked glory to get to the shower and then back to my clothing.

And I couldn't get past the guy I saw in the mirror. I hated him. I hated him with a deep passion. Until one day, suddenly—no magic, no bizarre drug experience—I looked in the mirror and the guy who looked back at me was a young athlete. And in that instant, everything changed. A switch flipped in my brain.

I'd been struggling, exercising, forcing myself out in the cold winters of the northeast, and trying to discipline my eating, but it wasn't working. But in that instant, when I recognized the young athlete still inside me, everything changed. My exercise became easy; my eating habits became those of a young athlete. I took good care of the guy in the mirror, whom I suddenly liked again.

And there I was, this Western scientist who'd just had a switch flick in my brain. And I wondered, How do I do that? How did that happen in my head, and how do I help that happen in everybody's heads? Everybody who's stuck, everybody who's stopped, everybody who's trapped has the power in their brains somewhere to flick a switch and change their lives.

And so, my lifelong commitment to helping people attain personal mastery through Compassionate Neuroscience was born.

Following the unexpected and life-changing moment when I stared into the eyes of that young athlete, I delved into research, inquiry, and contemplation of the role of my brain. Before long, I had developed my compassionate Neurocentric Coaching approach, which combines human experience with the latest scientific research and includes my *Brain Operating System* (BOS) methodology.

This methodology has profoundly transformed the lives of many of my high-achieving executive clients. These men and women have reinvented themselves—personally and professionally—by upgrading their brain structure.

I witnessed unstoppable in action—a gold-medal moment.

During the early stages of my profession as a sports physician and scientist, I had the privilege of working with Olympic athletes. It was my job to bring the best science to guide them toward their Olympic dreams.

As part of this work, our research team performed extensive testing on athletes in a high-performance laboratory. The tests pushed the athletes to their extreme limits, to define and then shift their physiologies to become premier world-class athletes in their category.

Read on to hear about an eye-opening experience that motivated me to share this transformational work with the world.

This defining moment propelled me to share the science of the unstoppable state.

So, I went through medical school, worked in family medicine for a period of time, and then specialized in exercise science and sports medicine. And I worked with elite athletes, with Olympians. My job was to bring cutting-edge science to help them to reach the Olympic Games, hopefully reach a final, and even more hopefully get onto the podium and hang some hardware around their neck. And I loved that part of my work.

I had an experience there one day that changed the future of my professional interest forever.

I did a lot of work with rowers. One of the reasons that rowers like working with exercise scientists is that we can put them in a laboratory, on a rowing ergometer, and track how their body is working through the course of their exercise.

And I took this elite, elite rower—already two Olympic golds, going for her third—and my job was to break her. My job was to push her to her extreme. And I was very good at it.

So I hook her up with all the measuring devices: IV, oxygen, breathing apparatus. I'm pushing, pushing, pushing, pushing her. And I'm struggling. She is putting so much power in this ergometer that it's almost taking off, almost hovering it's going so fast. And she's pumping and pumping, and I'm watching her electrolytes changing, her oxygen saturations, and her lactate going up. And finally, finally—I thought I was not going to get there—she finishes. And she drops the handle, which recoils and slams into the machine. She rips the mask off her face and collapses on the floor. And then she lets out the most death-defying roar I have ever heard.

Literally, the walls of the laboratory shook, and it didn't help that the lab next door was a sleep lab. All the professors from there came through and said, "What's going on, Roddy?!"

And I realized: Nothing I measured had any relevance to her being **unstoppable**, compared to that roar. That's what gave her two golds, ultimately three golds, best in the world over a 12-year period.

And I realized more: This is where it is. This is where it's at.

In Search of Personal Mastery

Once you've mastered your brain, you've mastered your biology.

How many hours, days, and years have you spent figuring out modern technology to enhance your life? The answer to this question may be quite a large figure, especially considering the time and effort you've devoted to understanding how to operate computers, smartphones, and other electronic devices. Yet most people haven't spent any time mastering the operating system of their own brains—because they haven't been taught how.

Nature gifted you with a state-of-the-art supercomputer with advanced functionality. Once you understand how to operate this computer—your brain—you'll realize that you can command your brain to serve you. You will achieve personal mastery.

Modern science can teach us how to achieve personal mastery through knowledge of our complex neurobiology, personal insight, and hard work. Just as skeletal muscles can be trained to achieve peak performance, so your intellectual and emotional muscles can also be strengthened and developed to unlock your full potential.

Your brain is perfectly designed to serve you.

The brain is the only organ that we're not in complete control of.

Did you know that? Why is that? It's stupid! It's just an organ; it's just a lump of biology in my head, no different than my beautiful heart, no different than my liver, my spleen, my muscles. It's a gift given to me to operationalize my life. And yet, somehow, my brain rules me day to day to day. My life is full of stuckness. Where does this stuckness come from? It comes from in my brain.

If I want to get up and get something, I simply send commands and orders to my body, and my muscles start working. Right? They obey me. If I want to exercise, climb a hill, I say to my heart, "Pump faster!" I say to my lungs, "Breathe deeper!" And they respond.

But my brain? It's telling me what I can't do; it's not serving me. When we wake up in the morning, we think, Oh, it's going to be a terrible day today; I feel miserable today. And what happens to that day? It's terrible, right?

We are designed perfectly, over 400 million years of iterative design. And iteration after iteration, Nature has designed us perfectly...so if we're living imperfect lives, whose bad?

My bad.

It's not really my bad, because nobody's taught you this, right? We should be teaching this to kids, coming out of school, making sure every college graduate knows this stuff.

Unpack Unstoppable

 **What is unstoppable?**

Unstoppable. That's a big word. I think it might be the biggest word that I know—not in length, but in raw power. And when I started putting this coaching engagement together, based on my understanding of the human brain, I had all sorts of titles that I thought about, but I couldn't get away from this word: Unstoppable. And truly, I think that you're going to see this is Nature's gift to us: being unstoppable. But as so many of us have reflected, we stop ourselves all the time. So, if we can learn to get out of our own way and use this magnificent gift—wow! We're ahead of 99.5% of everybody else.

 **Throughout life, you've experienced peaks and valleys.**

There have been times when you've felt stuck, like nothing was going your way. Maybe things didn't fall into place, no matter how hard you worked. Or you let that nagging voice of doubt get the best of you. Whatever it was, you felt like you were being held back, unable to progress.

 **Other times, you've felt unstoppable.**

Feelings of love, fearlessness, inspiration, intuition, motivation, compassion, focus, energy, fulfillment, and victory point to the state of unstoppability.

You may have experienced these when you fell in love; graduated or won an award; received a promotion, title, or salary increase; accomplished a personal achievement; or stood up for something or someone you believed in. You may know the highs of adventurous travel, loving relationships and having children, excelling in your profession, or thriving in adversity. **Unstoppable** success also includes bursts of creativity and the experience of an effortless flow state.

At any given moment, you're either unstoppable or you're not. You can't be both at the same time.

To be truly **unstoppable**, you must first know what's holding you back.

 **EXERCISE 1**

Times You've Felt Stoppable

ACTION 1 OF 3

Brainstorm

Spend five minutes writing down times you've felt stoppable.

ACTION 2 OF 3

Choose

Choose one stoppable time from your list. Circle it.

ACTION 3 OF 3

Reflect

Reflect on the time you chose. Spend five minutes writing down your responses to the following questions:

- What did it look like?
- What did it feel like?
- What were you doing?
- What were you *not* doing?
- What were you saying?
- What were you *not* saying?
- What were you hearing?
- How were people reacting to you?
- How did it feel on the inside?
- What would I have seen if I was watching you?

We can all relate to feeling stoppable.

The exercise may have brought up some difficult emotions. Identifying these experiences increases your awareness of stoppability and begins to reveal your **unstoppable** state.

Go deeper to experience nine common states of stoppability. Take time to absorb your reactions.

Anxious

Feeling anxious or on edge can trigger a stress response that makes it difficult to think clearly and make quality decisions. This anxiety can escalate to fear or panic.

Afraid/Fearful

Fear is a natural response to threat, but it can spiral out of control and become immobilizing.

Stuck

We can become stuck in a rut. We may lack motivation and feel unable to move forward.

Discouraged

Unmet expectations can lead to discouragement and disappointment. We may become hard on ourselves (and others) and lose confidence or enthusiasm.

Overwhelmed

Overwhelm goes hand in hand with extreme stress. We may feel we lack time, resources, or know-how.

Scarcity minded

Guarding time or resources is common if we're in a scarcity mindset. We can feel insecure or falsely believe there's not enough. We struggle to gain access to abundance.

Unfulfilled

There are times we're just going through the motions of life. We may feel dissatisfied, confused, lost, or disconnected from our purpose.

Hostile

Sometimes we hold grudges, thinking that we've been wronged. Anger or hostility surface.

Resentful

Resentment might look like a combination of frustration, judgment, anger, and envy.

You'll learn the tools to flip from stoppable to unstoppable.

Becoming Unstoppable

This woman reflects unstoppable!

Look into her eyes. Imagine her thoughts and feelings. What do you see? What do you feel?

 EXERCISE 2

Times You've Felt Unstoppable

ACTION 1 OF 3

Brainstorm

Spend five minutes writing down times you've felt **unstoppable**.

ACTION 2 OF 3

Choose

Choose one **unstoppable** time from your list. Circle it.

ACTION 3 OF 3

Reflect

Reflect on the time you chose. Spend five minutes writing down your responses to the following questions:

- What did it look like?

- What did it feel like?

- What were you doing?

- What were you *not* doing?

- What were you saying?

- What were you *not* saying?

- What were you hearing?

- How were people reacting to you?

- How did it feel on the inside?

- What would I have seen if I was watching you?

What unstoppable feelings did you experience during the reflection activity?

You may have experienced positive feelings of success, compassion, confidence, drive, passion, or fearlessness—to name a few.

*Go deeper to explore common **unstoppable** states. Notice your reactions and which states resonate most with you.*

Fearless

Fearlessness helps us find the courage to take big leaps into the unknown. It can help us build bridges to places that we want to go and step into our ideal future.

Determined

Determination is part of a winning mindset. It empowers us to have an unwavering belief in what's possible—despite challenges.

Driven

Drive inspires action. It propels us forward. We have the power to persist and adopt a "no excuses" policy.

Passionate

Passion is deep emotional energy. It propels us toward our ideal future.

Present

Present-moment awareness gives us the power to utilize the fullness of every moment to accomplish our goals without being distracted by the past or the future.

Composed

In a composed state, we are clear, calm, and purposeful—even on the rough days.

Intuitive

Trusting our intuition provides us with the clarity that enables us to make confident, clear, and calm decisions.

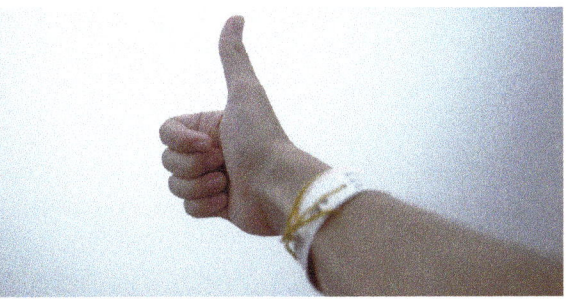

Energized

Energy fuels our dreams and enthusiasm. It gives us the mental and physical drive to succeed.

Define Your Ideal Future

 **Believe and feel in your heart: It's possible to live the life of your dreams.**

I'll lead you through a practical process to define your ideal future. For now, however, hold off on writing anything down.

Reflect and write.

When you're ready to sit down to work through the exercise, I encourage you to set aside ample time and approach it with a deep sense of both attention and intention. Imagine a clean canvas—you can create anything that your heart desires. But sometimes, a blank canvas can be intimidating, and if that's the case for you, rather than diving into the future, think about your current life.

Begin by reflecting on the aspects of your life today that are working well for you. Take note of how you feel about these positive aspects. Consider other experiences in your life that elicit similar positive feelings. Now, with this as the foundation, stretch your imagination. Cultivate the courageousness to take these and imagine one area of your life that is limitless—free from any constraints. And soon, as you begin to work on this, you'll be ready to write down the first draft of your desired future.

Now, you don't have to create your vision all in one go. In fact, I quite strongly recommend that you come back each day to work on it, taking it a little bit further in clarity and depth every session.

Now remember, the people, the experiences, and the obstacles that have held you back or kept you small before have no place in and no influence over this exercise. This is your perfectly imagined, ideal future. Those challenges are behind you. Expand your imagination. Let it guide you forward.

- *What would you do if money were no object?*

- *Who would you spend your time with?*

- *Where would you be?*

- *What would your physical body feel like?*

- *What would you do for fun?*

- *What would you see, feel, and sense when you woke up in the morning and when you fell asleep at night?*

- *What do you dream of having in your life?*

Your future has yet to unfold, and the now—as you think about it—is full of possibility, and is waiting for your intention to create something new, something bold, something beautiful, and something that's yours.

I hope you enjoy this exercise.

 EXERCISE 3

Define Your Ideal Future

Create a clear vision for your future.

Describe what you want for your life.

Don't worry about getting it done perfectly now. It's an iterative process you'll revisit regularly. If you have an hour available now, begin writing your first draft. Alternatively, you may familiarize yourself with the process now and work on it over the next few days.

Either way, spend at least two hours describing, modifying, expanding, and revising your future vision before you begin the next session.

Though I've provided ample writing space below—and I believe there is power in handwriting your future vision—you may want to create a digital version of the document as well so that you can easily make revisions as you work your way through this coaching process.

Action 1

Imagine and Write

Write a draft of your ideal future—anything and everything you want in the future.

Start by choosing a time three or more years from now. Once you've decided on a date, imagine you're there, living in the moment. Visualize your life exactly as you want it to be. Add as much color and detail as possible. Make it so colorful that a movie director could pick up this working draft and create an inspired, compelling film based on what you've described.

Here are the areas you may want to include:

- **Purpose**: Values, beliefs, why you're doing what you do, the impact you make on the world, and how you feel about your life

- **Career and finances**: What, where, why, how, and how much (or little) you do, with whom, and what you earn

- **Daily life**: Where you live, with whom you live, your material possessions, your daily rituals, your behaviors, your pet(s), and your activities

- **Physical and emotional health**: Quality of sleep, nutrition, energy level, state of mind, and habits you're proud of

- **Recreation**: How you spend your leisure time, what you do for fun, and where you go to travel, adventure, relax, or volunteer

- **Relationships**: Family, friends, team members, colleagues, community, mentors, and other significant people in your life

- **Spirituality**: Mindful awareness, faith, creativity, or situational responsiveness

There are two essential guidelines for writing your first draft:

1. Write in the first person.

2. Write in the present tense.

For example:

- "I am 85 years old, sitting in a well-worn leather chair, surrounded by my family…"

- "I am selling my digital marketing company today for $27 million…"

- "I'm waking up in a log cabin in the mountains of Switzerland…"

In the space below, describe your ideal future as best you can—for now. Then, move on to Action 2.

Action 2

Revise and Enrich

Revise your vision to make it even more vibrant and colorful.

You can do this by adding:

- Descriptive details, such as adjectives and adverbs.

- Sensory information, such as sights, sounds, sensations, smells, and tastes.

I'm confident you've done a wonderful job of describing your ideal future. Now, put yourself in the middle of your future and notice how you feel physically, emotionally, energetically, and spiritually. Look at who you spend time with and how they make you feel. Recognize some of the habits you've mastered and others you've abandoned. See how you handle stress, receive compliments, and share your joy. Your values and beliefs are at the forefront of your vision. Notice the full range of your positive emotions as you reread your vision, and ask yourself:

- How inspired do I feel? Do I admire myself and my dream life?

- Have I enlivened all of my senses?

- Am I feeling all of the positive emotions I wish for myself?

- Have I written my dream big enough to leave a legacy? Or is it so small that it may not push me to my full potential?

Revise your ideal future, as needed, to vividly describe your dream life. Then, move on to Action 3.

Action 3

Confirm and Streamline

Confirm your ideal future description to ensure it aligns with your dreams. Then, craft succinct statements capturing its essence.

This action serves multiple purposes, providing immediate value and enhancing clarity around your vision. As you reread and immerse yourself in your ideal future, envision yourself test-driving it.

- Is it the right size?

- Does it feel good to you?

If you wish to expand an area, spend a few extra minutes revising and refining it. Then, you'll proceed to create three to five consolidated summary statements.

To write your summary statements:

1. Identify the prominent aspects that stand out to you.

2. Group together similar aspects or related goals.

3. Summarize each aspect or goal into a concise, first-person statement written in the present tense.

Now you have a vivid vision of your future and three to five summary statements to carry with you through the rest of the coaching.

Confirm and streamline your ideal future in the space below.

Well done!

You've created a dynamic, living document of your ideal future, one that you'll continue to build on and refer to for the rest of this coaching—and your life.

As you gain knowledge during the coaching, you'll be prompted to go back to your vision and refine it, because once you've completed the coaching, this written document will serve as your **unstoppable** road map to achieve your dreams.

Mastery Missions

Congratulations!

You've finished the first session, and now you're ready for your Mastery Missions. As a recap, your Mastery Missions are activities, exercises, reflections, and other tasks to help you go deeper and harness the power of time between sessions. They will accelerate your mastery of your *Brain Operating System* (BOS).

Use the space below to guide your missions. Plan to spend one hour, minimum, completing these before beginning the next session.

MASTERY MISSION 1

Prioritize Planning

ACTION 1 OF 2

Schedule

Review your weekly schedule, and designate dedicated time to fully engage with the sessions. For best results, allocate a minimum of two hours each week to accomplish one session. Aim for slots where you can concentrate fully on the sessions. When the time arrives on your calendar, prioritize it to firmly commit to your journey toward becoming **unstoppable**.

ACTION 2 OF 2

Plan

Create a safe, inviting space where you can comfortably engage in the sessions and exercises without distractions. You may choose to add special objects, such as a photograph, a piece of art, a favorite quote, a candle, plants, materials, or supplies to fill your space with joy and creative inspiration. Think outside of the box, and brainstorm your ideas here. Most of all, have fun with this action.

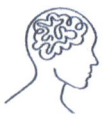

MASTERY MISSION 2

Recognize Unstoppability

ACTION 1 OF 2

Identify

To consolidate and deepen your understanding of your stoppable and **unstoppable** states, recognize instances of these states in your daily life. An effective way to do this is to choose one particular time of day, every day, when you commit to becoming mindful of your reactions and responses. For instance, just before you begin work, look at your daily to-do list or consider your goals or objectives for the day.

Identify the state you're in and the feelings you're experiencing. Perhaps you're feeling anxious, discouraged, passionate, or energized. Answer the question: Do I feel stoppable or **unstoppable**?

ACTION 2 OF 2

Observe

Observe stoppable and **unstoppable** states in other people. Note the words they use, their body language, and the subtleties of their responses. Reflect on what makes them either stoppable or **unstoppable**.

 **MASTERY MISSION 3**

Explain Unstoppability

ACTION 1 OF 1

Explain

Explain the stoppable and **unstoppable** states to family, friends, or colleagues. Try a game where you kindly and respectfully recognize and mirror each other's statements and reactions during everyday conversations to see whether they fall under the stoppable or the **unstoppable** category. Reflect on your experiences here.

Supplemental Science

 You're invited to delve into the supporting research on the topics covered in this session. Keep in mind that exploring the supplemental science is optional. You can return anytime to read more about the underlying science of the *Brain Operating System* methodology.

History of the *Brain Operating System*

At the start of this session, I shared my lifelong commitment to helping people achieve personal mastery through my compassionate Neurocentric Coaching approach. To learn more about the development of my coaching approach subsequent to my life-changing mirror experience, I invite you to read the following interview transcript.

In this interview, I discuss the early neuroscience that is foundational to my *Brain Operating System* model and explain my rationale for building my methodology on this groundwork. I also share my unique approach to simplifying and translating complex neuroscience in an engaging and memorable way, making it easy to apply to everyday life and empowering anyone who wants to become **unstoppable** to realize their dreams.

Interview Transcript

Podcast Interviewer: Thanks for sharing about your life's journey, especially your transformational mirror experience. Let's dive deeper into what happened for you after that. Can you tell us a bit about the development of your *Brain Operating System* methodology?

Roddy: Sure. So, I had two motivators: one, my determination to understand the neurobiology behind what happened to me, so I could replicate this in my own life, and two, I wanted to figure out how best to help others realize they, too, have life-changing potential in their brain. It's there—it's just waiting to be harnessed. A big aha moment for me was when I realized that people are stuck or stopped because they don't know how to operationalize their brain…simply because, like me, they haven't been taught how to do so. Another aha moment was when I realized I could help to change that!

Podcast Interviewer: So this is the origin of your Compassionate Neurocentric approach that empowers people to reach their full potential?

Roddy: Yes! And at the heart of this approach is my commitment to integrating scientific knowledge with human experience to the benefit of people striving to lead better lives. As an applied scientist, I'm interested in science that's useful, science that has value and meaning for my life and the lives of those I coach.

So, as I researched, questioned, and came to understand the role of my own brain in my own life-changing experience, I realized the importance of being able to distinguish and work with thoughts, feelings, and fears—where they originate in the brain and how they relate to one another and influence our behavior. I was especially interested in the role of belief in success because I realized that was the key shift for me—when I truly believed that I could again be that young athlete, I became **unstoppable**.

Layer onto this that I'm fascinated by evolutionary biology…and so I was drawn to explore the evolutionary origins of thoughts, feelings, and fears to understand their behavioral impacts.

Podcast Interviewer: So, what did you learn?

Roddy: Well, let's start back with some science done around 1960. Paul MacLean, who conducted his research at both Harvard and Yale, proposed what became known as the *triune brain concept.* Now, I'll quickly add that his work has received some criticism, mainly because our understanding of the science has moved on in far greater detail than even he would probably have imagined. But, if you've read MacLean's work closely, you'll know that a strong driving force behind the development of his triune brain concept was the search for a neurobiological explanation of human behavior. He wanted to provide answers to profound questions about the human brain-behavior link. As I dived deeper, I found in the triune brain a well-researched neurobiological perspective on the human brain that I could relate to my own experience, as well as one that provided an explanation—with a behavioral focus—of the evolutionary development of the human brain. So, it soon became clear to me that the triune brain concept provided a foundation on which to develop my Neurocentric Coaching to help others use their brain to achieve transformative and lasting life changes, and it became an integral part of my *Brain Operating System* methodology.

Podcast Interviewer: I'm familiar with MacLean's work and that the triune brain concept continues to enjoy wide application. Before we met today, I ran a Google Scholar search using the keyword *triune brain model*, and the result yielded a lot of recently published articles. What's fascinating is that MacLean's concept is used in a diversity of fields, ranging from neurosurgery to marketing to education, even architecture. So it seems that MacLean's work continues to impact and influence pure and applied thinking and research about many aspects of what it means to be human and the varied endeavors of humankind. I guess this is not surprising, given MacLean's aim to research and develop a neurobiological explanation of human nature and behavior.

Roddy: Absolutely, and MacLean's focus on the brain-behavior link is one of the reasons I use it as a foundation of my work. You see, the triune brain concept provides a system-level, generalized model for understanding the immensely complex workings of the human brain.

This is really important because the full complexity of the human brain and its functions is so vast that it can seem literally beyond our intellectual grasp. This creates a substantial challenge for a practitioner like myself, who's motivated to define straightforward and practical guidance for their clients. Pure scientists may know a whole lot about brain structure and function at the detailed network and cellular levels, but so what? What does this mean to me in my own very real life? How does this knowledge inform human behavior? Because it's ultimately our behavior that influences how we live our lives and whether we achieve success, whatever that looks like for us.

Don't get me wrong; there's massive value in detailed research on the human being. It is the most rapidly advancing field in biology. But I'm greedy, and anxious to understand my brain, to enhance my life and help my fellow humans optimize their relationship with their own brain.

So, I realized that, in order to teach others how to master their brain, my job is to understand the key elements of the complexity and then, like any good teacher, find ways to simplify it, to make the essential knowledge easy to understand and, more importantly, easy to apply. My solution, as an applied scientist, is to use conceptual models to achieve this. These are powerful tools for communicating key concepts to nonscientists, enabling them to operationalize what would otherwise be incomprehensible volumes of deep and detailed scientific knowledge.

Podcast Interviewer: So, essentially, you've done the challenging job of getting to grips with the complex brain science and then you've synthesized and simplified it into a methodology that your clients can apply in their lives every day?

Roddy: I'm aware there's a trade-off in simplification, and I acknowledge that this modular brain model imperfectly reflects the vast complexity of human brain functionality. But it's precisely because of the complexity of the interplay between brain structure, function, and behavior that I've reached for simple conceptual models. Application of a modular brain model, which largely describes the internal relationships between key functional regions within the brain, enables the human brain owner to more easily understand the links between their neurobiology and their behavior, and to gain the clarity and confidence they need to overcome their fears and reach their full potential. What we lose in complexity and detail, we gain in utility and applicability.

Podcast Interviewer: So, MacLean's triune brain concept is integral to your *Brain Operating System* methodology, but from what I understand, you've built on it further to create your own *Brain Operating System* model. Can you tell us a bit more about this development?

Roddy: Of course. Initially, I focused on the three brain regions as MacLean did. Then, through an iterative process of application and reconceptualization, as I developed my *Brain Operating System* coaching methodology, I realized the importance of teaching about two other brain regions that I came to see as vital to peak performance and brain mastery. So, I expanded the triune model into my five-region *Brain Operating System* model. And I'm confident that this model enables even high-level business leaders and Olympic athletes to understand how and why their brains behave as they do…and it enhances their success when they understand and apply the model. Sure, it's a simplification, but that's part of its beauty and efficacy; it makes important concepts accessible to brain users, empowering us all to exercise authority over our brains to achieve personal mastery and to live a fulfilling and successful life.

Podcast Interviewer: I love that you've had the courage, as a strong and respected scientist, to take poetic license with the story, while sticking to the underlying evidence, so that the individual can apply the knowledge in a meaningful way in their life.

Roddy: Yes, I'm a storyteller by nature, and a strong believer that learning should be fun, and these aspects shape my work and teaching. As an educator, I believe we must engage our audiences with stories. When you hear me talking about the science, helping people to understand and apply it, you'll hear me applying scientific knowledge of the brain's development in a deeply engaging way. When we realize that we're each part of a scientific story, and one that started millennia ago, it brings the underlying science to life in a powerful way. The models come to life in the mind of the learner, and they are empowered to now participate in their own optimization. What I learned many years ago in front of that mirror is that we don't have to sit back and accept our condition. When I studied to be a doctor, I was told that the adult human brain was fully formed. Not so today. We understand the brain very differently. We're each able to make substantial changes in the way it operates. If we choose—and let me repeat this critical phrase—*if we choose*, we can each secure the fulfillment and success that we have been designed for.

Commitment

Between this session and the next, I commit to the following:

☐   Writing my ideal future and consolidating it into three to five summary statements.

☐   Observing stoppable and unstoppable states on a daily basis.

Next up, in Session 2: *Understanding Your* Brain Operating System, we'll unpack how you can gain control of your brain to access the state of unstoppability. You'll learn about the natural wiring of your magnificent brain. Plus, you'll discover how to modify beliefs, attitudes, and actions to reach your ideal future.

> "We are designed to be successful. Nature has gifted us all with the capacity to be unstoppable."
>
> —DR. RODDY CARTER

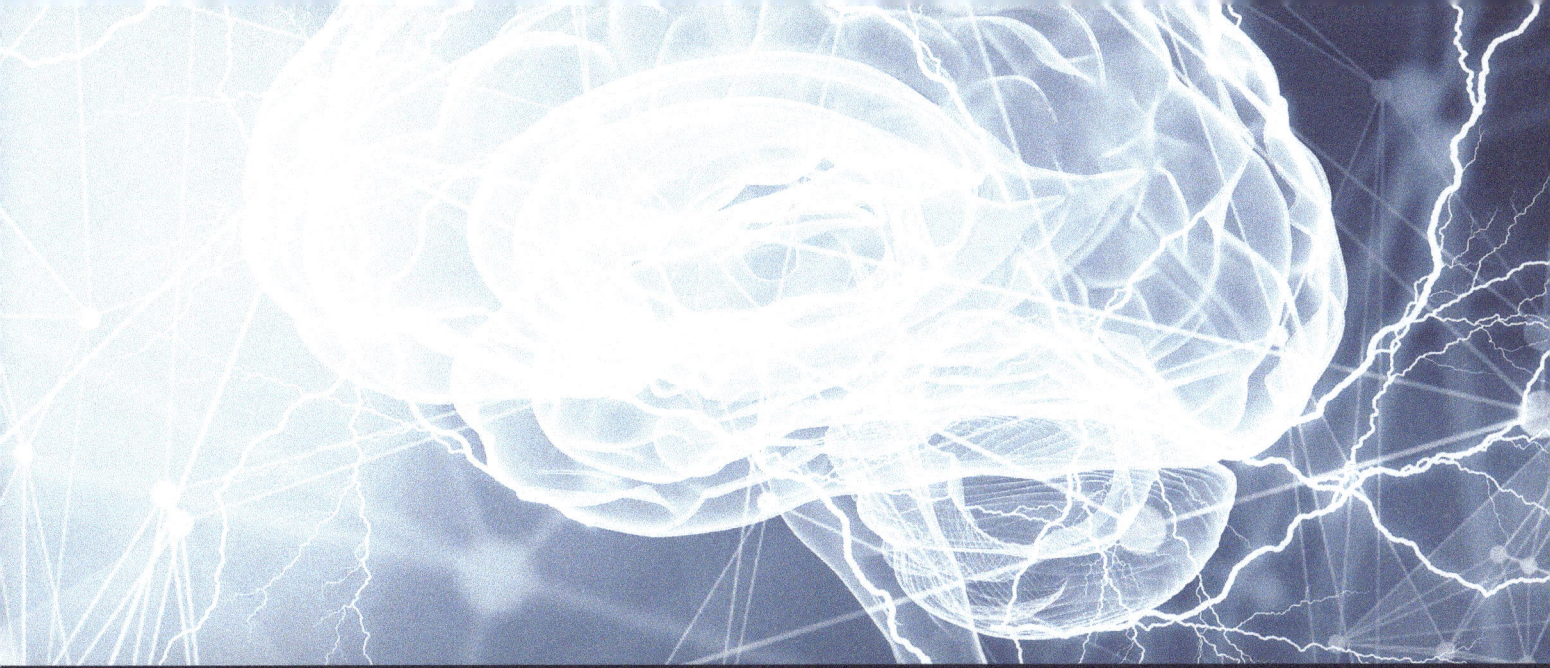

UNDERSTANDING YOUR
BRAIN OPERATING SYSTEM

Welcome to Session 2! Now that you've explored what it means to be **unstoppable** and crafted a clear vision of your ideal future, let's begin our deep dive into the evolution of your magnificent brain.

This session's content and activities will take one to two hours to complete. Spend an additional hour working through your Mastery Missions before moving forward. Exploring the Supplemental Science is optional.

In this session, you will:

- Embark on an exploration of your brain's structure, functioning, and evolution.

- Uncover the groundbreaking science behind the key regions of your *Brain Operating System* (BOS), and understand how your brain is wired to move past limiting beliefs to realize your ideal future.

- Discover a powerful 5-action sequence that uses each region of your brain to overcome personal challenges keeping you stuck.

The Evolution of the Human Brain

 **Four Billion Years Ago...**

There's very good evidence that 4 billion years ago, more or less, life started. And then it took a really, really, really long time of not much going on, until about 400 million years ago. The very first forms of life—life as we really understand it; not the little unicellular or multicellular organisms—the very first insects started to form on this planet. About 300 million years ago, something more interesting happened: What we call reptiles developed. And think about Nature's task, right? She started with a few chemicals. Those chemicals started aggregating into molecules. Those molecules grew into bigger things called organic molecules, like proteins and sugars. And she started packaging them into what we call cells, the fundamental unit of life.

Chemicals → Molecules → Proteins, Fats, and Sugars → Cells → Fundamental Unit of Life

And that's where life started, way back in those individual little packages. And then she started putting lots of cells together to get multicellular organisms, these kind of wobbling jellies of many cells that were identical to each other. And then she said, "Hey, it'd be kind of cool if these little wobbly things could move around." So she elongated them into these little wormlike things, and they started doing these cool driving movements to move around the planet.

Cells → Multicellular Organisms → Complex Organisms

And as these organisms got more evolved and intricate, she started running into problems because they got bigger and their movements needed to be coordinated. And so we see the central nervous system emerging for the very first time early in evolution. And Nature took those reptiles, those long little wiggly worms that had started getting arms and legs—early crocodiles or lizards or things like that—and she gave them a spinal cord that connected everything together, this long spiral cord that went down the body.

Cells → Multicellular Organisms → Complex Organisms → Central Nervous System → Spinal Cord

And she spoke to a scientist in the laboratory—and this is where I get poetic—and she said, "You know what? I think we can go one step beyond these slithering, crawling, creeping reptiles. Let's evolve a little bit better. Let's make them better at survival. What can we do?"

And the scientists came back after a long night, and they said, "You know what? If we tie the spinal cord into a little, scraggly knot at the top there—if we just take those nerves and we tie them into a little knot—we think we can give those things a brain."

And she said, "Well, with a bit of foresight, I think the brain is going to be the greatest gift we ever give life. Let's start!"

The milestones of human brain evolution—beginning 4 billion years ago.

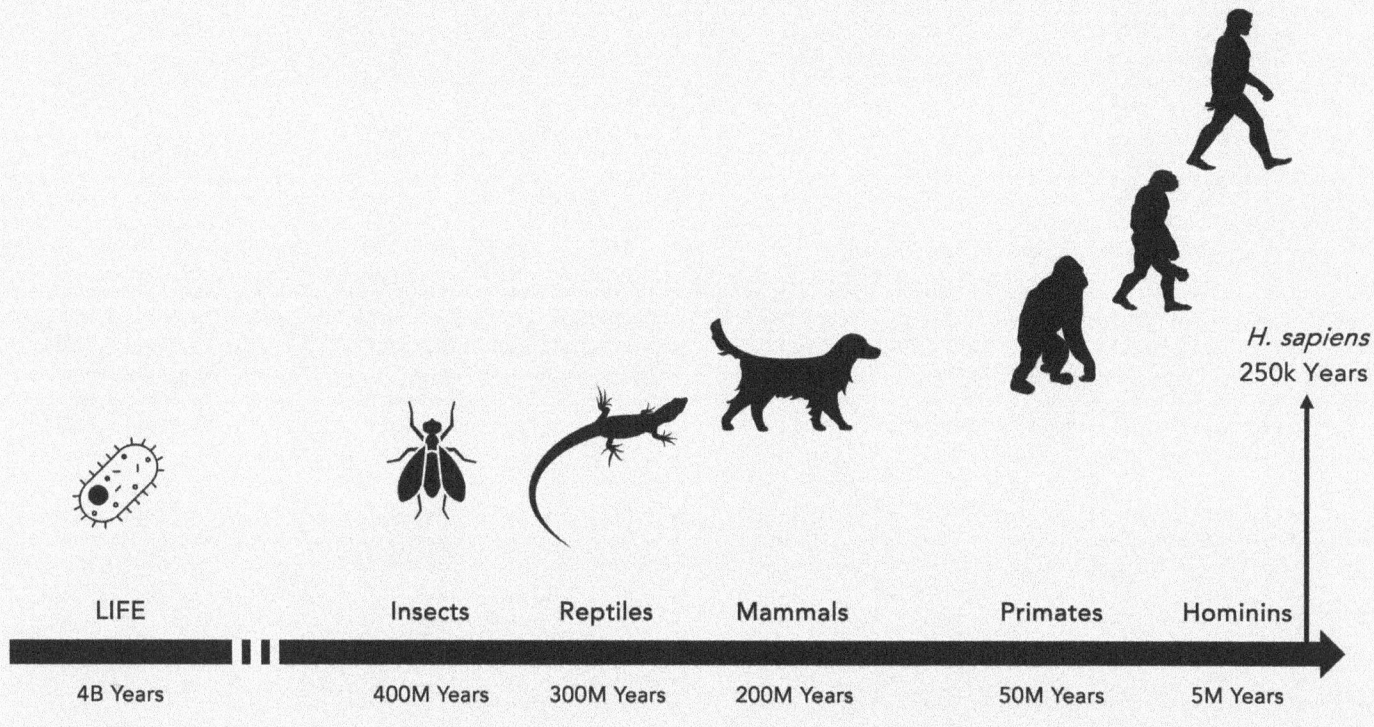

H. sapiens
250k Years

LIFE	Insects	Reptiles	Mammals	Primates	Hominins
4B Years	400M Years	300M Years	200M Years	50M Years	5M Years

- **LIFE:** Evidence shows that the earliest and simplest forms of life appeared on Earth about 4 billion years ago in the form of microscopic organisms, more commonly known as *microbes*.

- **Insects:** Gradually, more complex organisms began to evolve. Land insects, for example, date back to around 400 million years ago.

  An increase in the complexity and size of organisms resulted in the development of a central nervous system to coordinate life processes and activities, such as movement.

- **Reptiles:** The central nervous system design became more complex over time, and around 300 million years ago, early land-dwelling vertebrates—four-limbed, lizard-like creatures—developed a primitive brain. This brain region controlled critical survival instincts.

- **Mammals:** Over time, a second brain region emerged, enhancing the capabilities and survival capacities of the early mammals that possessed it. This additional brain region, which appeared around 200 million years ago, enabled nurturing of offspring and collaboration with others.

- **Primates:** As mammalian evolution progressed, a third brain region developed, introducing the capacity for thought and reason. In advanced mammals, this region bestowed higher faculties and abilities that enabled highly complex adaptations to environmental challenges.

- **Hominins:** The ongoing evolution of advanced mammals resulted in the development of another two brain regions: a complex filtering mechanism and the prefrontal cortex.

Homo sapiens has all five brain regions, which together endow modern humans with the most sophisticated brain design on the planet.

The Five Brain Regions

 **The reptilian brain: Fight, flight, or freeze**

Nature started with a little reptilian brain. And what did that reptilian brain do for the creeping, crawling, slithering things? It gave them survival!

And how were they enabled to survive? What did they do? They feared!

So, the reptilian brain was the very first organ of fear, and it enabled the earliest creatures to fight (strike to protect themselves), flee (slither away to escape), or freeze (lay low to avoid detection). I always think about rattlesnakes that meet a human in a road; it's the same design. This is all they have: a little knot at the top of their head that enables them to coil up and strike to fight, or to slither away—flight—or to just lie very quietly, hoping the human walks by and doesn't see them.

And this was the start of the human brain.

The reptilian brain:

- Triggers primitive **survival responses.**

- Governs **fight, flight, and freeze** responses.

- Is the **default brain** used in times of crisis.

Driven by fear and adrenaline, this region of the brain compels you to flee from danger, to turn to meet it with aggression, or to lie low to escape detection. You need your reptilian brain, but if that were all you had, you'd be a cold survival engine—like the snakes and lizards.

 **The emotional brain: Care and collaboration**

So these little reptilian-brained critters were popping out a million babies at a time. They didn't know their names; they didn't know if they survived. They just hoped one would survive to give them a next generation. That was hopelessly inefficient.

So Nature said to the scientists, "Hey, you know that cool little brain you started? I think you should upgrade it." And they came back and said, "You know what? If we can put another little layer on the outside of this brain, we think we can make it much better."

And so they added the emotional brain, and the currency of the emotional brain is love—deep connection and affiliation—and that enabled these creatures to nurture offspring, which meant taking care of them for a longer period of time instead of just spawning them out into the currents of the ocean. It meant training and educating them, showing them what was dangerous and what was safe.

And so the survival rate went up dramatically, and the creatures were able to collaborate with other adults within their species. They were now connected, so they started forming collective groups—the earliest tribes—and survival rates went up again.

So Nature got to version 2.0 of the brain, and survival had dramatically advanced.

The language of the emotional brain is love—a level of deep connection and affiliation.

The emotional brain gives species with that brain region the ability for two important functions:

1. **Care** for their offspring.

2. **Collaboration** with others.

As a result, survival rates for these species increases substantially.

 ## The cognitive brain: Thought and reason

This brain is much bigger today, we know, than it was in version 2.0. And, by the way, it's beginning to reach its energetic limits. It's a huge drain on energy. But before the brain reached that point, Nature added another part of the brain.

What did this do?

Logic, thought, and reason.

The cognitive brain introduced thought and reason!

Around 200 million years ago, the earliest mammals started arriving, and they had cognition. Having added the emotional brain, Nature added the tiniest little thin rim of a cognitive brain. And still today, dogs and horses and dolphins have a thin rim of cognition. And Nature rapidly advanced toward the first near-humans, 50 million years ago.

And the primates started expanding this cortex—the cerebral cortex—which is responsible for thought and reason, and Nature was nearly done...

The cognitive brain introduced thought and reason.

In modern humans, the cognitive brain is three times the size of that of our closest mammalian relatives. It is a supreme gift that clearly differentiates us from other animals. In addition to **thought** and **reason**, this gift gives us three things:

1. Memory

2. Planning

3. Strategic computation

 **Attention Focusing Consortium: Stops data overload**

But Nature was not yet done, because now she had a massive problem.

Now we had this massive influx of data. This huge influx of data was coming in; this cognitive-brain computer was able to take in a billion sensory inputs per second. And this powerful, powerful brain was beginning to struggle with data overload.

And Nature said, "If we don't bring in one other modification, we're going to be in trouble. This computer is going to be stuck; the servers are going to go down." And so she incorporated the next major brain introduction.

And it's a filter. It's a barrier. It enables the powerful cognitive brain to select out the noise that it doesn't care about, because if you look around you, there are an infinite number of lines, colors, dots, and pixels of light—never mind all the other information coming in.

And we can't handle that! No, we need to see the things we care about. We need to see faces and people, the things that we can react to.

And so we have this filter built into the brain that helps us manage data overload. And it's a complex, beautiful filter that stops the brain from being swamped.

The brain has a complex filtering mechanism that stops it from being swamped by masses of data.

A neural network in the brain stem known as the reticular activating system (RAS) is a key part of this complex filtering mechanism, but neuroscientists now know that other brain components, closely associated with the RAS, are also involved in data filtering. For ease of description, I refer to all the filter components collectively as the Attention Focusing Consortium (AFC). The mission of the AFC is to:

- **Prevent data overload** by filtering out information deemed not relevant in the moment.

- **Focus attention on data that it important**, thus prioritizing crucial information.

The prefrontal cortex: Awareness of awareness

The great apes—the gorilla, the orangutan, Australopithecus—big, hairy, knuckle-dragging guys—all have these backward-sloping foreheads.

Now think of Homo sapiens, the modern human being, with our big, square, buttressed-out foreheads. That's because Nature 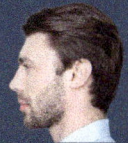 *and her scientists came back, and they put something in the front of the brain. That looks more like your brain, right?*

And this new addition is called the prefrontal cortex. It gives us awareness of our awareness. We have these gifts of fear, feeling, and thought that are going on in the back of our brain. And this new piece gives us awareness of our awareness.

So if I go to the front of my brain, in my prefrontal cortex, I can look back into the rest of my brain and I can see: Those are Roddy's thoughts. Those are his feelings. Those are his fears.

Can you see how powerful that might be?

So that was the full completion of our brain. And I'm telling you that the only thing that differentiates you from the great apes is the prefrontal cortex. And you don't even know you have it, and you don't know what it does. Which means that most of us are no better than those great apes.

True?

Not really true, because we're using our prefrontal cortex anyway. But wouldn't it be so cool to understand exactly what it was and what it did and how it worked? To be able to better operationalize the rest of our brain?

We're going to learn how to do that.

The prefrontal cortex lies at the front of the brain.

It's the latest part of the human brain to develop, and the most sophisticated. This part of the brain differentiates us from the great apes—it's what makes us the modern humans we are today.

The prefrontal cortex is a supreme gift that:

- Gives us **self-awareness**.

- Plays an important role in **higher brain functions**.

- Is a critical part of the brain's **executive system**, enabling **planning**, **reasoning**, and **judgment**.

In relation to the three levels of the brain, the prefrontal cortex enables us to be aware of our thoughts (**cognitive brain**), feelings (**emotional brain**), and fears (**reptilian brain**).

Observe Your Brain Levels

EXERCISE 1

Observe Your Brain Levels

Observe your fears.

Look at the image below. Notice what you **fear** as you study it. What if your lifelong friend was hanging off the side of this cliff? Notice all of your fears.

Observe your thoughts.

Look at the image below. Notice your **thoughts** as you study it.

Observe your feelings.

Look at the image below. Notice the **emotions** you feel as you study it.

Your experience looking at the images offers insight into your brain.

You might have observed that you can consciously shift the seat of your awareness from one brain level to another. Your prefrontal cortex makes this possible. And as you use your prefrontal cortex to shift your awareness, the intensity of your fears, feelings, and thoughts also shifts.

ACTION 1 OF 3

Reflect on fears

While looking at the climber high up on a cliff face, some experience a spontaneous and involuntary sensation of **nervousness** or **anxiety** in their stomach.

What involuntary sensations did you experience? Did you:

- Get a queasy stomach?

- Feel weakness, tingling, or subtle energy shifts in your knees or feet?

- Notice unexpected or involuntary sensations arising in other parts of your body?

These involuntary feelings are evidence of your **reptilian brain** in action. Even though you aren't the one hanging on the rock face with a sheer drop below, your **reptilian brain** still dominates your experience: "Attention! Attention! High-risk situation! What if the climber falls hundreds of feet to the ground?" These instinctual, fear-based thoughts activate your primitive survival response, and fear kicks in.

ACTION 2 OF 3

Reflect on thoughts

Fewer people tend to experience fear responses while looking at the climber on the training wall. This is because, in comparison to the climber on the cliff face, the one on the training wall is not in a high-risk situation—he's not far off the ground, he's firmly attached to a safety rope, and he has plenty of holds to choose from, so his climb is easier.

Instead of fears, you probably experienced a multitude of thoughts. What were your thoughts as you looked at the climber in a practice session? Did you:

- **Wonder** about the climber's age or experience?

- **Observe** the climber's process or gear?

- **Focus** on the colors and shapes of the holds?

- **Pay attention** to the climber's position?

All these thoughts demonstrate your **cognitive brain** in action.

Reflect on feelings

What feelings did you experience while looking at the hiker who'd reached a high point on his journey? Did you feel:

- **Enthusiasm** or **excitement** seeing him on the rock?

- **Triumph** or **empowerment** seeing him with his arms in a gesture of victory?

- **Unstoppability** seeing his hands in the air?

- **Pride** in his feat?

As you shared in the hiker's success, you experienced your **emotional brain** in action.

Hierarchical Structure

These three levels of your brain are intimately connected.

Millions of nerve junctions enable messages to pass between the regions of the brain. Your overall behavior is the composite effect of the three brain levels. In the absence of a higher function, the reptilian brain is the voice that screams the loudest. You hear messages of fear: "Run. Hide. Fight!"

The voice of the reptilian brain is useful when you are in true danger, but more often, it is a disruptive influence holding you back.

Fortunately, the three brain levels are wired hierarchically so that the cognitive brain, together with the emotional brain, can override the compelling, strident, and fearful voice of the reptilian brain.

The brain has an override mechanism to switch off fear.

Once Nature had the brain all set up, she had to coordinate its functionality. The coordination evolved during the building, but I'm going to pretend that she came to wire it afterward.

So, here was a noisy orchestra in the brain. She now had three centers—a center of fear, a center of emotion or love, and a center of thoughtfulness—all wanting to drive this great ship she was building. And that was a little messy. Who was the real leader of the supercomputer? Who was the real boss?

It was a loud mess that Nature had to sort out, and so she deliberately wired a hierarchical structure in that brain.

Which has the loudest voice of those three centers? The reptilian brain. Why? Because if your life is in danger, it's going to shout louder than anything else in the whole world. If a tenth-story window opens and you stand on the ledge, that reptilian brain is going to scream so loud that you can't ignore it.

So Nature created the reptilian brain to have the loudest voice. And that's a powerful driver in this brain, a powerful, powerful driver. But then she had to be able to silence it. Right? Because not everything is terrifying. After all, when you realize the window is closed, it's not quite as frightening.

Nature wired the brain in a very deliberate way, such that the cognitive brain has domination over both the emotional and the reptilian brains. She built an override mechanism into this beautiful computer that was able to switch off the voice of fear, because otherwise we'd be going nowhere.

Your brain is wired with a "wise override" system.

The reptilian brain serves its purpose and is crucial when facing life-threatening danger. However, in our modern world, fear frequently arises from perceived threats rather than genuine dangers.

Fortunately, your brain is wired hierarchically in a way that enables you to silence the compelling, fearful voice of the reptilian brain—when it's safe to do so. I refer to this as "wise override."

Wise override is possible because the cognitive brain has dominion over both the emotional brain and the reptilian brain.

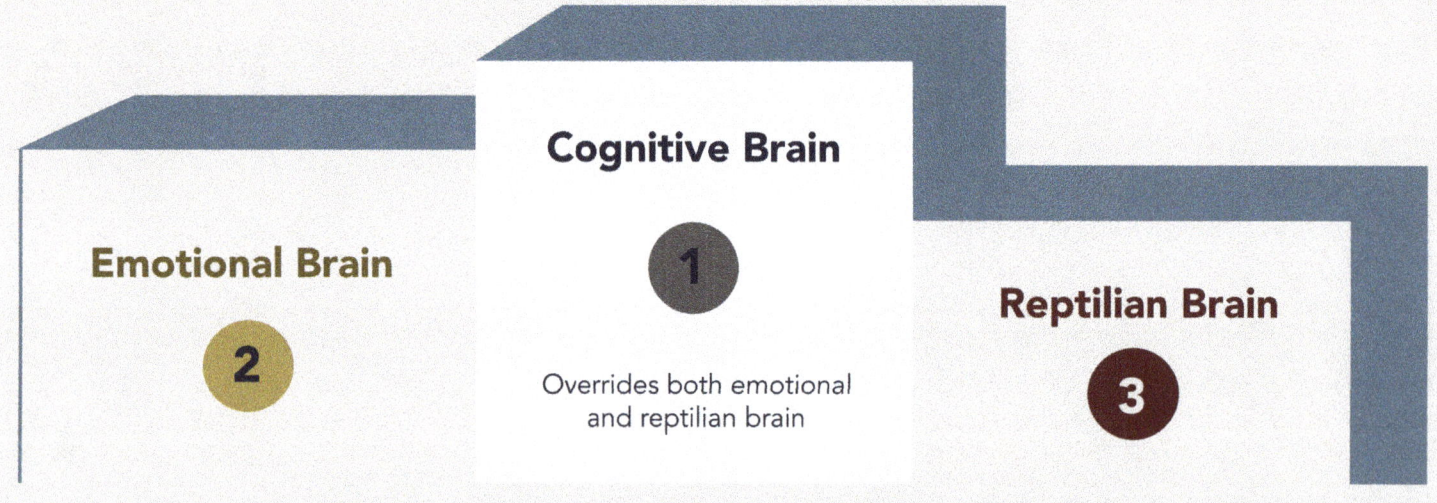

Emotional Brain

2

Cognitive Brain

1

Overrides both emotional and reptilian brain

Reptilian Brain

3

Experience Fear Override

 **EXERCISE 2**

Experience Fear Override

ACTION 1 OF 2

Immerse

There's an image below of a tranquil scene: the sunset at the end of a warm day. Rest your awareness on this visual, or imagine another scene that's calm and lovely.

As you mentally immerse yourself in this serene space, consider what you are thinking, feeling, and fearing.

Not everyone experiences instant peace and serenity simply by looking at a picture or visualizing tranquility. However, the prevailing messages in your mind are probably not "Run. Hide. Fight!"

Even if there are things in the back of your mind worrying you right now, the warm, emotional response evoked by the tranquil scene likely dominates those worries, leaving you feeling more relaxed and peaceful than when you began the activity. This shift from negative to positive feelings indicates that you've used your brain's hierarchical wiring to override the voice of fear.

ACTION 2 OF 2

Visualize

Now, imagine yourself playing a competitive game of chess. Gaining the advantage and securing victory requires unwavering focus, composure, and concentration. Your strategy and determination must be superior to your opponent's. One mistake will cost you the game.

As you visualize yourself in the scene, ask yourself what you're thinking, feeling, and fearing.

Your reptilian brain may respond to the stressful demands with: "Go back! That's not right. What a loser. Admit defeat. Resign! You've been outplayed."

However, you know you're well prepared for this match. You've beaten players stronger than yourself before. You know your powers of logic, reason, and strategy can prevail, so the thoughts emanating from your cognitive brain strengthen your composure and suppress your reptilian brain's voice of fear. Using your brain's hierarchical wiring, you're able to maintain your focus and concentration by overriding the voice of fear. This empowers you to ultimately win the game.

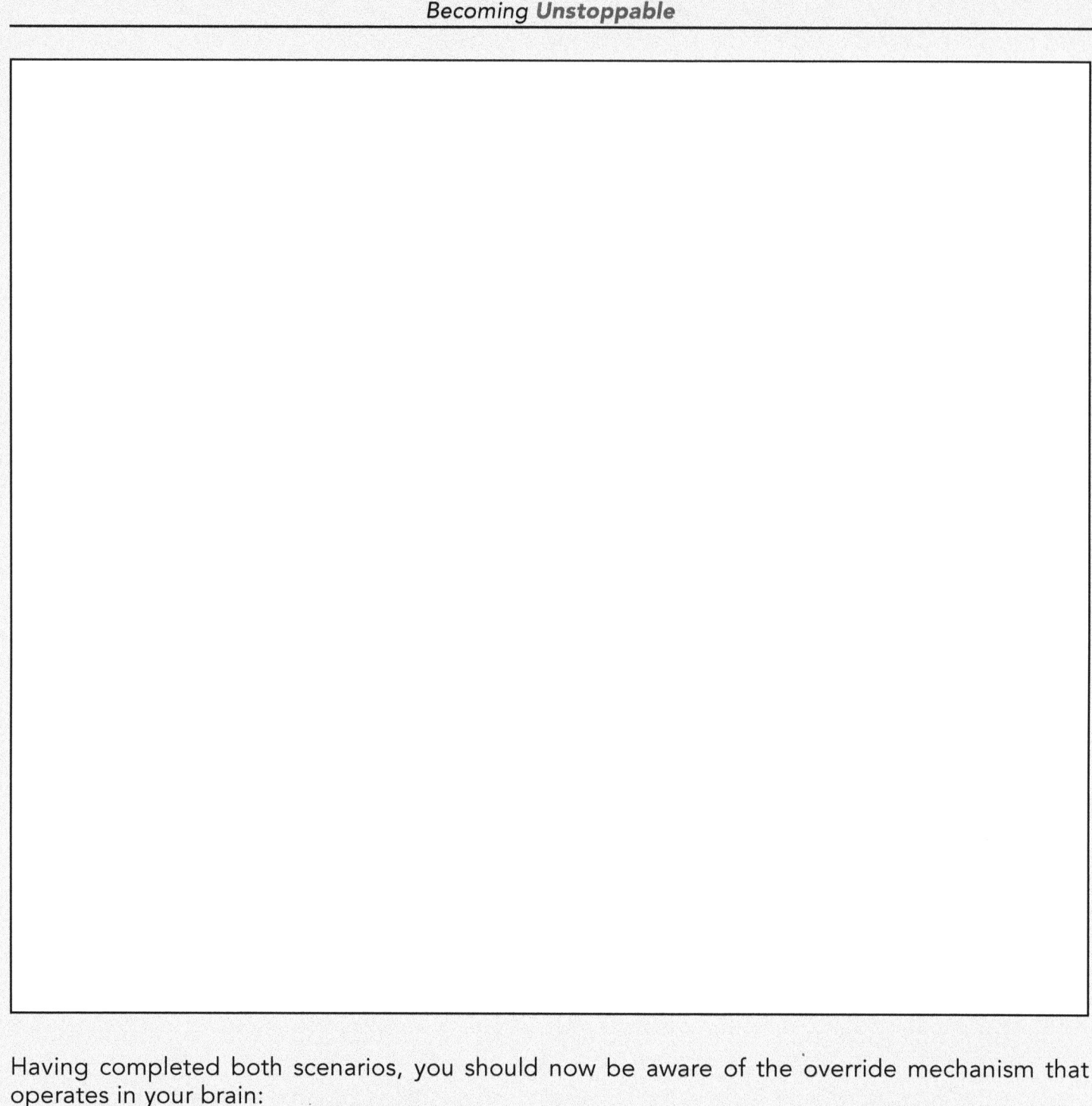

Having completed both scenarios, you should now be aware of the override mechanism that operates in your brain:

- A positive outlook (**cognitive brain**) and positive feelings (**emotional brain**) can silence the voice of the **reptilian brain**.

- Logic and reason (**cognitive brain**) and composure and determination (**emotional brain**) can silence the voice of the **reptilian brain**.

But why is it essential for you to understand this hierarchical system? Because it holds the secret to your success!

The Success Formula

 **Your limits come from inside your brain.**

Have you ever been blocked by fear?

Where do our limits come from?

Our reptilian brain!

But you've been wired to silence the voice of fear.

So, how do we do it?

We just think about it!

It's that easy. It doesn't sound easy, but that's how we're wired. I promise you: It doesn't get any more elegant or extravagant than this.

We just have to think our way past fear.

To become unstoppable and reach your ideal future, do one thing: Think about it.

When you think you can, you can. When you engage your cognitive brain to think an **unwaveringly positive thought**...and think that thought **so much** that you not only think you can, but you *know* you can...**it becomes true**!

Some will say this is far too simple. But the science explains why it's true.

Sometimes thought is enough, but when you leverage all levels of your brain, you achieve unstoppable success.

Thoughts originate in the cognitive brain. As soon as a thought or idea comes to mind, a mental image is created—either consciously or unconsciously. This idea can drive modest action, but you can do more to achieve success.

We're going to spend our time together across the next eight sessions learning how to enhance and co-opt the positive influence of the cognitive and emotional brains to work against the voice of fear. I'm going to teach you the critical role of the prefrontal cortex in this and how it's vitally important to keep the filter of the Attention Focusing Consortium clean for maximum gain.

As a preview of what's to come, here is the Success Formula:

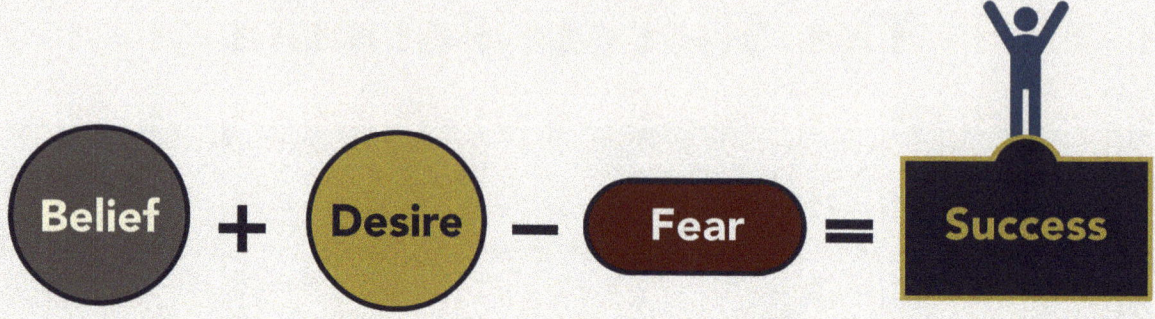

- **Belief:** Belief originates in the cognitive brain. To drive believe, think a positive thought.

- **Desire:** Desire originates in the emotional brain. It can flip between positive and negative depending on whether belief or fear is dominant.

  You'll learn how to recruit your emotional brain to get behind your thoughts with positive emotions.

- **Fear:** Fear originates in the reptilian brain and is frequently experienced as doubt. However, you'll learn a systematic process you can use to quiet the voice of fear.

The BOS Action Sequence

You'll learn to master all regions of your brain to achieve success.

In order to optimize the Success Formula and move ever closer to unstoppability, we must employ the BOS action sequence. During this coaching, you will acquire systematic knowledge to leverage each region of your brain to become **unstoppable**. This potent 5-action sequence draws together all the brain regions to equip you to overcome any obstacle and achieve your ideal future, building belief and desire while removing fear to bring you success—however you define it!

1. **Occupy the Office of the CEO:** The first action is always to step into the "Office of the CEO"—to **pause** and take a few deep breaths to shift the seat of your awareness from the competing voices of your reptilian, emotional, and cognitive brains into your prefrontal cortex. This gives you the clarity and perspective to confront any problem, challenge, or dilemma.

2. **Program your filter:** The second action is to check the settings of your **Attention Focusing Consortium** to ensure accurate evaluation of your current situation, avoiding distorted perceptions of reality. This empowers you to make optimal, **unstoppable** decisions for both your personal and your professional life.

3. **Conquer fear:** The third action is to **overcome fears** rooted in your reptilian brain. You'll learn, practice, and apply a 7-step process to conquer your fears.

4. **Drive belief:** The fourth action is to flood your brain with **positive thoughts**, ensuring that the voice of your cognitive brain shouts louder than the voice of fear, thereby driving belief.

5. **Activate desire:** The fifth and ultimate action involves powering up your emotional brain to simultaneously **activate desire** and **boost belief**.

Mastery Missions

Congratulations!

You've finished Session 2. I trust you've completed the two exercises—*Observe Your Brain Levels* and *Experience Fear Override*—as you worked through the session. Now you're ready for your Mastery Missions.

Between this session and the next, dedicate at least an hour to working on the following four missions. You'll utilize the responses from these missions in future missions.

MASTERY MISSION 1

Shift Your Sensory Experience

ACTION 1 OF 1

Experience your AFC

Completing this mission will help you to experience your Attention Focusing Consortium (AFC) in action. As you move through your day, stop from time to time to connect with your senses.

- Focus on what you can **hear** in the moment.

- Become aware of the **scents** around you. If you're outdoors, you may discover very different scents than what you find inside your house or workspace.

- Note what grabs your **visual attention**. What colors stand out?

- Are you feeling **hungry** or **thirsty**?

- Pay attention to the rise and fall of your chest as you **breathe**.

As you shift your focus from one sensory experience to another, you're experiencing the collaboration between your AFC and your prefrontal cortex. In the space below, reflect on your experiences. Become aware of how, when you're focused on one sense (e.g., hearing), your AFC filters out the multiple messages reaching you through your other senses. For example, when you're focused on listening intently, you won't be fully aware of the rise and fall of your chest as you breathe.

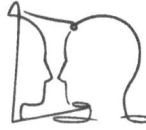 MASTERY MISSION 2

Observe Becoming Aware

ACTION 1 OF 1

Become aware

Recall or revisit the mountain-climber activity where you used your prefrontal cortex to become aware of your thoughts, feelings, and fears. Now, apply the same awareness practice in your daily life.

A good time to practice this skill is during life's natural pauses, such as making (or waiting for) your morning beverage, after an exchange with family members or colleagues, during the time between one task and the next, or while showering or brushing your teeth.

- Engage first with your fears (if any).

- Become aware of your feelings.

- Finally, grow mindful of your thoughts.

Choose one everyday experience during which you will commit to practicing this exercise, and record it here.

 MASTERY MISSION 3

Identify Thoughts, Feelings, and Fears

ACTION 1 OF 3

Identify thoughts

As you practice honing your awareness skills in Mastery Mission 2, take time to reflect on one specific exchange or experience that was particularly challenging or memorable. Mentally revisit this interaction, and identify and document your **thoughts** throughout the exchange.

ACTION 2 OF 3

Identify feelings

Identify and document the **emotions** you were feeling during this exchange.

[ ]

ACTION 3 OF 3

Identify fears

Fears can be subtle. If you noticed any negative emotions or experienced physiological changes in your body, you've touched on a fear. Take sufficient time to explore and document any potential **fears** you may have had during this interaction.

[ ]

 MASTERY MISSION 4

Modify Your Ideal Future

ACTION 1 OF 1

Modify

Describing your ideal future is an iterative, dynamic process. In Session 1, you created three to five consolidated summary statements. This mission requires you to revisit what you wrote to modify, expand, and refine your vision of your ideal future and edit your summary statements. In particular, use your **cognitive brain** to add new thoughts and ideas.

In addition to making edits in your writing spaces from Session 1, you can use the space provided below to write your any revised sections of your ideal future and summary statements. You can also make changes to the digital versions of them, if you chose to type them.

Supplemental Science

 You're invited to delve into the supporting research on the topics covered in this session. Keep in mind that exploring the supplemental science is optional. You can return anytime to read more about the underlying science of the *Brain Operating System* methodology.

Human Brain Scan

This image[1] is a sagittal cross section of the normal adult human brain as imaged by magnetic resonance imaging (MRI). In this image, you can clearly see the delicate neurological tissue that makes up our magnificent human brain cradled within the protective bony skull. The spinal cord runs through the spinal column, carrying vital information from and to the body.

Reptilian Brain

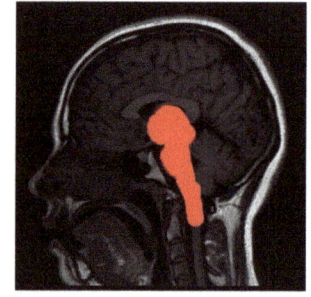

The image to the right shows an approximate delimitation of the region described in this work as the *reptilian brain*. From an evolutionary perspective, the brain first appeared as a complex gathering of nerves at the head end of the early reptiles. (Note that the rough anatomical representations here could never accurately capture the enormous complexity of the human brain.)

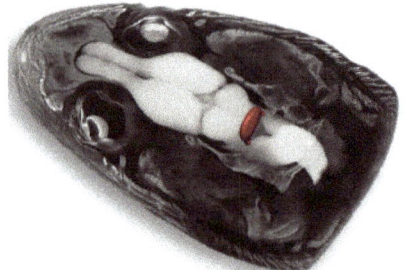

To the left, find the gross morphology of a reptile's brain to compare to the region in the adult human brain described as the reptilian brain above. The lizard brain reconstruction was computer generated from a microCT scan of a lizard.[2]

Emotional Brain

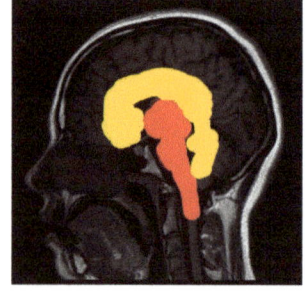

The image to the right shows the approximate delimitation of the region described in this work as the *emotional brain*. This region is a prominent feature of the brain of the early mammals.

Cognitive Brain

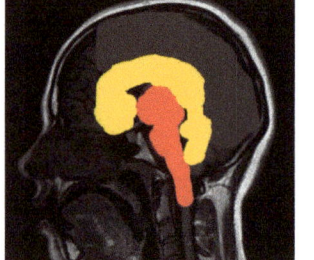

The image to the left shows the approximate delimitation of the region described in this work as the *cognitive brain*. Colloquially known as the *gray matter* because of the way it appears to the human eye, this is the region of the brain that is the home of thought and reason.

Prefrontal Cortex

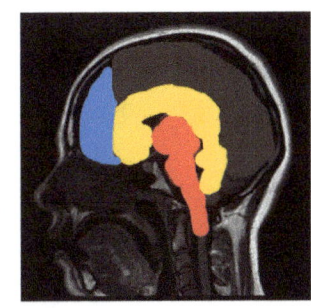

The image to the right shows the approximate delimitation of the region described in this work as the *prefrontal cortex*. Not only was this region the last to appear from an evolutionary perspective, but it is also the last to develop in the individual human, coming into play through adolescence and early adulthood.

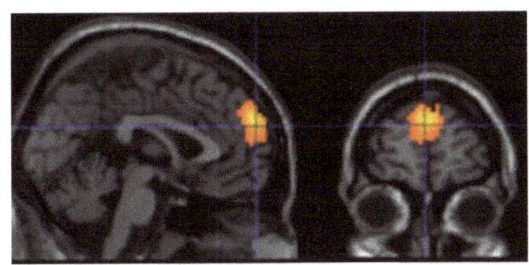

The yellow and orange hues in the functional magnetic resonance imaging (fMRI) scan to the left show nerve activity in an area of the prefrontal cortex.[3] To obtain an fMRI scan, the human subject is placed in an MRI scanner. During scanning, areas of the brain with incremental blood flow associated with increased nerve activity "light up" on the scan. Such fMRI scans can be used to research resting-state brain activity or brain activity during task performance. Using this imaging technology, scientists are able to understand the functional roles of different parts of the brain. (This image was chosen to illustrate the use of fMRI to record nerve activity in an area of the prefrontal cortex.)

Attention Focusing Consortium

The Attention Focusing Consortium (AFC) represents a functional (rather than anatomical) association of a number of nerve centers, and so could never be delineated against a simple radiological image. It is depicted as a linear "filter" in the body of the session for demonstration purposes only.

Components of the AFC, including the reticular activating system and the superior colliculus, are located in the brain stem. Other subcortical structures (i.e., nerve centers below the level of the cortex or cognitive brain region) that contribute to the function of the AFC include the thalamus and the basal ganglia.

In the session, the story of the evolution of the brain is told as if the AFC was added after the human brain was built; however, the complex filtering mechanism actually evolved in parallel with the development of the other regions of the brain.

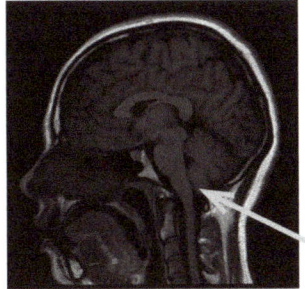

Brain stem

Scientists around the world are collaborating to map out the entire human brain and its estimated 85 billion neurons. The images below, a (side view) and b (view from below), show some of the vast multitude of connections in the brain of a healthy adult human. The connections were visualized using diffusion imaging tractography (a noninvasive application of MRI to generate elaborate three-dimensional images of individual nerve tracts with greater precision than regular MRI techniques).

The AFC plays a central role in focusing attention through a number of nerve centers that form electrical relay stations in this vast system. Picture an old-fashioned railroad engineer who was able to open and close specific railroad tracks, enabling trains (nerve messages) to pass through, or not. This crucial functional consortium protects us from the considerable peril we would otherwise face due to data overload and enables us to focus on critical (often survival-related) data.

a: 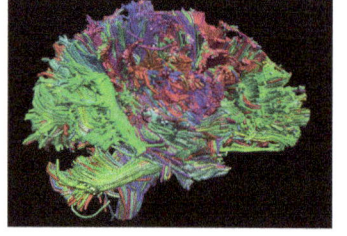   b: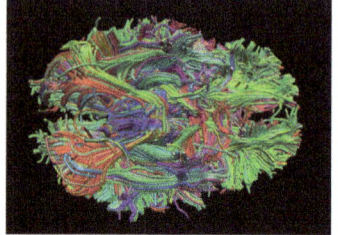

[1]Case courtesy of Frank Gaillard, Radiopaedia.rog, rID: 37605.

[2]Image modified from Macrì, S., Savriama, Y., Khan, I., & Di-Poï, N. (2019). Comparative analysis of squamate brains unveils multi-level variation in cerebellar architecture associated with locomotor specialization. *Nature Communications, 10,* 5560. https://doi.org/10.1038/s41467-019-13405-w (CC BY 4.0).

[3]Image modified from Zhang, Z., Luh, W. M., Duan, W., Zhou, G. D., Weinschenk, G., Anderson, A. K., & Dai, W. (2021). Longitudinal effects of meditation on brain resting-state functional connectivity. *Scientific Reports, 11,* 11361. https://doi.org/10.1038/s41598-021-90729-y (CC BY 4.0).

[4]Henrietta Howells, NatBrainLab (a: https://wellcomecollection.org/works/wb89yez7; b: https://wellcomecollection.org/works/vf6cqn2h) (CC BY 4.0).

Brain Operating System Model

The five-region *Brain Operating System* (BOS) model, foundational to this coaching, is an adaptation of the triune brain concept developed by Paul MacLean, an American physician and neuroscientist. MacLean developed this concept to provide a neurobiological and neuroevolutionary explanation of human psychology and behavior—he wanted to answer profound questions about the human brain–behavior link. MacLean conceptualized his triune brain concept based on extensive research and published it in detail in 1990 in a book titled *The Triune Brain in Evolution: Role in Paleocerebral Functions.*[1] In the Neurocentric Coaching BOS model, the brain regions referred to as the *reptilian, emotional,* and *cognitive* brains are based on MacLean's triune brain concept.

The other two BOS components, the prefrontal cortex and what is defined as the AFC, were added to incorporate the important roles these brain regions play in the attainment of personal mastery. There is much published research about the structure and function of the prefrontal cortex and the complex filtering mechanism, and about their influence on behavior. Two articles are listed below for optional further reading (prefrontal cortex[2] and AFC[3]).

[1]MacLean, P. D. (1990). *The triune brain in evolution: Role in paleocerebral functions.* Plenum Press.

[2]Dahl, C. J., Wilson-Mendenhall, C. D., & Davidson, R. J. (2020). The plasticity of well-being: A training-based framework for the cultivation of human flourishing. *Proceedings of the National Academy of Sciences, 117*(51), 32197–32206. https://doi.org/10.1073/pnas.2014859117

[3]Alves, P. N., Forkel, S. J., Corbetta, M., & de Schotten, M. T. (2022). The subcortical and neurochemical organization of the ventral and dorsal attention networks. *Communication Biology, 5,* 1343. https://doi.org/10.1038/s42003-022-04281-0

Hierarchical Structure

Top-Down Regulation

The brain's hierarchical structure enables voluntary control of emotions. This means that, by choice, cognition can be used to override fear. This process is referred to as the *top-down regulation* of emotions.

Automatic Fear Response

In the face of a perceived threat, the brain activates a fear response (fight, flight, or freeze). This activation is automatic—it is an adaptive safety reflex. Perceived threat can take many forms, including a sensory experience, a scary memory, or an anticipated event, any of which can quickly and easily activate the fear response. Because this adaptive, natural, reflexive response to threat is part of human biology, it cannot be prevented. However, it is possible to influence its behavioral effects, limiting the downstream impact of the fear messages being sent from the brain to the body.

Cognitive Override

Proactive engagement of the executive and cognitive functions of the brain can regulate the fear response within the brain itself. This process is termed *cognitive override* and can be applied when it is wise to do so, for example, when the perceived threat is not associated with real danger or when the unmodified fear response drives more risk than benefit.

Cognitive override involves putting the thinking brain in charge to assess the perceived threat. In doing this, thoughts are used to gain perspective on the threat and enable decisions about how best to respond to it. Application of this top-down process makes it possible to reconceptualize or give new meaning to a reflexive fear response, thus modulating its behavioral effects centrally.

The experience of having an anesthetic injection prior to dental work provides an example of the application of cognitive override. Anticipation of the pain, discomfort, and aftereffects of the injection is likely to activate a flight or freeze response, which may motivate avoidance of a dental appointment or at least engender negative feelings about a pending visit to the dentist. Cognitive override is applied by choosing to think about the positive benefits and outcomes of dental treatment. Thus, cognition is used to rationalize and reconceptualize the reflexive fear response to dental work, thereby taking control of it and preventing it from blocking necessary action to promote dental health.

Commitment

 **Between this session and the next, I commit to the following:**

☐ Becoming aware of how information is filtered through my AFC.

☐ Practicing shifting my awareness from one brain level to another.

☐ Revising my ideal future summary using all regions of my BOS.

Next up, in Session 3: *Understanding How Your Brain Talks*, you'll learn the three languages of the brain and how to use them to release yourself from the grip of fear.

"The greatest discovery of any generation is that human beings can **alter their lives** by **altering the attitudes of their mind.**"

—ALBERT SCHWEITZER

SESSION 3

UNDERSTANDING HOW YOUR BRAIN TALKS

Welcome to Session 3! Now that you understand your *Brain Operating System* (BOS), let's explore how your brain communicates with you.

Set aside two hours to complete the session content and work through the activities. Spend an additional hour on your Mastery Missions before progressing further.

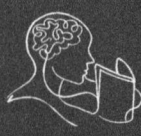

In this session, you will:

- Discover the three distinct languages of your brain.

- Realize the inherent challenges in differentiating thoughts, feelings, and fears—a vital *Brain Operating System* (BOS) skill most are never taught.

- Begin to recognize your own thoughts, feelings, and fears with the understanding that they come from different levels of your brain and that mastery of this task is the first step to becoming a brain master.

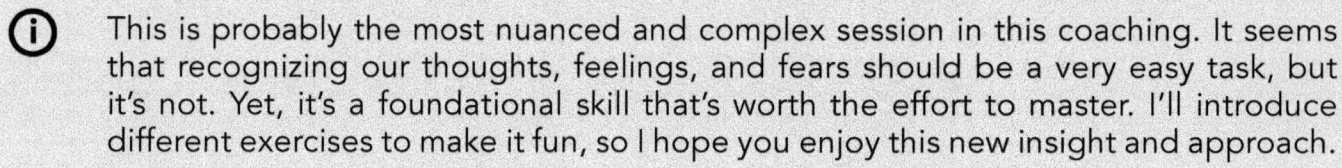

(i) This is probably the most nuanced and complex session in this coaching. It seems that recognizing our thoughts, feelings, and fears should be a very easy task, but it's not. Yet, it's a foundational skill that's worth the effort to master. I'll introduce different exercises to make it fun, so I hope you enjoy this new insight and approach.

The Three Languages of the Brain

Thoughts, feelings, and fears are the three languages of the brain.

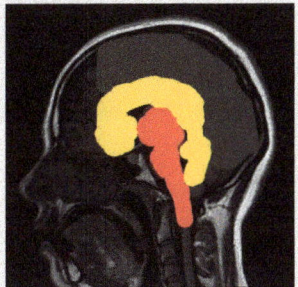

1. The **reptilian brain** uses the voice of **fear**.

2. The **emotional brain** speaks through **feelings** or emotions.

3. The **cognitive brain** expresses itself via **thoughts**.

Let's begin with an activity to test your understanding.

Decide whether each statement is a thought, a feeling, or a fear. Then, circle your answer. There are 24 statements.

I fear I've reached the end of my rope.	Thought Feeling Fear
I feel like a failure.	Thought Feeling Fear
I deserve more.	Thought Feeling Fear
I'm scared they'll think I'm a fraud.	Thought Feeling Fear
I wonder if I'll ever succeed.	Thought Feeling Fear
I'm afraid of consequences out of my control.	Thought Feeling Fear
I'm afraid my decision will aggravate the situation.	Thought Feeling Fear
I'm haunted by the idea of a life without purpose.	Thought Feeling Fear
I can't sleep because my mind is racing.	Thought Feeling Fear
I'm feeling helpless.	Thought Feeling Fear

I have a deep sense of calm.	Thought Feeling Fear
I'll never get my dream job; I don't have what it takes.	Thought Feeling Fear
I'm filled with excitement for my future.	Thought Feeling Fear
My heart aches after hearing the bad news.	Thought Feeling Fear
I can visualize what the future holds.	Thought Feeling Fear
I'm ready to make my dreams come true.	Thought Feeling Fear
I see no reasonable alternative approach.	Thought Feeling Fear
I cannot decide.	Thought Feeling Fear
I feel stuck.	Thought Feeling Fear
I'm tuned in to my personal strengths.	Thought Feeling Fear
I'm proud of myself for speaking up.	Thought Feeling Fear
I need more willpower.	Thought Feeling Fear
I'm worried it's an uphill battle.	Thought Feeling Fear
I feel terrible about the way I spoke to my partner.	Thought Feeling Fear

Some of the answers may surprise you!

Here's a summary of how I categorize each of the statements you just worked through:

THOUGHTS	FEELINGS	FEARS
I'm tuned in to my personal strengths.	I'm proud of myself for speaking up.	I wonder if I'll ever succeed.
I cannot decide.	My heart aches after hearing the bad news.	I'm afraid my decision will aggravate the situation.
I'm ready to make my dreams come true.	I'm filled with excitement for my future.	I fear I've reached the end of my rope.
I see no reasonable alternative approach.	I'm feeling helpless.	I'm afraid of consequences out of my control.
I deserve more.	I feel like a failure.	I'm scared they'll think I'm a fraud.
I can visualize what the future holds.	I have a deep sense of calm.	I'll never get my dream job; I don't have what it takes.
I need more willpower.	I feel stuck.	I'm haunted by the idea of a life without purpose.
I can't sleep because my mind is racing.	I feel terrible about the way I spoke to my partner.	I'm worried it's an uphill battle.

Differentiating thoughts, feelings, and fears is not easy.

I love doing this activity in big workshops. Generally, participants get about 74% of the answers wrong, and the beauty of this is that, **when we're wrong, we learn**.

If you're feeling a bit confused right now about how to distinguish **thoughts**, **feelings**, and **fears**, don't worry! I'm about to teach you how to do this. We'll consider each brain language in detail, and then I'll give you some feedback on the activity you've just completed.

I invite you to read the transcript of a real-life discussion from one of my workshops. One participant ("Ari") shares a feeling. *But is it really a feeling?*

As you observe how I guide Ari through this discussion, consider how you would categorize his statement. Is it a feeling, a thought, or a fear?

Identify Thoughts, Feelings, and Fears

 **Is it a feeling, a thought, or a fear?**

Roddy: *Who wants to share a feeling about your dream?*

Ari: *One of the feelings I was having was the state I want to be in for myself in the future. I feel like I really strongly want to be that person. More than I am now.*

Roddy: *"I feel that that person is somebody I strongly want to be." Is that a feeling?...I'm not answering. Is that a feeling?*

Ari: *I mean, I could tell you it's not.*

Roddy: *Why is that not a feeling?*

Ari: *It's a thought.*

Roddy: *Tell me why you think it's a thought. Repeat exactly what you said.*

Ari: *I said I feel strongly about wanting to be that future version of myself.*

Roddy: *Pause. Why is that a thought and not a feeling?*

Ari: *Because it's coming from the cognitive.*

Roddy: *How do you know that? Why is it not coming from your heart?*

Ari: *I don't know why!*

Roddy: *So, you just sense that it's not a feeling?*

Ari: *Well, if you think of a feeling words list, I can't hear any of the feeling words.*

Roddy: *Okay, you can't hear the words we normally associate with a basic feeling.*

Ari: *It's tough, but if it's in the future, is that more a thought? And if you're feeling it's in the now?*

Roddy: *That's an interesting observation. Me, I felt nothing when you spoke. I felt nothing! Was there any temperature to your statement? Was there any warmth? Passion? Emotion? Love? How was your voice? Flat.*

Ari: *Well, the word "strongly" feels like...*

Roddy: *"Strongly!" You put the word in there. You used your very smart intellect. You said, "Roddy wants a feeling, so I'm going to put in a kind of emotion word there." But it came from your brain. Did you see that? You tricked us.*

Most of us aren't able to distinguish whether we're thinking, feeling, or fearing.

While reflecting on the process of writing down his desired future, Ari categorizes "I feel I really strongly want to be that person" as a feeling statement.

I prompt him to consider further: Is the statement a feeling, a thought, or a fear? Pretty soon, you see Ari change his mind; he says, "No, I can tell you it's not [a feeling]"—although he isn't sure why. Eventually, I explain that it *is* a thought. But why?

A more straightforward way to explain why this is a thought is to first talk about **what a feeling is**.

For the purpose of learning the three brain languages, you're learning how to categorize a "pure thought." In truth, statements may include input from two brain levels at the same time and are often hybrids of thoughts, feelings, and fears.

Thoughts and fears are both streams of logic:

- A **fear** is a negative logic stream that evokes a **negative emotion**.

- A **thought** is a positive logic stream that evokes a **positive emotion**, or at least not a negative one. A neutral thought can quickly evoke fear.

Feelings

Feelings have five qualities:

1. Feelings have an **emotional temperature**.

2. Feelings are expressed using **descriptive words** that symbolize the presence of emotion.

3. Feelings may be directed and **felt in one or more parts of the body**. You often put your hand somewhere on your body, maybe over your heart, throat, or belly (usually away from your head), when you describe an emotion.

4. Feelings **draw you deeper into conversation**. You may lean forward to listen intently, hanging on every word, eager to find out what happens next. You may also notice more nonverbal cues.

5. Feelings often **resonate deeply with others**. We have special nerves in our brains called "mirror neurons" that enable us to empathize—to feel the pain of another as though it were our own actual pain.

Feelings can be either positive or negative.

To distinguish between the two, you have to go behind the emotion:

- When you go behind a positive emotion, you can anticipate finding a **thought** (cognitive brain).

- When you go behind a negative emotion, you can anticipate finding a **fear** (reptilian brain).

 **Feelings can have a negative emotional temperature.**

Rae: Can I share a feeling? I'm nervous! So, the fear would be the fear of failure. But the nervousness, it's like, I can feel it in my stomach. It's...it feels real.

Roddy: About your dream?

Rae: About the dream, yeah.

Roddy: Is it a feeling?

Rae: Nervousness...is negative?

Roddy: It's negative, for sure. She even showed me! She made a face. She said, "Ahhh! This is grabbing me by the guts, Roddy! I'm noticing a feeling inside of me. I just put this beautiful dream out there. Ahhh...I'm not sure I can make it." Did you see that? I'm extrapolating. I'm a little wilder than she was in the moment. But, did you see that? That was a feeling. How would she have stated that as a fear?

Rae: I'm afraid it won't happen, or...

Roddy: I'm afraid that I'm going to be embarrassed in front of myself when I don't reach my dreams. Is that a feeling? It evokes feeling pretty quickly, but it's not a feeling. That's just a statement—a negative statement. There's a fear behind it.

"I'm nervous" is a negative emotion.

Rae expressed a feeling statement with the following qualities:

- A negative emotional temperature

- An uncomfortable sensation in her stomach

- Nonverbal cues: wrinkles on her forehead, eyebrows up and drawn together, eyes opened wider, fists clenched, body hunched over

- An evocation of empathy in the other workshop participants

The negative emotion Rae experiences tells us that she's operating from her reptilian brain.

Fears

Fear has three qualities:

1. Fear initiates a **fight**, **flight**, or **freeze response** to keep you safe in potentially dangerous situations.

    There are a range of intensities to the traditional fight, flight, and freeze responses. You don't need to be propelled into immediate action. A fear may present with the following reactions:

    -   **Fight**: Disagree, resist, push back, argue, dominate, attack, pulverize

    -   **Flight**: Back off, turn away, melt away, escape, bolt, flee

    -   **Freeze**: Hesitate, quiet down, evade, stop, go to ground, disappear

2. Fear triggers **physiological changes in the body**, such as tightening of muscles, shortness of breath, dilating of pupils, increased heart rate, trembling, sweating, and sometimes a strained or higher-pitched vocal tone.

3. Fear is a deeply negative thought. It quickly evokes **negative emotion**.

It's human nature to avoid fear, but continuing to do so will only leave you at fear's mercy, stuck doing the same things only to achieve the same results. To attain your ideal future, you must learn to **override your reptilian brain** and **manage your fears**.

Do you remember from Session 2 how to take control of your fears? **Think your way past fear—** it's simple, but it's not easy.

Here's a moment I will never forget...

During a live workshop, Geoff, one of the participants, spoke up. What he didn't realize at the time was that he was spontaneously articulating the full impact of mastering the *Brain Operating System*...

> "The more I thought about it,
>
> the more I didn't have to worry."

Thoughts

Thoughts have four important characteristics:

1. Thoughts are **positive statements** with no temperature.

2. Thoughts are **concepts** we use to relate to one another using the cognitive part of our brain. Thoughts translate ideas into words that we can share.

3. Thoughts use a **matter-of-fact, emotionless tone** that shows little or no emotion.

4. Thoughts can be used to start the **positive feeling response** in the emotional brain.

Example: "Matter-of-fact" thought

 **I have the resources and knowledge to make it happen.**

Roddy: Who's got a thought? Somebody?

Participant: I have the resources and knowledge to make it happen.

Roddy: Is that a thought? Yes! Why is that a thought?

Participant: Because it's not a feeling and it's not a fear.

Roddy: Definitely not a fear. It's a positive statement. Did it have any temperature to it? No. She said it in the most matter-of-fact way: "I have the resources and the knowledge to make it happen."

Example: Thought disguised as a question

 **How do I get there?**

Participant: So, I wrote down, "How do I get there?"

Roddy: "How do I get there?" Is that a thought? How did she say it?

Participant: I said it matter of fact. I think it's a thought.

> **Roddy:** No temperature, right? And definitely, I don't feel a negative temperature. Now, you could absolutely ask that in a way that said: "How am I going to get there? I don't know how I'm going to get there. How do I get there?" And it's going to evoke a response, something like this: "When I have the resources and knowledge to get there."
>
> "How am I going to get there?" Well, we can draw a little line from A to B, and then B to C, and then we're going to pursue that line.
>
> It's a thought. It was a statement. It happens to have a question mark at the end. That's a different kind of thought. But it wasn't laden with emotion. And it definitely wasn't a fear.

Thought 1: "I have the resources and knowledge to make it happen."

The participant shared this statement using a matter-of-fact tone. It is a thought because it's a positive statement with no temperature.

Thought 2: "How do I get there?"

Two main ideas make this question a thought:

1. A matter-of-fact tone indicates the absence of temperature. This thought is likely to elicit a logical and reasoned response.

2. The statement is not laden with emotion.

Because it poses a question, this statement is a different kind of thought—but a thought, nevertheless.

Revisit

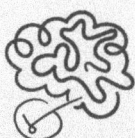 **Now that we've covered the three languages of the brain in detail, think back to the thought/feeling/fear categorization activity you did earlier in the session.**

It's time to elevate your understanding of how to differentiate thoughts, feelings, and fears. Review each section below to better understand why specific statements were categorized as thoughts, feelings, or fears.

Thoughts

I wake up at night feeling heart palpitations.

This statement is a thought because you use it to share your experience with another person, perhaps your doctor. Even though you may experience heart palpitations as a fearful fight, flight, or freeze response, this statement has no temperature. You're simply using these words to communicate a fact. If you look deeper, you may uncover a fear that triggers your heart palpitations, but this statement, itself, does not convey emotion or fear.

I see no reasonable alternative approach.

This statement is a thought because it does not convey emotion and it has no temperature. It communicates that you have engaged reason and logic (using your cognitive brain) to explore all your options and that this is your conclusion.

However, you could supplement this thought with a feeling statement. For example, "I see no reasonable alternative approach [thought], and I'm feeling confident about my decision [feeling]." Or, "I see no reasonable alternative approach [thought], and I'm scared about the future [fear]."

I'm ready to make my dreams come true.

This statement is a thought because it communicates a decision and intention to reach for your dream life. It's a positive statement that could start a positive feeling response in your emotional brain, evoking such feelings as empowerment, determination, motivation, or inspiration. However, this thought statement itself does not convey emotion.

105

Feelings

I'm filled with excitement for my future.

This statement communicates a feeling because it has an emotional temperature. The presence of the word "excitement" signifies an emotional state. The specific emotion may lack clarity, as it could be a positive emotion like joy or a negative emotion like anxiety. Nonetheless, both have an emotional temperature.

Feeling statements may have corresponding thoughts. For example, "I'm filled with excitement for my future [feeling] because now I have a plan to get there [thought]."

I feel terrible about the way I spoke to my partner.

This statement is a feeling. It carries emotional weight and communicates a negative feeling. You may even feel the physical sensation of the burden caused by this negative emotion.

However, this is not a fear statement because it reflects *how* you're feeling—terrible about the way you spoke—but not *why* you're feeling like this. A potential fear underlying this feeling could be, "I feel terrible about the way I spoke to my partner [feeling] because I'm sure my words have hurt them deeply [fear]."

I feel like a failure.

This statement expresses negative emotion. It reflects profound disappointment in yourself, which may literally manifest as a heavy-hearted physical sensation.

It is not a fear itself because you feel the emotion in the present moment. However, the statement may quickly evoke fear. An underlying fear associated with this could be, "I am a failure." The distinction lies in the subtle underlying fear of "I am"—being labeled as someone who consistently fails.

Fears

I'm worried it's an uphill battle.

This fear statement communicates deep negative emotion and points to the fight response. Words like "worried" and "uphill battle" suggest fear of an ongoing challenge, perhaps a conflict that may not have a straightforward resolution or a complex problem that will not be easy to solve. Your fight reactions could include disagreement, resistance, or pushback.

I fear I've reached the end of my rope.

This deeply negative statement points to an ongoing fear of hopelessness and helplessness. Fearing that you have no options, you may scream to be heard (fight), turn away from a challenge (flight), or stop trying completely (freeze).

I wonder if I'll ever succeed.

This statement communicates self-doubt and the fear of perpetual failure. Fearing that you'll never have what it takes, you may argue for your limitations (fight), withdraw from opportunities (flight), or try to make yourself invisible (freeze). These fight, flight, and freeze responses limit your chances of success.

The Subtle Voice of Fear

 **Throughout your journey toward unstoppable, your reptilian brain will speak up—probably quite often!**

That's okay. It's doing exactly what it's been trained over millions of years to do. But now you're much better at hearing the voice of fear because you've learned that the call to fight, run, or hide isn't always obvious. In fact, it's often quite subtle. Fear can be disguised as intellectual ideas or questions like:

- Now that I've failed, what happens?

- What will they think of me?

- Why would things change now?

- Why would my dream suddenly come true?

- Why should I be taken seriously?

- What's so special about me?

Subtle or obvious, soft or loud, your reptilian brain will make itself heard. It can keep you stuck even when there is no genuine threat. But **you can silence your fears**. Your brain is intricately structured, with a wise override mechanism designed to silence the voice of the reptilian brain. To do this, you need help from both your **cognitive brain** and your **emotional brain**.

> The key is to use your **cognitive** and **emotional** brains together to create a **belief** so powerful it overrides the fear and resistance arising from your reptilian brain.

The Great Flip Flopper

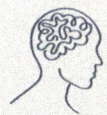

Here's a secret to using the cognitive and emotional brains together.

So far, we've discussed that a "pure thought" arising in your cognitive brain is a statement with no temperature.

But that doesn't mean thoughts lack power. Thoughts have power precisely because they evoke the emotional brain to pour out positive feelings. As a result, thoughts are quickly activated by adding the energy of emotion.

There are two inherent attributes of the emotional brain:

1. It serves as a **turbobooster** that magnifies the voice that triggers it.

2. It is a **diagnostic tool** that allows me (and ultimately you, too) to determine whether thoughts or fears are dominant in your brain at any one moment.

Right now, as you read these words, your emotional brain is actively listening to hear which voice is the loudest—that of positive thoughts (from the cognitive brain) or that of fear (from the reptilian brain). Then, it gravitates to the loudest voice. Thought evokes positive feelings; fear evokes negative feelings. For this reason, I call the **emotional brain** the "**great flip flopper**."

When the loudest voice is **thought**, emotions are positive, but they can flip to become negative quickly, as soon as the voice of **fear** dominates.

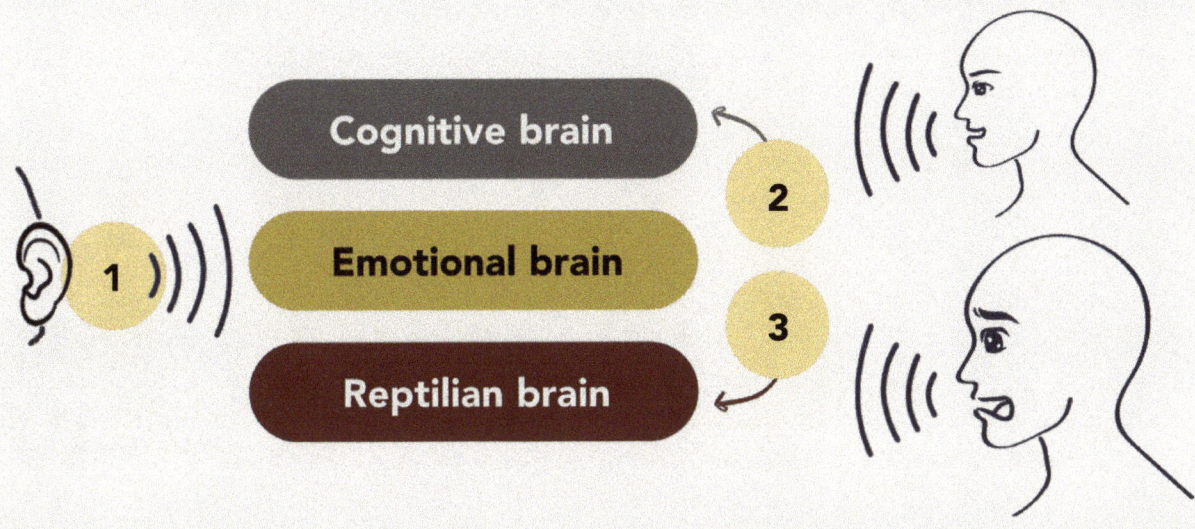

1. The emotional brain is listening.

Your emotional brain is always listening to your internal conversation. Which way will it flip?

2. The wise voice of an owl represents the cognitive brain.

When the voice of the cognitive brain dominates, it attracts the attention of the emotional brain and **exudes positive emotion**.

When this happens, you amplify and enrich **belief**. Messages from the cognitive brain continue to encourage you. The emotional brain magnifies your positive thoughts and propels you forward, urging you to move toward your dreams.

3. The voice of an alligator represents the reptilian brain.

When the swift, loud, and powerful voice of the alligator—the reptilian voice of fear—shouts the loudest, it overwhelms the quivering emotional brain and evokes **negative** emotion.

When this happens, you often experience **doubt**. You continue to hear the persistent warnings of the reptilian brain, alerting you to all of the potential risks and the looming possibility of failure if you venture beyond your comfort zone to pursue a new career.

And the boosting capacity of the **emotional brain** magnifies—sometimes enormously—the voice that triggers it.

When the voice of the **reptilian brain** is loudest, the emotional brain responds with a flood of negative emotion. It turboboosts the voice of fear to drive **doubt**.

When voice of the **cognitive brain** is loudest, the emotional brain responds with positive emotion. The brain has activated a turbobooster behind the positive thought to drive **belief**.

Remember, belief plus desire overrides fear and enables success.

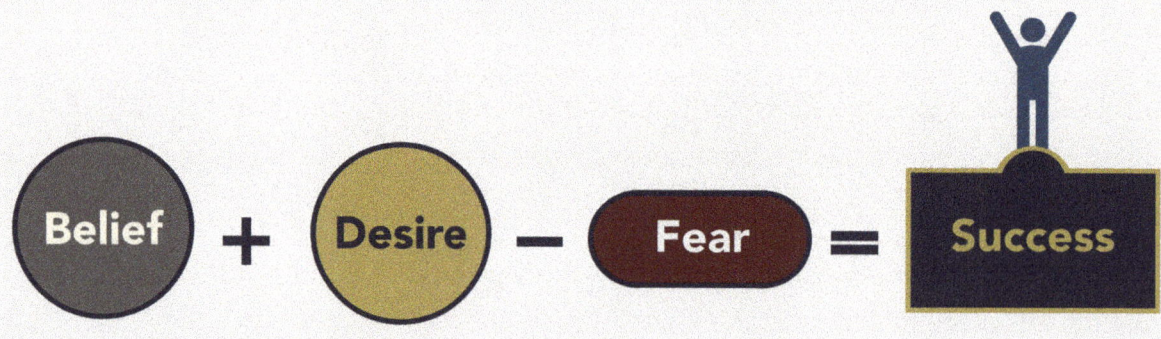

Belief + Desire − Fear = Success

Belief originates in the **cognitive brain** and can be turboboosted by desire.

Desire is activated when the **emotional brain** is harnessed to get behind your positive thoughts with positive emotions.

Enliven Your Ideal Future

 EXERCISE 1

Enliven Your Ideal Future

ACTION 1 OF 3

Reevaluate

Refer back to how you categorized your thoughts, feelings, and fears in your third Mastery Mission from Session 2. Were you able to recognize the three languages of your brain—and the parts of the brain they come from? Use the following points to determine whether you categorized your statements correctly.

Thoughts

- Do they lack emotional temperature?

- Are they written in a matter-of-fact tone?

- Are they positive statements, or at least not negative?

Feelings

- Do they have an emotional temperature?

- Do they elicit physical sensations?

- Do they include descriptive words?

- Would they naturally draw someone deeper into a conversation?

Fears

- Do you notice a negative emotional temperature?

- Do you feel any physiological changes, such as an increased heart rate?

ACTION 2 OF 3

Reflect

Reflect on the process of categorizing your thoughts (cognitive brain), feelings (emotional brain), and fears (reptilian brain).

- Did you find it easier to differentiate thoughts, feelings, or fears?

- Which language was the easiest?

- Which was the most difficult?

- Were you surprised by any aspect of your reflections?

Make notes below about your observations.

ACTION 3 OF 3

Revise

Use your knowledge of the three brain languages to revise your ideal future summary statements using the space below (or edit your digital document).

Focus on highlighting positive emotions originating from your emotional brain. To do this:

- Enhance the richness by incorporating sensory details, such as vivid sights, captivating sounds, delightful sensations, enchanting smells, and tantalizing tastes, immersing yourself deeply in the feelings of your envisioned reality.

- Elevate the emotional temperature of your thought statements by incorporating uplifting adjectives like *radiant*, *limitless*, *vibrant*, *joyful*, and *thriving*, as well as adverbs such as *boldly*, *wholeheartedly*, *brilliantly*, *effortlessly*, and *abundantly*.

If you notice any fear statements in your ideal future, use your cognitive brain to replace them with neutral or positive thoughts.

Well done!

As you reflect on your ideal future statements now, your thoughts, feelings, and fears have likely shifted. Continue to come back to these statements and enjoy the soaring emotions drawing you toward your dreams.

Mastery Missions

Congratulations!

Well done in applying yourself to this complex new skill.

At the start of the session, I mentioned that this is the most complex session in the coaching. Some grasp the concepts quickly, but most require ample time and practice to master these skills. In learning to accurately label your thoughts, feelings, and fears, you are facilitating your overall brain mastery.

Now that you've completed the *Enliven Your Ideal Future* exercise, you're ready to start your Mastery Missions.

MASTERY MISSION 1

Revisit Thoughts, Feelings, and Fears

Before you begin this Mastery Mission, recall the defining characteristics of thoughts, feelings, and fears:

Thoughts

- Are positive statements with no temperature.

- Are concepts we use to relate to one another using the cognitive region of the brain.

- Use a matter-of-fact, emotionless tone.

- Can be used to start the positive feeling response in the emotional brain.

Feelings

- Have an emotional temperature.

- Are expressed using descriptive words that instantaneously elicit an emotional response.

- May be directed or felt in one or more parts of the body.

- Draw the listener deeper into conversation.

- Often resonate deeply with others.

Fears

- Initiate a fight, flight, or freeze response, associated with the following actions:
  - o Fight: Disagree, resist, push back, argue, dominate, attack, pulverize
  - o Flight: Back off, turn away, melt away, escape, bolt, flee
  - o Freeze: Hesitate, quiet down, evade, stop, go to ground, disappear
- Trigger physiological changes in the body.
- Are deeply negative thoughts that quickly evoke negative emotion.

ACTION 1 OF 4

Pause

Take a mindful moment. Pause to shift the seat of your awareness into your prefrontal cortex.

ACTION 2 OF 4

Identify thoughts

Identify the thought statements you wrote in the third Mastery Mission from Session 2. Write down all of them here. If needed, recategorize your statements by transferring any feelings to Action 3 and fears to Action 4.

ACTION 3 OF 4

Identify feelings

Now, locate your feelings in the third Mastery Mission from Session 2. Determine whether those statements are, in fact, feelings. If you uncover a fear, write it in Action 4. If you discover a thought, write it in Action 2. Categorize your emotions below.

Negative	Positive

ACTION 4 OF 4

Identify fears

Finally, locate the fear statements you wrote in the third Mastery Mission from Session 2. You've likely written a combination of fears and emotions. Identify your fear statements, and write them down on this page. If you spot an emotion, transfer it to Action 3.

 **MASTERY MISSION 2**

Practice Observing the Brain Languages

ACTION 1 OF 1

Practice daily

Engage in a daily, dedicated **practice** before starting the next session to master differentiating between thoughts, feelings, and fears. Use any of the suggested approaches, or create your own.

- **Ask and answer**: *What am I thinking? What am I feeling? What am I fearing?*

- **Monitor** your thoughts, feelings, and fears. Choose a time of day or regular task in your daily routine, such as brushing your teeth or stopping at a red light. This will act as a prompt to remind you to practice identifying your thoughts, feelings, and fears.

- **Reflect** regularly on your ideal future as a means to monitor your thoughts, feelings, and fears.

- **Track** how your thoughts, feelings, and fears gradually evolve over time. Keep your reflections in a daily journal.

Document your preferred strategies below.

Supplemental Science

You're invited to delve into the supporting research on the topics covered in this session. Keep in mind that exploring the supplemental science is optional. You can return anytime to read more about the underlying science of the *Brain Operating System* methodology.

Autonomic Nervous System

The human nervous system can be seen as two primary and integrated systems, one known as the *central nervous system* and the other the *peripheral nervous system*. The brain is part of the central nervous system, and if we know how, we can voluntarily take control of this highly complex nerve hub. In contrast, the autonomic nervous system (a part of the peripheral nervous system) operates outside of our voluntary control, regulating vital physiological processes 24 hours a day. Although it is possible to indirectly influence this system, it mostly functions outside of our conscious awareness.

The autonomic nervous system has two subsystems: the *sympathetic* and *parasympathetic* nervous systems. These subsystems control the same body functions but have opposite physiological effects. The sympathetic nervous system activates the body's reflexive "fight-or-flight" response, putting the body on alert, whereas the parasympathetic nervous system (known as the "rest-and-digest" system) deactivates the stress response, calming the body and maintaining body functions at their normal activity levels.

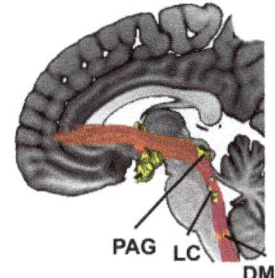

The images to the left and right show some of the subcortical neural connections (in color) and nerve centers (in yellow) that are associated with the autonomic nervous system (visualized using diffusion imaging tractography).[1]

Nerve centers in the reptilian region of the brain, including the periaqueductal gray (PAG), locus coeruleus (LC), and dorsal medulla seed (DMS), regulate involuntary body functions essential for survival, such as breathing, heart rate, balance, blood pressure, digestion, and reflexes (e.g., swallowing and blinking). As such, this brain region is an important component of the autonomic nervous system.

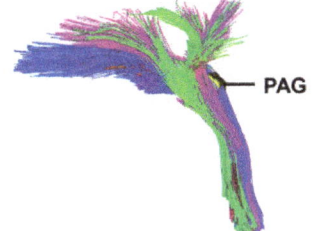

[1]Image modified from Reisert, M., Weiller, C., & Hosp, J. A. (2021). Displaying the autonomic processing network in humans – a global tractography approach. *NeuroImage, 231*, Article 117852. https://doi.org/10.1016/j.neuroimage.2021.117852 (CC BY 4.0).

Sympathetic Nervous System

When fear dominates, the sympathetic nervous system takes over.

Fight-or-Flight Physiological Changes

When the fear response is activated by the perception of a potential threat or danger, it takes microseconds for the sympathetic nervous system to take control and effect physiological changes that prepare the body to confront the danger (fight) or run from it (flight). Both these actions require heightened mental acuity and physical activity, so the sympathetic nervous system, via the release of stress hormones such as epinephrine (adrenaline) and cortisol, stimulates increased blood flow to the brain, heart, lungs, and skeletal muscles. This diversion of blood flow increases the supply of oxygen and glucose to these body parts, facilitating the metabolism of enough cellular energy to support alertness, physical strength, and rapid movement.

Maximizing Glucose and Oxygen Supply

Other changes that maximize the supply of oxygen and glucose to the brain and skeletal muscles include an increase in heart rate and blood pressure, more rapid breathing and dilated airways to increase blood oxygen uptake, and an increase in the production of glucose in the liver. In parallel with these physiological stimulations, some body functions (e.g., saliva production and digestion) are inhibited to divert energy resources away from physiological processes nonessential to the fight-or-flight response.

Other Changes

Other changes associated with fight-or-flight readiness include an increase in pupil dilation for visual acuity and a decrease in blood supply to the skin, linked to the diversion of blood flow to the vital organs and skeletal muscles.

Rapid Reaction, Then Restoration

All the fight-or-flight physiological changes enable and support rapid reaction to potential danger, thus increasing the chances of survival. Once a perceived threat or potential danger is no longer imminent, body functions are restored to pre-activation levels.

Parasympathetic Nervous System

When thoughts dominate, so does the parasympathetic nervous system.

After a stressful or scary experience, the parasympathetic nervous system automatically returns the body to a calm and relaxed state. Heart rate and other body functions stimulated into heightened activity by the sympathetic nervous system return to normal levels, and processes such as saliva production and digestion are reactivated.

Under control of the parasympathetic nervous system, the body is able to rest and recover from fear and stress. Physiological balance that supports routine day-to-day functioning is restored and maintained.

Although the parasympathetic nervous system activates automatically, the hierarchical wiring of the brain makes it possible to choose to use cognition to override the fear response and return the body to a state of calm. When the cognitive brain is in control and thoughts dominate, so does the parasympathetic nervous system.

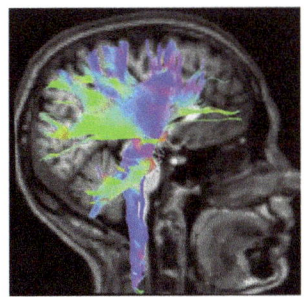

The image to the left shows some of the neural connections that run between the cognitive, emotional, and reptilian regions of the brain, enabling cognitive override of fear and restoration of the parasympathetic state of calm.[1] The structural connectivity between these regions was visualized using diffusion tensor imaging.

[1]Image modified from Liu, J., Likhtik, E., Shereen, A. D., Dennis-Tiwary, T. A., & Casaccia, P. (2020). White matter plasticity in anxiety: Disruption of neural network synchronization during threat-safety discrimination. *Frontiers in Cellular Neuroscience, 14*, Article 587053. https://doi.org/10.3389/fncel.2020.587053 (CC BY 4.0).

Chronic Stress

Ancient Versus Modern Stressors

The stressful situations our early ancestors faced were mainly physical and transient—running to escape or to hunt, or fighting to protect themselves. Modern humans face a very different stress landscape. Today, most of our stressors are mental or emotional in nature. We seldom need to physically escape, chase, or fight, and it is often the *anticipation* of a potential threat, rather than an actual danger, that activates our fear response. In addition, modern stressors tend to be experienced on a sustained basis.

The Modern Epidemic

Ancestral humans survived via acute stress. Their reptilian brain protected them by triggering the release of epinephrine (adrenaline) and cortisol, which activated their sympathetic nervous system. They were able to manage temporary crises by putting these stress hormones to good use to support physical reactions. Once a stressful experience was over, their stress hormone levels dropped and their parasympathetic nervous system calmed them down, restoring their physiological processes to resting levels.

In contrast, modern humans struggle with chronic stress. As with our ancestors, our reptilian brains respond to stress by triggering the release of epinephrine (adrenaline) and cortisol to activate our sympathetic nervous systems and enable us to manage stressful situations. However, in the absence of actual danger that requires a physical reaction, and under the influence of sustained stress, the prolonged and excessive action of the reptilian brain results in prolonged, persistent physical expressions of stress. Our parasympathetic nervous system is not able to restore and maintain a state of balance.

Chronic Stress Impacts Health and Well-Being

Our ancient design leaves us only modestly equipped to cope with the stressors of the modern era. We remain well suited to dealing with physical danger, but a surplus of epinephrine (adrenaline) and cortisol, the consequence of omnipresent mental and emotional distress, has significant negative impacts on our health and happiness.

Epinephrine (adrenaline) activates the cardiovascular system, even in response to mental and emotional stressors. However, to manage these types of stressors, we do not need an energized cardiovascular response to support physical reactions. Sustained epinephrine (adrenaline) production holds the cardiovascular system in an activated state, which invites serious health risks like high blood pressure and heart disease.

Excess cortisol, resulting from prolonged stress, has a negative impact on the inflammatory and immune systems, promoting inflammation and suppressing immunity. Chronic inflammation increases the risk of heart disease, diabetes, and cancer, while recurrent elevation in cortisol reduces the efficacy of our immune system—we become more prone to infections and take longer to recover from them.

Other physical effects of chronic stress include insomnia, digestive problems, headaches, and muscle tension and pain. Chronic stress can have a negative impact on our motivation, productivity, and outlook on life, leaving us feeling anxious, overwhelmed, and stuck.

Freedom From Chronic Stress

By mastering our BOS, we can free ourselves from the burden of chronic stress. The most important action is to recognize and address the pervasive negative emotions that alert us to the chronic activation of the reptilian brain. Once we have recognized the fears behind these negative emotions, we can use cognitive override to silence the voice of fear and free ourselves from the deeply entrenched modern ailment we call chronic stress.

You can also read more about stress and how to manage it wisely in my first book, *BodyWHealth: Journey to Abundance.*

Commitment

 **Between this session and the next, I commit to the following:**

☐ Practicing recognizing my thoughts, feelings, and fears on a daily basis.

☐ Enlivening my ideal future statements with descriptive and sensory details that evoke my emotional brain.

Next up, in Session 4: *Owning the Office of the CEO*, we'll dive deeper into the function of the prefrontal cortex and why it's essential to use this part of the brain to be the CEO of your life. Plus, you'll master a 5-step process to move past stoppable moments.

> "What we are today comes from our thoughts of yesterday, and our present thoughts build our life of tomorrow: Our life is the creation of our mind."
>
> —BUDDHA

OWNING THE OFFICE OF THE CEO

Welcome to Session 4! Now that you've practiced differentiating thoughts, feelings, and fears, you're ready to learn how to use your prefrontal cortex to achieve masterful clarity and gain perspective, empowering you to become the CEO of your own life.

Plan to spend at least two hours completing the session content and another hour working through your Mastery Missions.

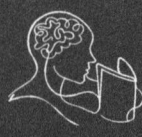

In this session, you will:

- Learn to harness the perspective and potential of your prefrontal cortex.

- Uncover the power of a pause to take refuge from the swirling chaos of thoughts, feelings, and fears and make clear, calm decisions with unwavering clarity.

- Master a 5-step process to work with (and not against) your *Brain Operating System* (BOS) to gain the clarity and perspective required to move past stoppable moments.

The Office of the CEO

To become unstoppable, you need to become the CEO of your life.

Becoming the CEO of your life means being the **boss of your life**, reclaiming the leadership role from your brain. Before learning about the BOS, you were enslaved to your brain. But after completing this coaching, you will be CEO of your own life, your BOS responding to *your* authority—and not the other way around. This, in turn, ensures you can:

- **Make quality decisions** about the major and minor aspects of life.

- **Optimize** your resources to **realize your dreams**.

- **Communicate clearly and compassionately** with friends, family, and colleagues.

- **Experience a state of flow** to achieve greater creativity, performance, fulfillment, happiness, and overall well-being.

Unfortunately, most people run their lives and businesses from the state of a chaotic mind.

Overwhelmed by stress, they lose sight of the bigger picture and become stoppable. They suffer mentally or emotionally. Their physical health may become compromised. Their reptilian brain dominates, and their excess of stress leads to:

- Poor decision-making.

- Reactivity, impulsivity, or reduced resiliency.

- Diminished creativity or an inability to solve problems quickly and efficiently.

- Deteriorating health and happiness.

However, when you are able to identify your thoughts, feelings, and fears, you know you've accessed your prefrontal cortex. I refer to this state as "operating from the Office of the CEO"—the brain's executive center, where you can make calm, clear decisions.

Explore a real-life scenario that illustrates the practical application of your BOS to access the Office of the CEO.

The Factory Floor

Charly, the CEO of Carbon Thermo Corporation, regularly walks the factory floor. She's developed good working relationships with the employees but can sometimes get caught up in the fast-paced, minute-by-minute pressures of the floor's frenetic activity.

Employees see her and expect immediate answers, but she can't effectively solve their meaningful problems in an instant. It's a chaotic space. In the past, she's misjudged situations, made snap decisions, and suffered the consequences.

The Office of the CEO

Charly steps away from the chaos and enters her

top-floor office—the Office of the CEO. It's an open, well-organized space with tall windows and lots of light. There's a big desk with plenty of room for Charly to work, think, and breathe.

Every day, people knock on her door. She listens to each person, thanks them, and then sorts their input into one of three categories: **Thoughts**, **Feelings**, or **Fears**.

- Lynn from Logistics sticks her head around the door. "Come in," Charly says. "What have you got for me?" Lynn explains that a shipment of parts was damaged in transit. "Thank you," Charly replies. She puts "We need to track the frequency of damaged parts complaints and, if necessary, reassess our shipment protocols" on the **Thoughts** pile.

- Chris from Marketing knocks. He wants to pitch a new marketing initiative. Charly notices his enthusiastic body language. She leans in to hear his idea. Charly feels good about targeting a new offshore market and puts it on the **Feelings** pile.

- Pam, the best project manager in the company, stands at the door. She's known to present innovative solutions, but today, she enters Charly's office with slumped shoulders and head hanging low. She struggles to explain why the current workflow process is failing. Finally, she throws up her arms and says, "No one's following protocol. We're doomed." Charly puts "Pam is afraid that the business is going to fail because of nonadherence to our workflow processes" on the **Fears** pile.

Now, Charly can sit back and evaluate all the items on the three piles calmly and critically. She can prioritize and solve business issues from a position of clarity and perspective.

Whether you're the CEO of a factory, a household, a family, a community, or a project, it's essential to have access to a calm space, both physically and mentally—a place where you can retreat to think clearly, gain perspective, and make sound decisions.

Thinking clearly and effectively while running a business or life can be challenging if you're caught up in the chaos of the "factory floor." Thoughts, feelings, and fears are constantly competing to be heard. However, when you access the Office of the CEO, you can make clear-minded, strategic choices to address problems and challenges.

The Prefrontal Cortex

Let's revisit a previous concept and delve deeper into understanding it.

The prefrontal cortex is the part of the brain that gives you **self-awareness**. It's where you gain perspective. It's the part of your brain that allows you to look back on your thoughts, feelings, and fears.

Your prefrontal cortex serves as a refuge from the swirling chaos of thoughts, feelings, and fears.

The prefrontal cortex is a vital part of your BOS that:

- Facilitates calm and dispassionate visibility of your thoughts, feelings, and fears.

- Empowers you to make clear and conscious decisions.

- Is active when you experience a state of flow.

Recall a time when you were completely engrossed in an activity where time seemed to stand still. Distractions held no power over you. You were fully present in what you were doing.

In times like this, you're operating from your prefrontal cortex. You're able to observe every passing moment—including what you're thinking, feeling, and fearing—without becoming entangled in the chaotic chatter of your cognitive, emotional, and reptilian brains.

A Lesson From Nature

The power of presence.

I live in a house with big doors that invite fresh air to wash freely through...and it's not uncommon for feathered visitors to dart inside as well.

I'm usually alerted to their entrance by the excited barking of my little dog, driven as much by curiosity as by instinct. The event erupts into chaos, with Skittles leaping and lunging after the frightened bird. The bird flaps hopelessly from wall to ceiling, leaving a trail of feathers behind.

When this happens, I work to calm down both the delicate little visitor and the excited dog before quietly shepherding the bird toward an open door to escape back to the great outdoors.

But one day—one bird—was different.

Although the bird was trapped inside, he was calm. He sat on the back of a chair, his head cocked to one side, and looked at me with an air of intrigue. Almost reluctantly, I steered him toward the open door. He settled confidently on the wooden railing of the deck outside.

We held each other's gaze for a while. In that moment of stillness, I realized that this little bird was a great teacher.

It's easy to panic and lose clarity of thought when things get busy or tough. Panic blinds us, and we can't always see the full range of possibilities. When this happens, we're operating from the reptilian brain, like a trapped bird desperately flying around. But the truth is, both the problem and the solution are inside our magnificent brains. When we realize this, we can solve the toughest problems.

Nature has given us an immense gift, the prefrontal cortex. This region of the brain allows us to think clearly and gain perspective. There's a systematic process steeped in neuroscience that will help you to tap into this powerful region of your BOS.

Before I teach you this process, let's go behind the scenes with the transcript of a workshop. You'll meet Lucy, one of the participants, as she wrestles with a major life decision.

Lucy in the Office of the CEO

 **Exploring thoughts, feelings, and fears can help solve personal dilemmas.**

Roddy: Who has a real-life dilemma that they're willing to share with us today?

Lucy: I'm deciding whether to buy a house that I really can't afford. And I'm afraid. I'm feeling afraid because I want to stay where I am, but I don't know what's going to happen if I have to move. So I'm wrestling with the decision to buy or not to buy.

Roddy: Beautiful. What a dilemma. We've all sat there sometime with some major decision in our lives. Should we? Shouldn't we? How do you feel about it?

Lucy: Nervous.

Roddy: Nervous. What does that mean?

Lucy: Or...scared.

Roddy: Scared. What does that mean?

Lucy: Just, there's a lot at stake. And I'm a single mom. I've got my son. If I don't make the right decision...there's a lot of risk, I guess.

Roddy: So, these are all fears you describe. What are you feeling?

Lucy: I feel...confused.

Roddy: Confused. Where do you feel it? Where do you feel confused?

Lucy: In my brain.

Roddy: "I feel confused here, Roddy. Things are jumping around. It's kind of crazy. I can't sort things out." Is that the only place you're feeling confused?

Lucy: A little bit in my heart. I want...I'm trying to trust my intuition. And in my heart, I believe I can do it. But my brain is kind of saying, "What, are you crazy? You can't afford that place," but my heart is saying, "I could do anything I want."

Roddy: That must be lousy.

Lucy: Yeah.

Roddy: You're almost on the edge. Should you? Or shouldn't you? Such a big decision.

Lucy: Yeah.

Roddy: That's a crappy feeling, right? What are you afraid of?

Lucy: My goal in life is to create an environment that's more...peaceful. I want to simplify my life. I want to have less stress. And I'm afraid that this is not going to result in less stress.

Roddy: What are the consequences of more stress?

Lucy: Less healthiness. Anxiety. Just being grumpy at my son. Working long hours. Body stress. No sleep. So, you know, there's a lot of repercussions for that.

Roddy: What does being grouchy with your son look like?

Lucy: Well, it feels...it's not pretty, and it doesn't feel good, either.

Roddy: What does it feel like for him?

Lucy: It feels...that doesn't feel good for him, too. "Why's Mom being like this? What did I do? That was an overreaction."

Roddy: What does he do in those circumstances? How does he react?

Lucy: He...a lot of times he'll echo me...he'll get upset. He'll yell. He'll get angry.

Roddy: So you're worried because this little angel of yours is going to be put through pain.

Lucy: Yeah.

Roddy: Anything else? What else are you afraid of?

Lucy: Just the scarcity, the fear of money and not having enough and changing my lifestyle.

Roddy: Afraid of running out of money?

Lucy: Yeah. It's scary. I know it's an irrational fear.

Roddy: I don't know. Is it irrational?

Lucy: I mean, no, but...I don't know. So, I have to move into a smaller place. You know, it's more like I don't want to sacrifice. I love my home. I want to stay there. I want to buy it.

Roddy: What happened in those last three statements? Did you see a shift of energy? What happened?

Lucy: A feeling.

Roddy: And how did that happen? Because I was sucking you down into your reptilian brain. I was holding you in fear. Did you see that? I was asking you to colorfully elucidate the fear. I was playing a game, deliberately keeping you in your reptilian brain. Where did you go? You went to your cognitive brain with a positive thought. You spontaneously, deliberately said, "But I think I can do it." Yeah! In an instant, you flipped your brain and your mindset. You said, "Roddy, I refuse to let you hold me there." You had a thought, which is positive—and it became the loudest noise in that beautiful brain. And the flip flopper went positive, just like that. Did you see? I didn't even have to finish the exercise.

What happened in the discussion?

Lucy took a journey through her brain. Over a matter of minutes, Lucy underwent a remarkable transformation by owning the Office of the CEO. Did you notice her initial fear? And the negative emotion that accompanied it? Her fears were real, but suddenly, there was an energy shift.

What caused the energy shift?

Lucy had a positive thought! She shifted from fear and confusion to clarity and confidence. What you probably didn't notice was that I was leading her through a 5-step process—which you're about to learn—using her prefrontal cortex to access a state of mindful awareness.

It took courage for Lucy to confront layers of fear, especially in a room full of strangers, but she did. She explored her feelings and fears and then spontaneously had a positive thought.

Despite my deliberate attempt to keep her anchored in her reptilian brain, her cognitive brain took over. Her emotional brain quickly followed, and positive emotions flooded her body.

When the cognitive brain becomes the loudest voice in the brain, the great flip flopper (the emotional brain) flips to positive emotions.

In a matter of moments, Lucy flipped her brain and her mindset. You may have noticed the empowerment and inspiration resonating in her words. Her cognitive and emotional brains worked together. They created positive emotions so powerful that they overrode her fear.

Why do you think I tried to keep Lucy in her reptilian brain?

Because fears hinder progress, they occasionally camouflage themselves behind other fears, forming layers that impede our journey. To become **unstoppable**, we must uncover all our fears.

During the conversation, I guided Lucy to listen to the voice of her reptilian brain. Then, I purposely tried to hold her in her reptilian brain to help her explore all aspects of her fears. I refer to this process as "sweeping the basement," which involves asking questions such as, "What else?" to assist her in searching for deeply rooted fears lurking in the basement of her reptilian brain.

Lucy explored many different fears. She recognized them for what they truly were—the voice of the reptilian brain—and gained a genuine understanding of their nature.

In a future session, you'll learn a comprehensive approach to conquering deeply rooted fears. But for now, there are three simple actions you can practice to set yourself up for success:

1. **Recognize** and **acknowledge** fear.
2. **Welcome fear** without silencing it or pushing it away.
3. **Make decisions** from the **prefrontal cortex**.

Only when Lucy had identified and welcomed all her lurking fears did she spontaneously flip to a positive thought in her cognitive brain.

Now let's go back to Lucy's dilemma for another look. What if she hadn't spontaneously introduced positive thoughts? What if she'd stayed stuck in fear?

Shift Out of a State of Fear

 **Here's what I would have done if Lucy had stayed stuck in fear.**

Roddy: So, I was trying to suck you in and keep you there for the exercise. But you spontaneously, deliberately said, "But I think I can do it." Yeah! But if you hadn't done that, where was my next point of call? I was going to say, "What do you think about it? What do you think about buying the house?"

Lucy: It's a good investment.

Roddy: So, it's a good investment. What else? What else are you thinking about?

Lucy: It's a smart decision. It's stability.

Roddy: Why is it smart?

Lucy: It allows me to have my son stay in the same school. I enjoy the neighborhood and the community that I have there. It's smart for me to be able to stay where I love.

Roddy: And your money is going to be growing, right?

Lucy: It's an asset.

Roddy: Can you afford it?

Lucy: I fear I can't, but…

Roddy: Right now it's on the edge.

Lucy: Currently, it's on the edge, yeah. Can I make changes to afford it? Yeah. Can I get a roommate? Yeah. Can I earn more money? Yes.

Roddy: How do you know that?

Lucy: Past experience.

Roddy: So you've gone through situations where you made more money?

Lucy: I always can find a way to make it work.

Roddy: You always can find a way to make it work. How do you feel right now?

Lucy: Unstoppable.

Roddy: What did we do? You were terrified you were going to ruin your little one's life—and you ended up in a place of empowerment. What we did is we took a journey through the brain. It's that easy.

Use questions to shift out of a fearful state.

To help Lucy find her way out of persistent negative feelings, I would have asked her: "What do you think about it? What do you think about buying a house?"

I asked her anyway. In response, a multitude of compelling reasons flooded Lucy's brain. She accessed her cognitive brain and manifested several innovative ideas, providing her with avenues to generate extra income if she needed it.

Over a matter of minutes, by owning the Office of the CEO, Lucy moved from "I'm feeling afraid...nervous...scared...confused..." to "...I love my home, I want to stay there...I want to buy the house I'm in..." to "I always can find a way to make it work!"

She felt empowered. She became **unstoppable**!

Before you try the process for yourself, take a moment to pause.

5-Step Process to Gain Clarity and Perspective

The first—but often overlooked—step to own the Office of the CEO is to pause.

An intentional pause instantly shifts the seat of your awareness from the swirling chaos of your reptilian, emotional, and cognitive brains into your prefrontal cortex. You become aware of your awareness. This present-moment awareness gives you immense power.

Pause. Take a deep breath now.

This diagram illustrates the 5-step process to gain clarity and perspective.

You can use the same 5-step process I used with Lucy to successfully confront and conquer problems, challenges, and dilemmas you encounter on your journey.

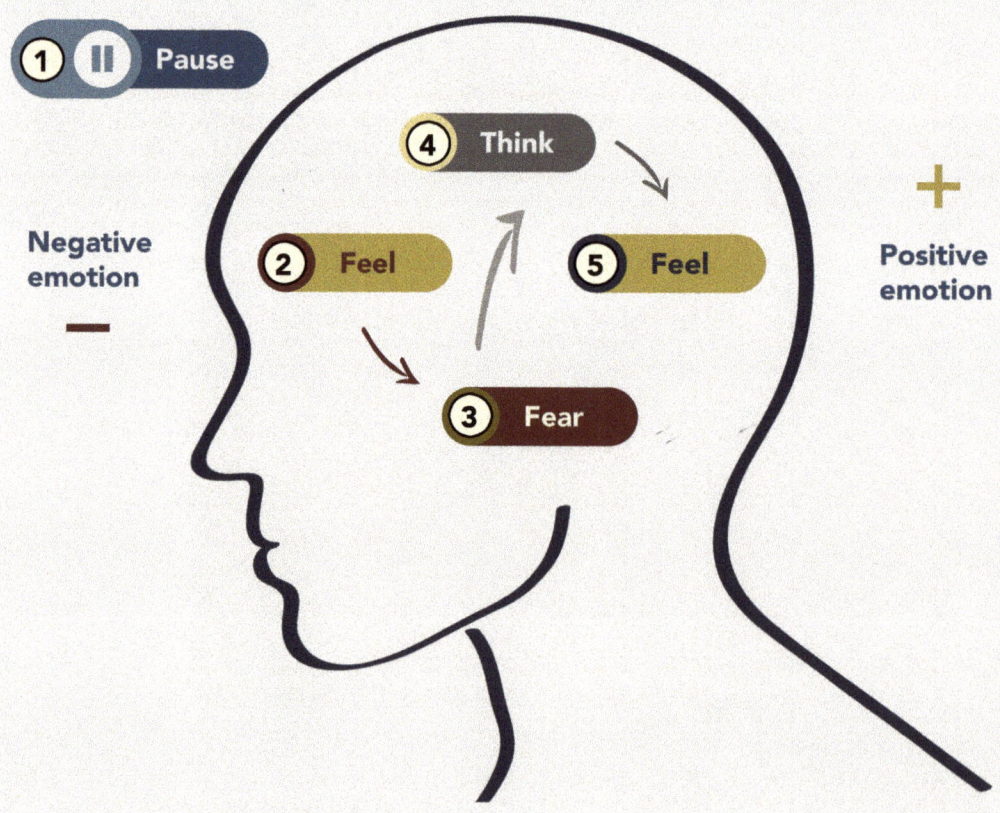

1. **Pause.** Begin with a brief pause—a mindful moment.

   An intentional pause instantly shifts the seat of your awareness into your prefrontal cortex and prepares you to journey through your brain.

2. **Feel negative emotions.** Become aware of the negative emotions you are experiencing.

3. **Explore fear.** Identify and acknowledge all of your fears.

4. **Think.** Notice positive thoughts as you begin to naturally rise above the reptilian brain of fear.

5. **Feel positive emotions.** Recognize and celebrate the positive feelings you have evoked by thinking, by using your cognitive brain to override fear.

 **Learn how to use this 5-step process.**

We simply step from feeling to fear to thought, which is positive, and always end again in feeling. If that feeling is negative, what do I do? I go back to the beginning. I know my work is not done yet, so I have to keep cycling. The negative feeling is a barometer that says, "The loudest voice in this head is still the voice of fear." That information tells us that we need to dig down into the fear more before going back up into the voice of thoughtfulness. And only when the voice of the cognitive brain is the loudest does the emotional brain finally flip flop, and your work is done.

To further your understanding of the 5-step process, go back a few pages to read through Lucy's dilemma again.

This time, look for the steps in the process as I guide her through it. First, I encourage her to pause (Step 1) by reflecting on the fact that we all face major decisions and dilemmas in our lives. Then, I encourage her to feel negative emotions (Step 2) by asking questions like "How do you feel about it?" and "Is that the only place you're feeling confused?"

Then, I encourage her to go deeper by exploring her fears (Step 3), asking questions like "What are you afraid of?" and "What are the consequences of more stress?" After we've acknowledged all of her fears, I help her move to Step 4 by asking what she thinks about buying a house.

And finally, Lucy makes the glorious leap to Step 5 (feel positive emotions), feeling **unstoppable** as she proudly proclaims, "I always can find a way to make it work."

Own the Office of the CEO

EXERCISE 1

Own the Office of the CEO

Practice the 5-step process to own the Office of the CEO.

Select a dilemma or obstacle you currently face. This could be something stopping you from realizing your ideal future.

Keep Lucy's journey in mind as an inspiring example to guide your own process.

STEP 1 OF 5

Pause

As you begin the 5-step process, pause for a moment and deliberately shift the seat of your awareness into your prefrontal cortex.

This intentional pause prepares you to journey through the levels of your brain. You become aware of your awareness.

Take three deeper-than-normal breaths before you move ahead.

STEP 2 OF 5

Feel negative emotions

Visualize the challenge, obstacle, or problem you chose to address, and then ask yourself, *How do I genuinely feel about this?*

Observe and acknowledge the emotions you feel as you contemplate the situation.

- Take note of your negative feelings.

- Pay particular attention to the details of any physical sensations, and pinpoint where they are in your body.

If, upon reflection, you discover that all of your emotions associated with the problem are positive, there's no need for further action. The voice of fear remains dormant. It has no power over you.

STEP 3 OF 5

Explore fear

Identify, acknowledge, and explore the fears associated with your problem.

Questions prompt deeper inquiry. Probe your position with incisive questions, and provide thoughtful answers:

- What am I afraid of?

- What could potentially happen?

- What are the consequences—for myself and for others?

- What does this mean?

- What does this look like?

- Who else is impacted?

Press yourself to expose unconscious fears hidden beneath more obvious fears. Continue to ask questions until you can't find any new fears.

STEP 4 OF 5

Think

Explore the thoughts coming from your cognitive brain.

Ask questions to discover your thoughts on the matter:

- What do I think about this problem or situation?

- What is the real story?

- What would others see or say?

If you find yourself experiencing negative emotions, it suggests that you're uncovering more underlying fears. Return to Step 3 to document and explore the newly found fears lurking in the "basement" of your mind. Once you have identified and explored all the fears associated with your problem, you can resume searching for positive thoughts.

You may notice that the first few thought statements are neutral or evoke only minimal positive emotion. As you progress through this step, you'll reach a pivotal moment when positive thoughts naturally, almost effortlessly, emerge. This occurs because your cognitive brain has taken the reins and is now more dominant, effectively silencing the voice of your reptilian brain.

Feel positive emotions

Deeply reflect on and celebrate the positive emotions you experienced while recording your thoughts in the previous step.

Consider the following reflective questions:

- What positive emotions did I experience?

- Where in my body did I experience these positive emotions? Pinpoint the location of any physical sensations.

- What empowering beliefs am I currently experiencing?

Once sufficient positive thoughts have surfaced, you'll experience a positive shift in your emotional state, flipping the great flip flopper—your emotional brain.

However, if you encounter negative emotions during this step, you'll know you've detected yet another fear. If this happens, take a moment to pause and revisit the previous steps before moving forward. Feel free to repeat the 5-step process, either now or later, until positive emotions have replaced all negative ones.

Reflect on your journey.

You just journeyed through your magnificent brain! First, you paused to own the Office of the CEO by engaging your prefrontal cortex. You recognized negative feelings and underlying fears. Hopefully, you shifted your fears to positive thoughts and ultimately experienced positive feelings—sequentially.

Did you notice an energy shift? Perhaps similar to Lucy's?

Continue to practice and apply this process to tackle any other challenges or obstacles that come your way. Prepare to witness its transformative power in shaping your journey toward **unstoppable** success!

Mastery Missions

Congratulations!

You've finished Session 4. Whenever you're feeling stuck, own the Office of the CEO—use your prefrontal cortex to apply the 5-step process to gain clarity and perspective. In doing so, you'll become unstuck and **unstoppable**.

It's important that you master the 5-step process. I encourage you to take ample time to go through the process again and complete these missions before moving on to the next session.

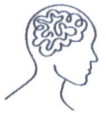

MASTERY MISSION 1

Master the 5-Step Process

ACTION 1 OF 1

Master

Strive to master the 5-step process. Try it again—perhaps on the previous problem you selected or perhaps on another challenge at work or at home.

- **Pause** to shift the seat of your awareness into your prefrontal cortex.

- **Feel** your **negative emotions** when you bring this issue to mind.

- **Explore** your **fears** associated with the issue. Keep going to uncover and resolve as many fears as possible.

- **Think** about the matter.

- Recognize and **feel** your **positive emotions**. They may spontaneously arise. Notice these positive feelings in your brain and body.

Repeat the 5-step process as frequently as required to remove fear and bring clarity to the issue.

The next time you feel stuck, overwhelmed, frustrated, disappointed, or confused, irrespective of the circumstances, begin with a mindful pause. Then, come back here and systematically work through the five steps. Whenever other issues arise, apply the same process to gain clarity and perspective on those, too.

 **MASTERY MISSION 2**

Apply the 5-Step Process With Others

ACTION 1 OF 2

Track

Apply the 5-step process with others as a practice opportunity. When someone comes to you with a negative emotion, guide them through the process without mentioning it to them. Observe their progress through each step.

In your own mind, keep track of where they are in their brain.

ACTION 2 OF 2

Reflect

Below, write down your reflections on guiding someone else. Reflect on the level of ease with which you were able to help them work through problems by guiding them through the 5-step process. What worked well? What would you do differently next time?

 MASTERY MISSION 3

Continue to Practice the Brain Languages

ACTION 1 OF 1

Persist

Continue to practice the skill of distinguishing your thoughts, feelings, and fears.

Persist in asking and answering the following questions: *What am I thinking? What am I feeling? What am I fearing?*

Practice anytime you find yourself waiting in line, for appointments, in traffic, or when someone is running late. Instead of instinctively reaching for your phone, utilize the time to practice differentiating your thoughts, feelings, and fears.

Below, document the strategies you've been using to remind yourself to practice, and also brainstorm new methods you'd like to use for self-reminders.

Supplemental Science

 You're invited to delve into the supporting research on the topics covered in this session. Keep in mind that exploring the supplemental science is optional. You can return anytime to read more about the underlying science of the *Brain Operating System* methodology.

The Neurobiology Underlying Controlled Breathing

The autonomic nervous system, composed of the sympathetic and parasympathetic nervous systems, regulates vital physiological processes. It operates automatically, but it can be influenced indirectly using breathing techniques. Intentional slow, deep breathing can be used to purposefully activate the parasympathetic ("rest-and-digest") nervous system and deactivate the sympathetic ("fight-or-flight") nervous system.

Proactively shifting to the parasympathetic state not only calms the body, but it also calms the brain to support clear, conscious, mindful execution of cognitive control. Research shows a positive association between the calm, relaxed parasympathetic state and prefrontal cortex executive function, goal-directed behavior, and emotional regulation.

Chest or Abdominal Breathing

Subconscious reflexes associated with the autonomic nervous system control breathing rate. In the fight-or-flight state, when the sympathetic nervous system is active, oxygen demand for cellular energy metabolism is high. Breathing is rapid and shallow because the lungs have to work fast to maximize oxygen supply to the working muscles. Chest breathing dominates under these conditions. In contrast, when the parasympathetic nervous system is in control and the body is in a calm, relaxed state, the metabolic demand for oxygen is low and breathing is slow and deep—ensuring that there is time for the lungs to fill up on each breath in. Abdominal breathing dominates under these conditions.

Although the breathing process is an automated body function, it is possible to override the autopilot and intentionally shift between chest and abdominal breathing. This means that breathing, unlike other automated functions, can come under our voluntary control.

Breathing and Stress Reduction

Breath control is a powerful way to manage stress. This is possible because breathing and stress are linked. When stress levels are high, chest breathing dominates. But the impact of stress can be countered by enforcing a pattern of slow, deep abdominal breathing. Voluntary, controlled breathing interventions enable a shift of unhealthy physiological responses toward more balanced, positive ones. Controlled breathing is especially effective in situations that are stressful but not life threatening, for example, when feeling anxious before a job interview or before speaking in public.

The Role of the Vagus Nerve

The vagus nerve is the main component of the parasympathetic nervous system. One of the 12 cranial nerves, the vagus nerve extends from the brain stem (part of the reptilian region of the brain) down through the chest to the colon and has connections to the heart, lungs, intestines, and other organs.

The vagus nerve is central to activation of the calming parasympathetic response. Vagus nerve stimulation reduces the heart rate. A slowing of the heart rate signals to the brain that fight-or-flight reactions are no longer needed, and the parasympathetic relaxation response takes over.

Enforcing a pattern of slow, deep abdominal breathing activates the parasympathetic nervous system via the vagus nerve because vagus nerve stimulation is linked to the breathing process. During breathing, inhalation is an active process driven by the diaphragm and chest muscles, whereas exhalation is passive, and it is particularly during exhalation that vagus nerve stimulation occurs.

Chest breathing maintains the sympathetic state because exhalations are short during rapid, shallow breathing; hence, vagus nerve stimulation is minimal. In contrast, slow, deep abdominal breathing supports long exhalations, which maximize vagus nerve stimulation and activation of the parasympathetic nervous system. The image to the right shows the three-way coupled oscillation of breathing, neurocognitive cortical processes, and subcortical modulation.[1]

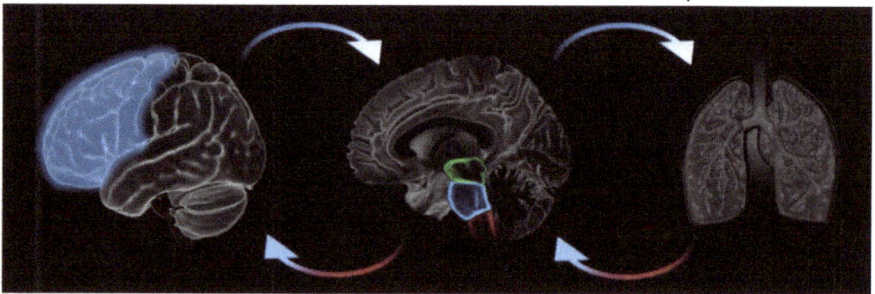

[1]Melnychuk, M. C., Robertson, J. H., Plini, E. R. G., & Dockree, P. M. (2021). A bridge between the breath and the brain: Synchronization of respiration, a pupillometric marker of the locus coeruleus, and an EEG marker of attentional control state. *Brain Sciences, 11*(10), Article 1324. https://doi.org/10.3390/brainsci11101324 (CC BY 4.0).

A Controlled Breathing Technique

A variety of breathing techniques can be used to activate the parasympathetic nervous system. These techniques involve slow, deep abdominal breathing with a longer exhale than inhale, and they all aim to promote physical/mental health and cognitive performance.

The slow, deep abdominal breathing technique described below is simple, easy to apply, and effective. Note that using this controlled breathing technique may feel a bit strange at first, but it will come to feel more natural and comfortable with practice.

In Through Your Nose, Out Through Your Mouth

Sit or stand in a comfortable position with your shoulders relaxed.

When first learning and practicing this technique, place one hand on your chest and one on your abdomen. This will help you to be conscious of whether you are executing chest or abdominal breathing.

Inhale though your nose, consciously using your diaphragm to draw air deeply into your lungs. You should feel your abdomen rise.

Purse your lips and exhale slowly through your mouth, as if blowing air out through a straw. Exhale gently—do not force air out of your lungs. You should feel your abdomen fall as you exhale.

Inhalation/Exhalation Ratio

Pay attention to your inhalation/exhalation ratio, and aim to make the exhale longer than the inhale. Because exhaling is what stimulates the vagus nerve, implementing a longer exhale than inhale maximizes this stimulation and the associated activation of the calming parasympathetic response.

Try inhaling for a count of two and exhaling for a count of four. You can also try inhaling for four counts and exhaling for six, or inhaling for six counts and exhaling for eight. Experiment to find a ratio that works for you, but always breathe out for longer than you breathe in to maximize vagus nerve stimulation.

Nose and Mouth Breathing

The nose is designed to warm, moisten, and filter the air that reaches the lungs, so it is important to inhale through the nose. Breathing out through the mouth with pursed lips is important because it helps to slow the breathing rate and control the length of the exhale.

When Should You Apply This Technique?

Intentionally implement abdominal breathing whenever you want to shift the seat of your awareness into your prefrontal cortex. Take three deep, slow, and controlled abdominal breaths to help you to pause and step into the calm space of the Office of the CEO.

Be mindful of your breathing as you go about your daily life. Anytime you feel stressed, take control of your breathing to shift your body and brain into a calm state.

Commitment

 **Between this session and the next, I commit to the following:**

☐ Dedicating at least one hour of focused practice time to work through a current problem or challenge using the 5-step process to gain clarity and perspective.

☐ Applying the 5-step process with someone else.

Next up, in Session 5: *Programming Your Filter*, we'll delve into your brain's complex filtering mechanism to help you manage the potentially crushing effects of data overload. Additionally, you'll discover the power of your prefrontal cortex in consciously programming your brain to achieve your ideal future.

> "Maintaining awareness of your awareness keeps your brain in its optimal state, giving you the **clarity** and **perspective** you need to **achieve your dreams**."
>
> —DR. RODDY CARTER

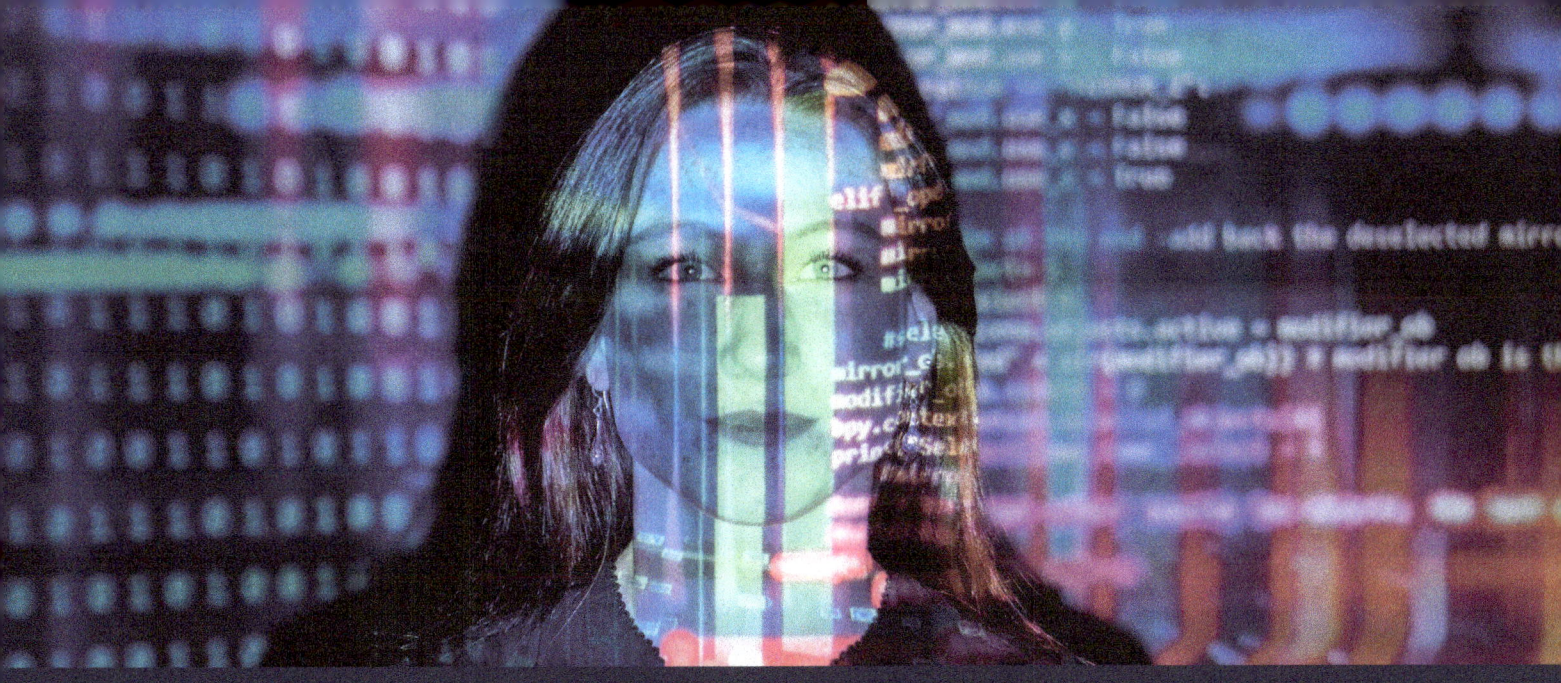

PROGRAMMING YOUR FILTER

Welcome to Session 5! Now that you've gained a deeper understanding of your prefrontal cortex and the 5-step process to gain clarity and perspective, you'll learn how to program your *Brain Operating System* (BOS) to focus your attention on targeted information to ensure you realize your ideal future.

Plan to spend at least two hours completing the session content and activities. Spend another hour on your Mastery Missions before continuing to the next session.

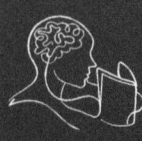

In this session, you will:

- Program your brain to focus on the most critical data to achieve the success you want.

- Discover the pros and cons of your Attention Focusing Consortium, and maximize how you use your attention, which is a precious and severely limited resource.

- Train your filter to accurately assess situations, remove biases, make quality decisions, and enhance your responses to unexpected events.

The Risk of Data Overload

Let's return to the evolutionary story of the human brain.

Completion of the human brain design endowed us with a supercomputer with immense complexity and power. While this remarkable development brought incredible computational capacity, it also presented a potentially life-threatening challenge. With the brain's ability to access huge amounts of data, humans were at risk of data overload.

The volume of data your brain has to process impacts everyday tasks.

Look at the picture to the right, and note how long it takes you to spot the glasses.

Now look at the picture to the left. Find the same glasses. How long did it take you to find them this time?

If you haven't found the glasses yet, don't worry. You're not alone. Many people don't see them at first.

This exercise demonstrates the impact of data excess on your brain. Finding the glasses in the second picture usually takes longer because your brain must process more information than for the first picture.

Whether you found the glasses is not the primary focus of this activity. It emphasizes the significance of your Attention Focusing Consortium (AFC).

Your AFC is vital in filtering out nonrelevant information (like books and papers) and selectively focusing on a subsample of data relevant to your search (the glasses).

Without your AFC, you'd be vulnerable to the crushing effects of data overload in this digital era. Fortunately, your AFC continually works behind the scenes, helping you sift through billions of sensory inputs to concentrate on what truly matters to you.

However, as a consequence, you're at risk of missing things—even huge, potentially important things. The scientific term for this is ***inattentional blindness***, being blind to unexpected things because the focus of our attention is elsewhere.

The Pros and Cons of the AFC

The magnificent advancement of having an AFC comes with benefits and risks.

There are five important points—both positive and negative—you need to realize about your AFC:

1. Your AFC enables you to **focus attention selectively**. As a result, it protects your brain from data overload.

2. Your AFC puts you at **risk of missing other important data**. Missing important things like this happens every day and impedes your success.

3. **Attention is a limited resource** managed by your AFC. The AFC is a powerful filter that maximizes the use of attention to your advantage. Still, when you focus your attention on a particular task or stimulus, other stimuli go unattended.

4. **The AFC is programmed** by other regions of the brain and manages attention accordingly. The AFC's programming determines which data it filters out and which data it attends to. How you program your AFC impacts your capacity to achieve success.

5. The AFC is programmed both **unconsciously and consciously**. Programming of the AFC generally happens automatically and unconsciously (below the level of awareness), enabling regular tasks to be automated into the sub- and un-conscious. For example, think about the automatic actions of an experienced driver behind the wheel.

   However, conscious, mindful programming of the AFC is also possible. Because you have complete voluntary control over your thoughts, you have control over the programming of your AFC.

To see these pros and cons in action, find the *Monkey Business Illusion* video online and, as you're watching, count the number of times the people wearing white shirts pass the ball to one another. After you've watched and counted, consider the following questions:

- Did you see the gorilla walk among the players?

- Did you see the color of the curtain change?

- Did you notice one of the black-shirted players leave the stage?

The Implications of Programming Your AFC

How you program your AFC matters.

How your AFC is programmed has implications for all aspects of your life.

We've all experienced or known someone who wakes up with a groan, exclaiming, "I'm so tired! I don't want to face this day." Negative thoughts seem to infiltrate even before fully waking up, and guess what?

It becomes a bad day.

Why? Because negative thoughts influence the AFC to focus attention on negative experiences.

Here's a modern analogy for AFC programming.

You know the Facebook algorithm that tracks your likes, clicks, and time spent on posts to customize your personal feed? Your AFC works in exactly the same way. It notices where you direct your attention, and then enriches your view with these things. Once it learns what you appear to find important, it then programs itself to deliver more of this to you, while filtering out everything else.

How you choose to program your AFC has the power to change all aspects of your life, so program it carefully.

EXERCISE 1

Observe How You're Programming Your AFC

ACTION 1 OF 1

Observe

Observe what you're filtering into your awareness.

1. What instructions have you been giving your brain? Is the self-talk in your head generally positive and reinforcing—or is it negative and discouraging?

2. When did you last pay attention to your AFC's filtering function?

3. Is the focus of your attention primarily on positive opportunities, or is it on challenges you may need to overcome?

It's all right if you don't have answers to these questions or haven't thought much about how you're programming your AFC. But now that you're aware of this part of your brain, you know you can consciously choose how you program it—and I'll show you how.

Thoughts Program Your AFC

A simple thought can program your AFC.

Visualize a duck.

Before you begin, take a pause. Using your cognitive brain, visualize a clear picture of a duck.

Once you've got the image in your mind, proceed.

Look at the picture of the duck below, and answer these questions:

- Which way is the duck facing?

- Is the duck's bill open or closed?

- Do you notice patches of white plumage on the duck's head?

Before proceeding, get a clear image of a rabbit in your mind. Then, look again at the image above. Do you see a rabbit now?

Now that you've seen the rabbit, answer these questions:

- Which way is the rabbit facing?

- Are the rabbit's ears together or apart?

- Do you notice the patch of white fur on the rabbit's cheek?

Your cognition influences information filtering. You looked at the same image two times, but it's likely that, when I asked you to program your AFC to:

- See a duck, you saw a duck.

- See a rabbit, you saw a rabbit.

The picture remains unchanged, as does the visual data entering your brain. Yet, from identical visual input, you perceive two different animals.

You can consciously choose whether you see the duck or the rabbit, using your thoughts to program your AFC to focus on specific duck or rabbit features.

However, not everyone can see both animals, and that's entirely normal. The duck/rabbit ambiguous figure has been extensively studied, with some individuals switching effortlessly between duck and rabbit perceptions while others struggle to see the rabbit or the duck.

The key takeaway of this activity is that perception is not solely based on what you see but also on what you are looking for.

(i) This activity was inspired by Mathewson, K. E. (2018). Duck eats rabbit: Exactly which type of relational phrase can disambiguate the perception of identical side by side ambiguous figures? *Perception, 47*(4), 466–469. The drawing, originally published in Jastrow, J. (1899). The mind's eye. *Popular Science Monthly, 54*, 299–312, is now in the public domain.

Now that you've experienced using your thoughts to program your AFC, let's consider what you can do to consciously clear and focus your filter to help you become **unstoppable**.

> ## A well-functioning AFC is the life raft
> ## you need to survive in a growing sea of data.

A Clear Filter Gives You Clarity

Clarity enables optimal decision-making.

You can program your AFC for clear vision rather than identifying with distorted—and potentially harmful—versions of your life experiences.

Seeing the full reality of each experience fosters success. Alternatively, a narrow perception of reality (what you may think you have experienced) can keep you stuck. Your lived experience—reality or perception—is strongly influenced by whether your filter is clear.

- A clear filter frees you from bias. You become aware that your filter may be giving you a biased view of the world.

- A clear filter lets you observe what's important. You are receptive to all important data.

- A clear filter empowers you to assess situations positively. You are able to assess situations from a positive mindset.

- A clear filter facilitates good decision-making. You are able to take the next right action.

- A clear filter minimizes negative reactivity. Your ability to respond rather than react to negative people, events, and circumstances is stronger.

Use your brain's executive and cognitive functions to clear and focus your filter and accurately program your AFC.

Prefrontal Cortex

Before you clear and focus your filter, step into the Office of the CEO. Begin with an intentional pause to instantly shift the seat of your awareness into your prefrontal cortex.

Using your prefrontal cortex, you can scrutinize the data being sifted through your filter. This enables you to be objective about what your brain is reporting as fact and to assess your filter's state.

So, whenever you want to program your filter, your first step is to pause. Sit quietly and breathe deeply for a few moments to help you step into the Office of the CEO.

Cognitive Brain

There are many different ways to use your cognitive brain to consciously program your AFC. The most effective approaches aim to answer one key question: Are you seeing your actual reality or a distorted (and maybe harmful) version of it?

Once you exercise cognitive control, your AFC will keep searching for and discovering abundant evidence that reinforces the positive thoughts in your mind.

Four Filter-Programming Methods

Filter-programming methods aim to answer one key question: Are you seeing your actual reality or a distorted version of it?

There are many approaches to program your filter. Let's explore four of them in more detail:

1. **Be aware you have a filter.**

   The first and most fundamental approach to programming your filter is based on your awareness that you have a filter—and that it can serve you well or poorly.

   Now that you **forever have this awareness**, take responsibility for programming your AFC to serve you well. Use your thoughts to focus your attention on what you need to see.

2. **Spot-check your thoughts.**

   The second approach to programming your filter helps you become aware of whether your thoughts are facts, opinions, or assumptions. Learn how to assess your thoughts to identify and acknowledge beliefs and assumptions, because they may be potentially harmful distortions that prevent you from seeing your actual reality.

3. **Use Socratic questioning.**

   The third approach is the Socratic questioning method. It challenges the accuracy of your thoughts about yourself and your life experiences using thoughtful questions to prompt deep reflection and honest inquiry.

4. **Seek calibration from others.**

   The fourth approach is calibration. It involves seeking input and feedback from others to broaden your perspective and to confirm that your interpretations are accurate.

Spot-checking thoughts is a quick way to verify your filter is clear and focused.

This filter-programming method is a simple approach that helps you determine whether your thoughts—about yourself and your experiences—are facts, opinions, or assumptions.

What's a fact?

A fact is a statement about something that has actually happened or really exists. Facts can be verified objectively and don't change over time.

What's an opinion?

An opinion is a subjective statement often linked to emotions. Opinions are views that are not based on facts, cannot be verified objectively, and can change over time.

What's an assumption?

An assumption is a statement about something that may be true, but for which there is no proof or verifiable evidence. Assumptions often include generalizations.

In spot-checking thoughts, you're programming your filter by becoming aware of whether you're operating from a basis of fact, opinion, or assumption. This awareness gives you clarity about your actual reality. You'll have an opportunity to practice the spot-checking method in a moment.

Socratic questioning is a filter-programming method using thoughtful questioning to prompt reflection and respectful, genuine, and honest inquiry.

The benefit of the Socratic questioning method is that it challenges the accuracy of what you think about yourself and your life experiences objectively, systematically, and thoroughly.

Here are questions you can use to help you identify your perceptions and clear and focus your filter. As you ask them, decide whether you're seeing your actual reality or a distorted version.

- Am I basing my interpretation on facts or feelings?

- Am I applying habitual thinking to the situation, irrespective of the facts?

- Could I be jumping to conclusions?

- Am I considering all the evidence, or could I be missing something important or misinterpreting the evidence I am seeing?

- Could I be demanding something of myself that is unrealistic or holding myself responsible for something that someone else should be doing?

- Am I focusing only on the negative, or only on the positive?

- Am I blaming myself for a situation that involves many factors that are out of my control?

- Am I making general assumptions about the future based on only one experience?

Calibration—seeking input from friends or family members with diverse perspectives—can help fact-check your beliefs.

In the fields of engineering, science, and technology, "calibration" denotes the procedure of measuring, fine-tuning, and comparing instruments or systems to guarantee their accuracy and dependability when evaluated against a standard (the truth).

Similarly for you, calibration is a valuable tool when you're at risk of overlooking essential details or struggling to see the full range of options available to you. You can't see everything, but your friends and family have the benefit of an external vantage point. Their unique perspectives can help you resolve difficult situations with greater objectivity and avoid dangerous pitfalls and blind spots. You'll have the clarity to move forward with a comprehensive understanding of the facts.

Practice

Practice spot-checking your thoughts, using Socratic questioning, and calibrating.

To practice spot-checking thoughts, identify whether each statement is a fact, an opinion, or an assumption. There are 18 statements.

She remembers to call people on their birthdays.	Fact Opinion Assumption
Sometimes I feel sad.	Fact Opinion Assumption
Only bad drivers become involved in car accidents.	Fact Opinion Assumption
I always mess up.	Fact Opinion Assumption
I didn't give money to a beggar.	Fact Opinion Assumption
I should always be cheerful.	Fact Opinion Assumption
I'm a lousy parent.	Fact Opinion Assumption
I'm a terrible friend.	Fact Opinion Assumption
I yelled at him.	Fact Opinion Assumption
I'm the only parent who feels frustrated at times.	Fact Opinion Assumption
I was involved in a car accident.	Fact Opinion Assumption
I'm a selfish person.	Fact Opinion Assumption

Emotionally strong people never feel sad.	Fact Opinion Assumption
Generous people always give away their money.	Fact Opinion Assumption
I'm sure I'm the only one who failed the exam.	Fact Opinion Assumption
I forgot to call my friend on her birthday.	Fact Opinion Assumption
I should stop driving.	Fact Opinion Assumption
I failed my exam.	Fact Opinion Assumption

Spot-checking thoughts is an appropriate filter-programming method when you need to quickly assess the state of your filter to determine whether your thoughts are facts or perceptions of reality. Before spot-checking, pause to shift the seat of your awareness into the Office of the CEO.

Use the following feedback to check your identifications.

FACT	OPINION	ASSUMPTION
I failed my exam.	I always mess up.	I'm sure I'm the only one who failed the exam.
I yelled at him.	I'm a lousy parent.	I'm the only parent who feels frustrated.
I was involved in a car accident.	I should stop driving.	Only bad drivers become involved in car accidents.
I forgot to call my friend on her birthday.	I'm a terrible friend.	She remembers to call people on their birthdays.
I didn't give money to a beggar.	I'm a selfish person.	Generous people always give away their money.
Sometimes I feel sad.	I should always be cheerful.	Emotionally strong people never feel sad.

Now, here's a scenario to practice the Socratic questioning method.

Bay is in charge of new employee orientation. She begins her presentation and observes someone dozing off. She begins to feel self-conscious. Use Socratic questioning to help program her filter.

When Bay notices someone nodding off, she's certain it's because she's boring and monotonous. Is Bay basing her interpretation on facts or her feelings?

- **Her feelings.** Bay's thoughts are biased. She's embarrassed, anxious, and self-conscious. She starts to panic because she's worried she'll get terrible reviews on her evaluation forms.

Could Bay be misinterpreting the evidence?

- **Yes.** Bay could definitely be misinterpreting the evidence! She was so focused on the one person dozing off that she didn't notice how attentive the others were.

Is Bay making any assumptions?

- **Yes.** Bay assumed they couldn't stay awake because of her boring presentation and delivery. This assumption is based on Bay's limited perception of reality. Her current filtering is negative.

What other interpretations of this situation might there be?

- **The person is sleep deprived.** It's possible they weren't able to sleep the night before starting an exciting new opportunity or for another reason unrelated to Bay.

Could Bay be jumping to conclusions?

- **Yes.** Bay makes assumptions about being boring and causing them to fall asleep, even though she doesn't fully understand their experience.

Is Bay focused mainly on the negative?

- **Yes.** Bay predominantly focuses on the negative by focusing on the person at the back of the room rather than on those who are engaged. Consequently, she's unable to perceive reality.

In summary, the Socratic questioning method enables Bay to approach the situation objectively, removing biases and perceiving reality. This helps her recognize the truth about her expertise and professionalism.

Now, walk through a calibration scenario.

Phil's been struggling emotionally and feels physically exhausted. He reaches out to his friend, Jan, seeking her input.

Phil: Jan, I'm exhausted. I haven't been sleeping; I have so much on my mind.

Jan: I'm really sorry to hear this, Phil. Thanks for reaching out. Tell me, what is going on? What's been keeping you up at night?

Phil: (pauses) I've been dealing with a lot of stress lately, and it's taking a toll on me. There have been some significant changes at work, including the departure of some longtime friends. Their absence is hitting me hard. I've been shouldering extra responsibilities and drinking too much caffeine to make it through the day. I've neglected my exercise routine. By the time I get home, I'm physically exhausted, but my mind refuses to rest. I lay in bed bone-tired, but awake. I'm struggling to make changes.

Jan: (nodding empathetically) I'm really sorry, Phil. It sounds like you're going through a challenging time, and I can't imagine how difficult it must be. What about your family?

Phil: Oh, I guess I didn't mention it because it's been painful to think about. The main concern weighing on me right now is how profoundly my family has been impacted by everything happening. I feel like I'm just a shadow of myself, and they can't depend on me.

Jan: Phil, it's clear this is taking a toll on you and your family. Have you considered talking to them about how you're feeling? They wouldn't want you to feel you had to carry all this alone.

Phil: (sighs) You're right, Jan. It'd be awful if they were going through this alone. I'd want to be there to help them. For some reason, I've always had this misguided notion that I have to be the hero and figure it all out before I can talk to anyone. Maybe I'll take a few days off to get away, and we can all have a long weekend together to recharge and reconnect. I always feel better after stepping away from work, and you're right: Talking to them, they might have good insights.

Jan: That sounds wonderful, Phil! Some relaxation can make a huge difference, and involving your family in navigating these changes could be really beneficial.

Phil: (nods) I'm so happy we spoke. For some reason, I was overlooking the most significant problem...it is strange how our mind conspires to protect us sometimes and how much this can prevent us from moving forward meaningfully.

Jan: Phil, I'm really glad you called. I'm here to support you every step of the way!

Calibration can bring clarity.

With Jan's help, Phil came up with a plan. Together, they realized the critical oversight of not involving his family. She was able to help him see this blind spot and move forward.

Mastery Missions

Congratulations!

It's time to practice training your filter and programming your AFC for clarity.

Now that you've completed the *Observe How You're Programming Your AFC* exercise, use Mastery Missions 1 and 2 to gain perspective on the fears you explored in the previous sessions. Mastery Mission 3 includes some fun ways to practice conscious programming of your AFC and conscious shifting and focusing of your attention.

MASTERY MISSION 1

Spot-Check for Biases

ACTION 1 OF 2

Check

Practice spot-checking thoughts for potential biases. Refer to the lists of negative emotions and fears you wrote in Session 3, Mastery Mission 1. Check each fear or negative emotion for potential biases by asking the following questions:

1. What are the facts about this fear or negative emotion?

2. What are my opinions about the issue?

3. Am I making any false assumptions?

4. Do I have an incomplete view of the truth?

ACTION 2 OF 2

Gain clarity

If you spot any lingering negative emotions, apply the 5-step process to gain clarity and perspective on the issues.

By becoming aware of your opinions and assumptions about your fears, you're clearing your filter of potential biases that could keep you stuck in a stoppable state. This awareness helps you to silence the voice of fear because you gain clarity to operate from the basis of your actual reality rather than your perception of it, which helps you become **unstoppable**.

 MASTERY MISSION 2

Use Socratic Questioning

ACTION 1 OF 1

Inquire

Practice the Socratic questioning method to prompt deep reflection and respectful, genuine, and honest inquiry. Select one of the biases you identified in Mastery Mission 1, or opt for a different situation upon which you desire to gain perspective through a clear filter. This could be something hindering your progress toward your ideal future.

Before you begin, pause to step into the Office of the CEO. Then, inquire using the Socratic questions provided below.

It's unlikely that all the questions will apply to the opinion, assumption, or situation you're reflecting on. If the relevance of a question is not obvious, move on to the next question.

- Am I basing my interpretation on facts or feelings?
- Could I be misinterpreting the evidence?
- Am I viewing the situation as black and white when it's actually more complicated?
- Am I making any assumptions?
- Could I be basing my judgment on opinions, not facts?
- What other interpretations of this situation might there be?

- Am I applying habitual thinking to the situation, irrespective of the facts?

- Could I be jumping to conclusions?

- Am I considering all the evidence, or could I be missing something important?

- Could I be demanding something of myself that is unrealistic?

- Am I focusing only on the negative?

- Am I automatically assuming a worst-case scenario?

- Could I be exaggerating what's true?

- Am I holding myself responsible for something that someone else should be doing?

- Am I blaming myself for a situation involving many factors out of my control?

- Am I making general assumptions about the future based on only one experience?

- Does this really happen all the time, or are there similar situations where things are different?

MASTERY MISSION 3

Program Your AFC

ACTION 1 OF 3

Search

Harness the power of time between sessions to practice conscious programming of your AFC in your daily routines.

Search for a distinct object or item in an exercise of deliberate exploration. If browsing through a store, create a mental image of a product you frequently buy. How long does it take for you to spot it? Alternatively, you can experiment with an online search. Type in a broad term, like "coffee," and observe how long it takes to find your favorite brand amidst the results.

ACTION 2 OF 3

Notice

Notice specific items, such as people wearing hats or baseball caps, or cars of a particular color or make—perhaps your favorite. Alternatively, observe people who exude unstoppability. Note their body language, and seek out similar traits in others, too.

ACTION 3 OF 3

Focus

Pay attention to your attention. Become aware that you're able to focus your attention on an ongoing conversation, effectively filtering out other conversations or background noise. This conscious experience demonstrates your AFC's capacity to protect you from auditory overload, allowing you to focus on crucial information in the present.

Supplemental Science

You're invited to delve into the supporting research on the topics covered in this session. Keep in mind that exploring the supplemental science is optional. You can return anytime to read more about the underlying science of the *Brain Operating System* methodology.

Selective Attention

The Attention Focusing Consortium (AFC) represents an association of neurological centers (located in the brain stem and other areas below the cortex or cognitive brain region) that function in a coordinated manner to channel, filter, and integrate all the external (sensory) and internal (thoughts, memories, and emotions) data the brain deals with every moment, enabling management and processing of these data without the risk of data overload. The filtering function of the AFC supports selective attention: the ability to selectively attend to and focus on subsets of data while filtering out a plethora of distractions.

It is important to note that much of the data filtering associated with selective attention is happening behind the scenes—subconsciously—so people who do not know about the AFC are unaware of what it is accomplishing every moment.

Some of the nerve centers of the AFC are located in the brain stem (labeled in the image below[1]) and include the reticular activating system and the superior colliculus. Other subcortical AFC nerve centers include the thalamus and basal ganglia.

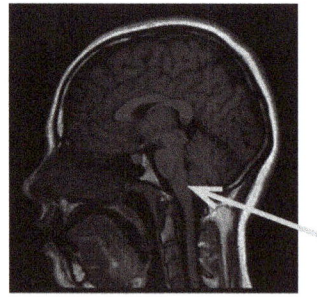

Brain stem

[1]Case courtesy of Frank Gaillard, Radiopaedia.org, rID: 37605.

Survival and Selective Attention

Millions of years ago, the continued existence of early humans as a species depended on the capacity of their brains to filter out, in the moment, less-relevant data to support survival in the wild. They needed the ability to selectively focus on a subsample of all the data they were taking in, so they could be alert to and avoid danger, as well as hunt, forage, and find a mate efficiently.

For example, when ancestral hominins were fleeing from a charging predator, their brains needed to be keenly focused on their escape route, not on the delicate beauty and fragrance of the flowers they trampled in their hasty retreat or on the serenity of the sunset or what they were going to have for dinner! If they selectively attended to nonrelevant information at a critical moment, their very survival was at risk.

Scientific research shows that modern humans (both adults and children) are more alert to potentially dangerous animals such as lions, snakes, and spiders than to harmless animals. This suggests that, although we live very different kinds of lives than our ancestors, we have inherited from them the survival imperative to instinctively pay more attention to animals that could potentially cause us harm.

The Risk of Data Overload

The Brain Constantly Deals With Large Volumes of External and Internal Data

The human brain constantly receives incoming data from the external environment via the senses. The human eyes, for example, are estimated to take in approximately one gigabit of raw visual data every second.[1] This amounts to a billion bits of data a second through our eyes alone. This volume of data is equivalent to 48 average-length (2.6 MB) Kindle e-books per second and would completely fill a 128 GB phone in just 17 minutes.

The human brain also constantly processes data in the form of memories, thoughts, and emotions. Scientists have recently estimated that, on average, we have over 6,000 new thoughts per day.[2] For an adult who is awake for 16 hours a day, that amounts to about 375 new thoughts every hour. In addition, our brain constantly processes all the internal data needed to keep our physical bodies functioning normally.

Data Overload in the Digital Age

Modern humans need the AFC more than ever. Although we do not often need to look out for dangerous animals or keep our wits about us when foraging for plants, we are faced with an even bigger data-overload challenge than that of our ancestors in the wild.

The amount of information bombarding our brains on a daily basis has increased substantially over time, particularly in relation to the advent and advancement of the digital age and the information era. It has been estimated that an amount of information equivalent to that generated between the dawn of human civilization and the year 2003 is currently created every two days.[3]

It has been reported that, for the average American on an average day, the estimated consumption of information in 2008 (outside of work hours) was 100,500 words and 34 gigabytes of data, and that this volume of data represented a doubling of that consumed on a daily basis over the period from 1980 to 2008.[4] Projecting forward to today (using a prorated 28-year doubling) puts these data volumes at 107,535 words and just over 36 gigabytes of data per day. It is anticipated that information generation and consumption will continue to increase, exacerbating an already widespread data-overload problem. Recently, 22.5% of respondents in a survey conducted in Germany indicated that information overload was one of their most frequent stressors.[3]

[1]Lee, K. H., Tran, A., Turan, Z., & Meister, M. (2020). The sifting of visual information in the superior colliculus. *eLife*, 9, e50678. https://doi.org/10.7554/eLife.50678

[2]Tseng, J., & Poppenk, J. (2020). Brain meta-state transitions demarcate thoughts across task contexts exposing the mental noise of trait neuroticism. *Nature Communications, 11*, 3480. https://doi.org/10.1038/s41467-020-17255-9

[3]Arnold, M., Goldschmitt, M., & Rigotti, T. (2023). Dealing with information overload: A comprehensive review. *Frontiers in Psychology, 14*, 1122200. https://doi.org/10.3389/fpsyg.2023.1122200

[4]Bohn, R., & Short, J. (2012). Measuring consumer information. *International Journal of Communication, 6*, 980–1000. https://ijoc.org/index.php/ijoc/article/view/1566/743

Energy Conservation in the Brain

The capacity to focus attention is a way to conserve energy in the brain. The human brain makes up just 2% of body weight but consumes 20% of the body's daily glucose supply, making it an energy-demanding organ. In general, nature works to conserve energy by limiting excessive energy burn. This applies to the brain, too, so the ability to filter out information not deemed relevant in the moment and to prioritize crucial information plays a role in conserving and maximizing energy usage in the brain. Research findings suggest that, when the brain is engaged in a challenging task, energy is actively diverted to neurons directly associated with the focus of attention.[1]

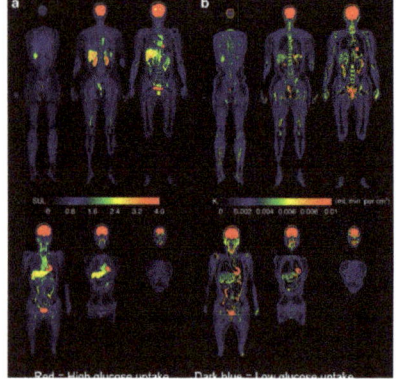

Total-body positron emission tomography (PET) scanning makes it possible to map resting-state whole-body glucose utilization in organs and other body parts, such as muscles and the skeleton. The glucose uptake maps to the left show the highest level of glucose uptake in the brain, followed by the heart, liver, and kidneys.[2] (The high glucose uptake level recorded in the bladder was attributed to the urinary clearance of the radiolabeled glucose substance used during PET scanning.)

[1]Bruckmaier, M., Tachtsidis, I., Phan, P., & Lavie, N. (2020). Attention and capacity limits in perception: A cellular metabolism account. *Journal of Neuroscience, 40*(35), 6801–6811. https://doi.org/10.1523/JNEUROSCI.2368-19.2020

[2]Image modified from Lu, W., Duan, Y., Li, K., Qiu, J., & Cheng, Z. (2023). Glucose uptake and distribution across the human skeleton using state-of-the-art total-body PET/CT. *Bone Research, 11*(36). https://doi.org/10.1038/s41413-023-00268-7 (CC BY 4.0).

Inattentional Blindness

Inattentional blindness happens to everybody. Here are some inattentional blindness research results.[1]

Even Experts Miss Things

Radiologists and non-radiologists were asked to identify lung nodules in a number of lung scans. The researchers included a gorilla 48 times larger than an average-sized lung nodule on the last scan. The results showed that 100% of the non-radiologists missed seeing the gorilla, as did a surprisingly high percentage of the experts (83%). They were all intently focused on finding lung nodules.

Nodules can be seen in the lung scan to the right.[2]

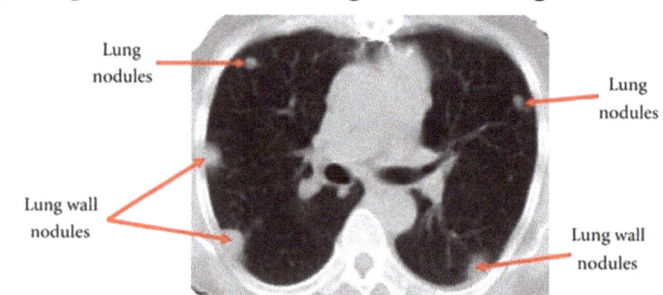

The Pull of Technology

The attention of modern humans is substantially impacted by the pull of technology. In a study where a person dressed in a clown suit unicycled around a college campus square, 75% of students who walked alone through the square while using their cell phone failed to notice the clown. In comparison, only 49% of students walking alone without a technology distraction missed the clown.

Technology Is Not the Only Distractor

In this experiment, researchers attached money to a tree branch overhanging a walkway. Of 63 pedestrians who were texting or talking on their cell phone when passing the tree, 94% did not notice the money. However, technology is not the only distractor. Of 333 pedestrians who were not using a cell phone at all when they passed the tree, 81% missed the money. What was distracting these pedestrians such that they did not see the "money tree"? They were most likely engaged in mind wandering—being focused on their own thoughts was enough of a distraction to cause them to miss the money.

[1]Wulff, A. N., & Thomas, A. K. (2021). The dynamic and fragile nature of eyewitness memory formation: Considering stress and attention. *Frontiers in Psychology, 12,* 666724. https://doi.org/10.3389/fpsyg.2021.666724
[2]Image modified from El-Baz, A., Elnakib, A., El-Ghar, M. A., Gimel'farb, G., Falk, R., & Farag, A. (2013). Automatic detection of 2D and 3D lung nodules in chest spiral CT scans. *International Journal of Biomedical Imaging, 2013,* 517632. https://doi.org/10.1155/2013/517632

Commitment

Between this session and the next, I commit to the following:

☐ Pausing for a moment every day this week to recap the day so that I can recognize when my AFC assessed situations positively.

☐ Being mindful of my negative emotions. Experiencing a negative emotion is a conscious reminder to introduce a positive thought (a factual statement rather than an opinion or assumption).

Next up, in Session 6: *Conquering Fear*, we'll go deeper into the BOS methodology to conquer fear and become **unstoppable**—again and again. We'll explore what it is to "conquer." Then, you'll dig deeper into your fears and practice a 7-step process to conquer one of the fears holding you back from your ideal future.

> ## "All that we are is a result of what we have thought."
>
> ### —BUDDHA

CONQUERING FEAR

Welcome to Session 6! In the previous session, you practiced consciously programming your AFC. Now, seize control of your magnificent brain to overcome deep-rooted, lingering fears lurking in the "basement" of your mind.

Allocate one to two hours to go through the session content and engage in the activities. To create positive and meaningful change, dedicate two hours to your Mastery Missions.

In this session, you will:

- Explore and expose the fears that are making you stoppable.

- Recognize the profound impact of exploring and confronting your fears head-on to achieve an **unstoppable** state.

- Master the 7-step *Brain Operating System* (BOS) fear-conquering process to overcome your fears.

Fears Hiding in the Basement

Mary was in tears. She'd come to me in desperation.

You wouldn't know that Mary was in trouble. Outwardly, she exuded joy and kindness. Her peers admired her unwavering optimism and exceptional productivity, but internally, she was plagued by stress and overwhelm. She constantly rushed, fearing she'd never have enough time and would let people down—despite clear evidence to the contrary.

Friends, colleagues, and even her partner were oblivious to her struggles. She masked her distress, concealing her inner turmoil.

Her coping mechanisms, which had served her well through many years of success, now seemed ineffective. Halfway through our conversation, she uttered a phrase I've encountered countless times: "Roddy, I'm just so tired of wearing the mask."

Behind every mask is a fear.

The voice of your reptilian brain shouts and convinces you that, if you don't hide behind the mask, you're in trouble—your weaknesses and failings will be exposed for all to see. We've all put on a mask to hide fears, a mask of happiness and confidence that belies our inner uncertainties.

What are some of the fears behind the mask?

FEAR OF FAILURE

You can't do it. You're an embarrassment.

FEAR OF CHANGE

You'll be out of control.

FEAR OF LOSS

You're worthless. Who will you be if you lose _____?

FEAR OF UNWORTHINESS

You'll never be as good as _____.

FEAR OF REJECTION

You're a failure, and that's all they see.

FEAR OF ABANDONMENT

When it's all over, you'll have nothing and end up alone.

FEAR OF INTROSPECTION

You're too weak to find out what lies behind the mask.

FEAR OF BEING A FRAUD

You're a fake. You don't know anything.

The consequences of wearing the mask are initially subtle, and we're often oblivious to them. On the surface, we may appear happy and successful, but the façade is temporary. Sooner or later, the mask stifles growth and leads to negative consequences.

Wearing the mask isn't sustainable. You're a dynamic, living being destined for growth.

When you grow, you expand. You make progress and move toward your ideal future—but your reptilian brain often perceives change or growth as a threat. It shouts in an effort to keep you safe. Its messages can be convincing:

- **Push aside intuition.** Be practical. You don't have what it takes.

- **Fake it.** Pretend it's true, even if it isn't.

- **Work harder.** Do whatever it takes—no matter the sacrifice or cost.

- **Never expose weakness.** No matter what.

- **Put others first.** Who do you think you are? Your needs are less important.

- **Put aside your dreams.** Do what's expected of you.

These and many more fears hold us in the stoppable state, but once we step back to examine them, the façade fades away and we reap the benefits.

The bold few who face their fears and dive into self-examination are rewarded.

If you're not living your full potential, it's because you haven't spent enough time with your fears.

Three Reasons to Face Fear

Here are three key reasons to face your fears:

1. You can harness fear's power.

Growth demands courage, especially when your reptilian brain shouts. However, by confronting each fear and taking action despite it, you empower yourself. Fears can also ignite energy and positive actions, guiding you to ask the right questions for greater clarity.

> View your fears as motivators and opportunities for growth. Use their power to drive transformation, and you'll be rewarded with greater resilience and self-confidence.

2. You can unlock new insights.

The natural tendency is to avoid fear, suppress it, or push it aside. However, your cognitive brain enables you to confidently face your fears and gain insight.

When you access the basement of your mind to explore fears, you see them for what they really are: the voice of the reptilian brain. New insights allow you to take huge strides toward liberation and success.

> Proactively explore your fears, acknowledging and befriending them. Your cognitive brain will help you understand why they're part of your life experiences, and once you understand them, they can transform into valuable gifts.

3. You can demand perspective.

Most fears feel real, but they rarely reflect the whole truth. A perfect example is when horrendous catastrophes come to mind when no actual danger exists. It's easy for the imagination to run wild, but most terrible things we imagine never happen.

These catastrophic scenarios are an important part of the reptilian brain's job: to protect you. If you succumb to the voice of fear and entertain worst-case scenarios, the fear intensifies in magnitude and perceived consequence. Even if initially unfounded, the imagined threat gains strength, reinforcing the voice of fear's belief in its saving you from disaster.

> Confront your fears, and use your BOS to distinguish actual threats from imagined ones. Awareness can free you from anxiety triggered by perceived dangers.

The Word "Conquer"

 **Conquer your fears to become unstoppable.**

*Now, anybody who knows me knows that I think a lot about words. I've told you about my love affair with "**unstoppable**."*

*"Conquer fears. **Conquer**."*

Whew, that's a big word. It means I'm the victor.

I've played with the word "destroy," but I really didn't like it because we never destroy a fear.

But conquest is something about, "I'm the boss."

You can say to fear, "You're there, but I'm the boss."

Expose Your Fears

 EXERCISE 1

Expose Your Fears

Bring your fears out of the basement.

Work through five deliberately designed actions that involve self-reflection to help you expose your fears. Later in the session, you'll discover a systematic 7-step process to conquer them.

ACTION 1 OF 5

Pause

Focus on your breath.

Shift the seat of your awareness into your prefrontal cortex by taking a deep, deliberate inhalation... and exhale slowly.

You may also take a moment to identify any areas of physical tension, such as in your neck or shoulders. Focus your attention on these areas with the intention of experiencing relaxation.

ACTION 2 OF 5

Identify

Leverage these questions to identify fears lingering in the basement of your mind:

- Are there aspirations or passions you deeply desire to embrace, but you find yourself hesitating or feeling held back?

- What's holding you back or preventing you from realizing your dreams?

- What common factors or circumstances tend to provoke negative emotions within you?

- What are some of the underlying causes or fears that might be triggering your negative emotions?

- What triggers feelings of anxiety or unease within you?

- Are there any recurring patterns you notice yourself encountering? What fear might be driving these patterns?

- What aspects of life do you avoid?

- Which areas of your life have caused you to feel trapped in unhappiness, unhealthiness, or dysfunction?

- What aspects of change scare you?

- What opportunities have you declined? Why?

- What stops you from saying yes to new opportunities?

Allow yourself ample time to respond thoughtfully.

ACTION 3 OF 5

Name and describe

Document the fears you exposed in the previous action. Give each fear a short name and description.

For example, if you recognize that you've held yourself back because you're seeking companionship, you may have uncovered a fear of being alone.

- Name it: "Fear of being alone."

- Describe it in your own words: "I'm terrified of being alone and excluded by others because people will see me as insignificant or assume I've lived a lonely life."

Sometimes, the description unveils a deeper fear. In this example, that could be "fear of rejection."

Write whatever comes to mind without overthinking or analyzing.

Draw inspiration from the common fears mentioned in *Fears Hiding in the Basement* as you name and describe your own fears.

ACTION 4 OF 5

Reflect

Reflect on your documented fears:

- How did you feel while you were exposing your fears?

- Can you identify your negative emotions?

- Can you describe the discomfort you experienced or pinpoint where you felt it in your body?

Elaborate on your negative feelings to reveal as much detail as possible. If you didn't experience negative emotions while exposing your fears, go deeper by repeating Action 2.

ACTION 5 OF 5

Assess

Assess the impact your fears have on you realizing your desired future.

Which of these fears may be keeping you stoppable—blocking you from achieving your ideal future?

To gain deeper insight into the intensity of each fear, assign a rating to each fear, with 1 representing the smallest impact and 3 indicating the most significant impact.

You did it!

It takes courage to proactively venture into the uncomfortable territory of your reptilian brain and expose deep fears. Not everyone opts to do this exercise. However, bringing your fears out of the basement is the first step toward conquering them!

Anne Conquers a Fear

Read an example of how you can use your BOS to conquer fear.

Let's go back to the workshop to join one of the participants (let's call her Anne). She courageously shares a deep-rooted fear of being unchosen. She feels she'll remain unchosen in her workplace, friendships, and relationships because she isn't likable.

The fear-conquering process won't be explicitly stated in this transcript, but notice how I guide Anne to use her cognitive and emotional brains to override the voice of fear that has been keeping her stuck.

 **Anne feels afraid of being unchosen.**

Roddy: *You said something beautiful. May I ask you about it?*

Anne: *Sure.*

Roddy: *"Unchosen." You know I like words. That's a big word, but that's not a very comfortable word. That doesn't sit nicely on me. What do you mean by that? Where is that coming from?*

Anne: *I think it goes back to the likability.*

Roddy: *Who's not choosing you?*

Anne: *Others in general, even in a workplace or friendships or relationships. The likability and the want to, um, not let them down.*

Roddy: *So you're not going to be chosen by a boss.*

Anne: *Right.*

Roddy: *And you're going to have no friends? And you're going to have no life partner?*

Anne: *Right.*

Roddy: *That's got to hurt. If that's deeply inside your heart, that's got to be worse than death. I receive it. How does it make you feel?*

Anne: *I can physically feel my heart and my voice shaking.*

Roddy: *It's grabbing you, right? I receive it. I receive it. Why does it make you so afraid, though? What is the fear behind that?*

Anne: *I think because I care so much about the people in my life that I would want them to want me as well.*

Roddy: *Why do you want them to want you? Because you care about them?*

Anne: *I don't know if I've asked myself that question.*

Roddy: *So there's a deep fear behind that, right? There's a fear of being alone, left alone.*

You know where our brain was born? On the plains of Africa. You go and look at the book, it shows that, to the best of our knowledge, Homo sapiens started on the plains of Africa. And we were kind of primates. Those are our earliest ancestors.

And I grew up in Africa watching wildlife, and I would watch a troop of baboons. Do you know what happened to the little one who was left behind?

Death. Something ate it.

If you were left on your own, outside of the troop, as a primate, it meant death.

Even today, with this brain with ancestral programming, there is still this deep fear, real fear, and the reptilian brain says, "This is as bad as death." And that's why it feels so terrible. It's real fear. It's real.

But I receive it. And I welcome it. And it's natural and healthy and powerful...why?

So you don't die on the plain! So that you live!

And you said something else: "I really worry about it because I care." And somewhere, your desire for survival and your caring for people around you got convoluted and intermingled. And so, it's a gift.

And I hope that, as you feel that pain, you're gonna recognize it as a gift.

How many friends do you have?

Anne: *It depends on what I would consider a friend.*

Roddy: *Okay, but they're there, right? How many good friends do you have?*

Anne: *I have a lot of good friends.*

Roddy: *You have a lot of good friends, lots of them. And what do they think of you?*

Anne: *I think that they like me.*

Roddy: *"I think...I just have a suspicion." You're right. They might like you. They might like you...they might like you a lot?*

Anne: *Mmmhmm.*

Roddy: *Really? They might like you a lot? Or am I imagining—am I pushing you there?*

Anne: *I think that they do.*

Roddy: *So do you have any evidence of times in your life when you were completely without friends? And without love and without affirmation and affection?*

Anne: *No.*

Roddy: *Do you want to think about it again?*

Anne: *I can't think of a time.*

Roddy: *Not one time. Zero.*

Anne: *Yeah.*

Roddy: *Not once.*

Anne: *Right.*

Roddy: *What do you think about that?*

Anne: *I think that's pretty lucky.*

Roddy: *You think it's pretty lucky, but what do you think about this fear? In the context of this massive successful relationship generation that you've done through your life? Are you telling me something is going to change tomorrow? Just suddenly mess it all up?*

Anne: *No. No.*

Roddy: *A little bit likely?*

Anne: *It's not going to happen tomorrow.*

Roddy: *So it's not going to happen tomorrow. Okay, so, we're good. Tomorrow is good, right?*

Anne: *Tomorrow is good.*

Roddy: *The day after? What about the day after? Two days until you have some fundamental shift? One year? Seven years? Twenty-seven years? Forty-eight years? No. So what are you worried about? Respectfully, you're wrong.*

7-Step Process to Conquer Fear

Here's a brief overview of the 7-step process to conquer fear.

Don't worry about working through the process with your fears yet. Read on for a high-level overview. Then, we'll walk through the process together.

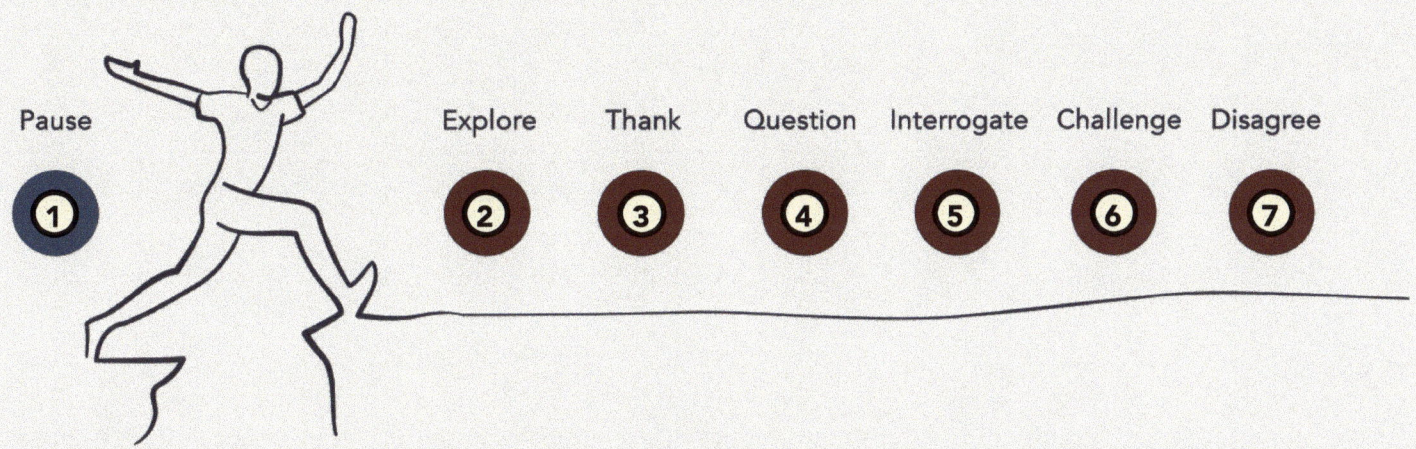

1. **Pause.**

   A pause shifts the seat of your awareness from your reptilian, emotional, and cognitive brains into your prefrontal cortex.

2. **Explore.**

   Once you've shifted your awareness to access your prefrontal cortex, you're positioned to explore your fear. Ask yourself, *What am I feeling? What am I fearing?*

3. **Thank.**

   Recognize the gift this fear has been in your life, and appreciate the positive intentions of your reptilian brain.

4. **Question.**

   Ask questions to gather as much data as possible about your fear, enabling you to better understand it.

5. **Interrogate.**

   Shift from amiable and polite questioning to a more assertive interrogation of your fear. Posture to demonstrate your determination, showing your fear that you mean business and that it has no place to hide.

6. Challenge.

Challenge your fear to prove why you should still listen to its voice.

7. Disagree.

Claim your victory and let go of the past—respectfully.

 **Let's break down what happened in the discussion.**

How did we get there?

Seven steps. What is my first step?

I just brought a pause. I paused to go into your prefrontal cortex, and mine. In the heat of battle, we pause. And when I'm in my free prefrontal cortex, I did what?

I started asking about feelings and fears. And then what did I do?

I said, "Thank you." I affirmed and acknowledged the fear.

That's what makes you beautiful. That's what keeps you caring about other people.

I affirmed and I thanked the fear.

I want to make the fear my friend. Otherwise, it scurries away in the basement and I don't find it—and it comes back and bites me you-know-where another day. So, I affirm it. I recognize the value in it.

And then I went on to the next step, which was? Questioning.

I just started questioning. I asked questions.

You kind of picture that you're two people.

You picture that you're negotiating with yourself, that you're in conversation with yourself. And you start gentle. "Just help me understand. You've told me something big and real; I want to understand it." I'm pulling data. I'm not biasing the data. I'm just pulling thoughts.

What followed the questions? I stepped it up. I went from easy questions to interrogation. Did you feel me coming at her? I wasn't going to let her squirm away.

Everything changes. And I even stand tall. I'm getting this part of my brain to really lean over that little guy in the bottom and say, "You know what? I've paid you attention. I've heard you. I've heard all the good reasons that you're shouting. And I've said thank you for them, but I'm not so sure that you're helping me now.

"You're actually hindering me."

Next step: challenging. "Prove to me how you're going to be such a bad guy. Prove to me how you're going to suddenly change overnight and not have any friends."

Questioning to interrogation to challenging. And then what did I did in the end?

I said, "Respectfully, you're wrong."

Seven steps.

Using seven deliberate steps, I carefully led Anne through her BOS to explore and overcome a lifelong fear.

Anne courageously confronted her fear of being unchosen. She took the upper hand and reclaimed her self-confidence, self-acceptance, and sense of belonging. In a matter of minutes, her feelings of inadequacy dissolved.

Let's revisit the initial conversation with Anne to deepen your understanding of the fear-conquering process. I systematically guided her through each of the seven steps. Go back a few pages to read through the transcript, and observe the questions I ask Anne throughout the process.

Notice how I first encourage her to pause (Step 1) on the word "unchosen." Then, I ask probing questions to encourage her to explore all aspects of her fear (Step 2). Once Anne has explored, we pause together on Step 3, thanking her fear—"I receive it."

Next, we move to questioning her fear (Step 4): "Why do you want them to want you?" and "How many friends do you have?" After, we go deeper, interrogating it (Step 5) with firm questions like "Am I imagining? Am I pushing you there?" Then I help Anne challenge her fear (Step 6): "Are you telling me something is going to change tomorrow? Just suddenly mess it all up?" And finally, when we see her fear fail in the face of that challenge, we disagree with it (Step 7): "Respectfully, you're wrong."

Conquer Your Fears

 EXERCISE 2

Conquer Fears

Learn the 7-step fear-conquering process.

To work through this exercise, choose one of the fears you identified in Exercise 1.

For your first time, select a less-intense fear to use as you familiarize yourself with the process. As you gain proficiency, you'll be able to master and apply the process repeatedly, effectively working through all the fears you identified.

As you practice the process, consider Anne's journey as a guiding example.

STEP 1 OF 7

Pause

Before confronting any fear, take a moment to pause.

Shift the seat of your awareness into the calm space of your prefrontal cortex—the Office of the CEO. This grants you immediate access to the executive control necessary to conquer your fear.

STEP 2 OF 7

Explore

Explore the emotions behind the fear you've chosen. Ask:

- What am I feeling?
- What am I fearing?

Notice:

- The range of emotions you experience as you explore the fear from different angles.

- The temperature of your feelings.

- Descriptive words that best capture your emotions.

- Sensations you feel in your physical body.

Negative feelings	Positive feelings

If you don't experience strong negative emotions, here's what's happening: Either you're not delving deep enough into your feelings or it isn't a true fear. You can choose to explore deeper questions about your feelings or select another fear to conquer.

Once you've explored your emotions, delve deeper to fully understand the fear.

- Can you see a link between this fear and other fears you have?

- What are you actually fearing, deep down?

- Are there one or more fears hidden behind this one?

STEP 3 OF 7

Thank

Recognize the gift this fear has been in your life, and thank it.

In this step, you understand and accept that there's an underlying reason for this fear. It has safeguarded you for many years. With genuine thankfulness, express gratitude for your fear and write it a thank-you statement in the space provided below.

When you affirm, acknowledge, express gratitude for, and befriend your fear, it often leads to an aha moment!

STEP 4 OF 7

Question

To better understand all angles of your fear, engage in a series of questions. Gather as much data and as many facts as possible. By shedding light on your fear, you unveil inherent flaws in the logic.

During this step, it can be helpful to imagine yourself having an amiable, nonjudgmental conversation with yourself, gently probing what your fear is all about. While the specific questions will vary depending on the fear, use the following as a starting point:

- Is this a new fear or one I've had for as long as I can remember?

- Can I pinpoint the possible origin of this fear?

- Does this fear pertain solely to my life or the impact I might have on others?

- In what ways is this fear holding me back?

- In what ways is this fear protecting me?

- Am I afraid of a process or an outcome?

- Is this fear linked to my self-worth, confidence, or competence?

- Is this fear linked to unrealistic expectations I have of myself?

- Am I afraid because of what I've witnessed happening to someone else?

- Is my fear based on other people's opinions of me?

- Am I afraid of losing something or someone precious?

- Am I afraid of having to compel myself to do something I don't want to do?

Select the questions relevant to your fear, and feel free to create your own. Questions wield power. They serve as tools to unravel almost any fear, exposing its core.

Below, write your own questions and record all the information you gain from your chosen line of questioning.

STEP 5 OF 7

Interrogate

Shift from polite, amiable questioning to interrogating your fear.

You're preparing to conquer—step in with confidence. Envision the CEO of your brain leaning over to interrogate the fear, demonstrating your resolve. It cannot hide.

Engage in a firm line of questioning. Demand that it answer these tough questions:

- Is this true? Is this *really* true?
- Is there evidence?
- How much damage have you (the fear) caused so far?
- What else are you hiding?
- What is the accurate probability that there will be irreparable damage?
- If there is damage, is it true that it couldn't be remedied?

STEP 6 OF 7

Challenge

Challenge your fear—your reptilian voice—to prove why you should still listen to it.

Insist that your fear provide concrete evidence to support its claims; do not back down. Demand answers.

Say to your fear:

- Justify your argument.

- Prove you're helping me.

- Provide hard evidence that substantiates your position.

- Identify a time when I've failed to overcome an obstacle of similar complexity and difficulty.

Persist with direct, pointed questions that challenge every claim your reptilian brain shouts.

STEP 7 OF 7

Disagree

Claim your victory. Let go of the past, and respectfully disagree with your fear.

This is a moment of immense power to relinquish your fear once and for all. You might stand in front of a mirror, look yourself in the eyes, and proclaim, "Respectfully, I disagree."

Sometimes, however, the voice of fear persists despite solid reasoning. When this happens, it's time to employ your mental strength and respectfully wrestle your fear into submission. Say (preferably out loud) things like:

- I will no longer heed your arguments.

- Your voice will not drive my actions.

- You have yet to consider all the facts. You lack the vision to see the tremendous upside.

- Respectfully, you're wrong!

- That's enough. No more shouting.

Celebrate your victory.

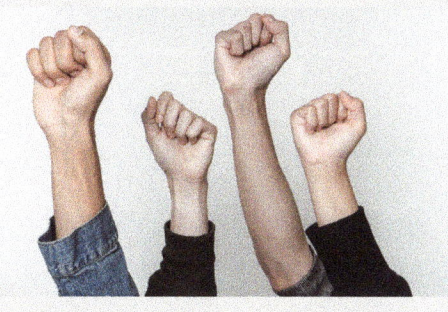

Each time you work through the 7-step fear-conquering process, celebrate or ritualize your conquest. It takes immense courage to press through your fears, but now you have the tools.

You used the full magnificence of your brain to conquer fear and pave the way to pursue your ideal future with unwavering persistence and passion.

Celebrating your victory can be as simple as visualizing the disempowered fear in your hand and then releasing it through a window or door, symbolizing its departure from your life.

Conquering Fear Is a Dynamic Process

While the 7-step process isn't foolproof, it undeniably works!

Depending on the intensity of a particular fear and how long it's been part of your life, **conquering a fear might not require completing all seven steps.** Simply understanding the fear through the information gathered during the fourth step: *Question* could be enough to reveal it as an overstated force and disempower it.

Conversely, you might need to **go through the 7-step process multiple times for intense and deeply rooted fears**. You can work through back-to-back iterations in the same session or step away for a moment, or even longer, before returning to 7-step the same fear until you address and resolve it adequately.

What if you don't conquer your fears right away?

Sometimes, you may work through the 7-step process and feel frustrated by not conquering the fear immediately.

If you find that you haven't conquered a fear in one sitting, step away. Temporarily ignore the voice of this fear. Engage in activities like exercising, walking in nature, driving, watching a movie, listening to a podcast, or spending time with your family.

This recommendation to ignore your fear might seem contradictory to what you know about facing fears. However, I'm not suggesting that you push the fear away permanently. Instead, consider a temporary distraction to enable productive progress when you work through the 7-step process again.

Tell your fear, "I'm going to step away and ignore you right now, but I'll be back with refreshed energy, new clarity, and perspective."

When you're ready to face the fear, begin again and work through the seven steps.

Mastery Missions

Congratulations!

Great work on completing Session 6 and the two exercises: *Expose Your Fears* and *Conquer Fear*. Now that you've bravely confronted one of your fears, practice the 7-step process with the other fears on your list.

For maximum transformative impact, allocate two hours to complete these missions.

MASTERY MISSION 1

Commit to Conquering Your Fears

ACTION 1 OF 2

Repeat

Continue to practice the fear-conquering process with other fears you named and described—approaching it each time with a fresh and focused mind. Allocate time to recap and reflect on each step as you progress through the process.

Ask yourself:

- Did I pause and shift the seat of my awareness into my prefrontal cortex?

- From the Office of the CEO, was I able to identify and describe my feelings and fears?

- Was I able to recognize and appreciate the gift of my fear? Did I thank it?

- Could I go deeper? What other fact-finding questions could I ask?

- Did I lean in and change to a hard line of questioning to interrogate my fear?

- Did I challenge my fear to try to prove to me why it is correct?

- What emotions did I experience during the final step, "Respectfully, I disagree…"?

Ignore

If you don't conquer a fear in one sitting, step away temporarily and ignore it. Find activities you enjoy that will help you relax, recharge, and gain clarity. For example:

- Take a leisurely walk outside.

- Listen to calming music.

- Engage in a creative hobby, such as gardening, cooking, drawing, or writing—something you haven't done in a while.

- Spend time in nature. Practice mindful awareness.

- Exercise, even if it's three minutes doing a series of push-ups.

- Spend time with children, animals, friends, or loved ones.

Be mindful that deeply rooted fears may require revisiting the process multiple times. Repeat the 7-step process as often as necessary, not only for existing fears but also for new ones that arise.

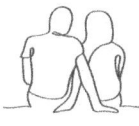 MASTERY MISSION 2

Journey Together

Teach

Journey toward conquering fears and achieving personal growth with someone you trust or who trusts you.

If facing one of your fears feels daunting, enlist the help of a friend or partner. You don't have to do it alone. Teach your friend the 7-step process, and work through your fear together, one step at a time. Always begin with a pause!

ACTION 2 OF 2

Guide

Guide someone at home or work through the 7-step process to help them conquer simpler frustrations or fears. Don't worry about getting it perfectly right. Start with a mindful moment, and if all else fails, ask deeper questions. Questions encourage them to reflect on various aspects of their fear.

As you progress through the practice sessions, observe the level of the brain you and/or the other person are operating from. When you began the process, did you notice a subtle shift when you took a pause?

Supplemental Science

 You're invited to delve into the supporting research on the topics covered in this session. Keep in mind that exploring the supplemental science is optional. You can return anytime to read more about the underlying science of the *Brain Operating System* methodology.

Stuck in Overdrive: Chronic Stress

The autonomic nervous system, composed of the sympathetic and parasympathetic nervous systems, regulates vital physiological processes. These two subsystems control the same body functions but have opposite physiological effects. The sympathetic nervous system activates the body's reflexive fear ("fight-or-flight") response, putting it on high alert, whereas the parasympathetic nervous system (known as the "rest-and-digest" system) deactivates the stress response, calming the body and maintaining body functions at their normal activity levels.

Hormones, particularly epinephrine (also termed *adrenaline*) and cortisol, play a key role in activating and sustaining the physiology that supports the fight-or-flight response and are commonly known as the "stress" hormones.

Action of the Stress Hormones

When the brain detects a potential threat or danger, it activates the sympathetic nervous system by sending a signal to the adrenal glands to release epinephrine (adrenaline) into the bloodstream. Through cellular-level processes, epinephrine stimulates the physiological changes that support the fight-or-flight response. These include an increase in heart rate and blood pressure; a diversion of blood flow to the brain, vital organs, and skeletal muscles; an increase in breathing rate and opening of the airways; and an increase in blood glucose levels. These physiological changes support heightened physical action (if needed) by maximizing the amount of oxygen and glucose available for cellular energy production in the brain, heart, vital organs, and skeletal muscles.

The initial release of epinephrine (experienced as the proverbial "adrenaline rush") is sufficient to rapidly activate the sympathetic nervous system; however, a cortisol boost is needed to sustain the fight-or-flight physiology. If the brain detects that a threat or danger is still present after the adrenaline rush, it signals to the adrenal glands to release cortisol (this signaling happens via the pituitary gland and involves two intermediary hormones). A key role played by cortisol in sustaining the activity of the sympathetic nervous system is through its effect on the maintenance of energy supply to the brain, vital organs, and skeletal muscles. Cortisol increases blood glucose levels by stimulating the metabolism of stored energy and counteracting the effects of insulin. As an energy-conserving mechanism, cortisol also slows down body functions that are nonessential to the fight-or-flight response (e.g., digestion).

Once the threat or danger has passed, cortisol levels decrease and the parasympathetic nervous system takes over regulation of vital physiological processes, shifting the body to a relaxed state.

The Negative Impact of Chronic Stress

The human body evolved to function mostly under parasympathetic nervous system regulation, with the capacity to rapidly shift to sympathetic nervous system control when needed for survival of unpredictable acute-stress experiences. However, the more prevalent mental and emotional stress that characterizes modern existence means that most people experience stress on a sustained basis. Although many modern stressors do not require a physical fight-or-flight response, they are nevertheless experienced as fear and elicit the reflexive fear response—the release of stress hormones to activate and sustain the fight-or-flight physiology. Prolonged exposure to stressors leads to chronic stress, which is the underlying cause of many modern-day ailments.

Epinephrine (adrenaline) is produced only when it is needed to activate the sympathetic nervous system in response to a perceived threat or danger, whereas cortisol (one of the glucocorticoid hormones) is involved in a number of vital physiological processes. These include the regulation of fat, carbohydrate, and protein metabolism; blood glucose levels; blood pressure; and inflammation. Consequently, cortisol is always present in the bloodstream and, under parasympathetic control, the cortisol level is maintained to support optimal functioning. Under conditions of chronic stress, however, prolonged periods of an above-optimal cortisol level can have long-term negative health consequences.

Most body tissues have cortisol receptors. Consequently, long-term exposure to sustained excess cortisol can potentially affect many different body systems and functions, leading to a number of health issues including high blood pressure, diabetes, muscle weakness, weight gain, obesity, headaches caused by chronic muscle tension, fatigue, and digestive problems. Excess cortisol can also negatively impact the immune system. Under normal conditions, cortisol suppresses the immune system to regulate immune system activity (e.g., to control allergic reactions). However, prolonged elevation of cortisol associated with chronic stress leads to immunosuppression that leaves the body compromised in its ability to detect and fight infections and diseases such as cancer. Recurrent elevation of epinephrine (adrenaline) in the body (e.g., in response to anxiety-based panic attacks) also has negative health consequences, particularly impacting the cardiovascular system and leading to ailments like heart disease, artery damage, high blood pressure, and strokes.

Freedom From Chronic Stress

Chronic stress is a symptom of unmanaged fear, linked to persistent activation of the reptilian brain. When we know how to recognize the pervasive negative emotions that signal chronic reptilian brain activity, we can intentionally use cognitive override to silence the persistent voice of fear. Application of the 7-step fear-conquering methodology empowers us to manage more intrusive fear and meaningfully reduce the burden of chronic stress, a deeply entrenched modern ailment.

Acute Versus Chronic Stress Responses

The graphs to the right illustrate the activation over time of the parasympathetic and sympathetic nervous systems under acute and chronic stress conditions.[1] In particular, note the return to normal shown in graph (a), where, once the perceived

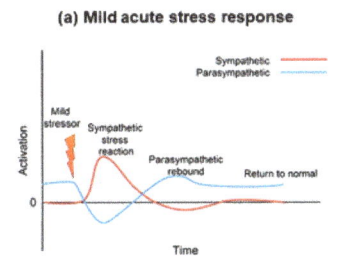

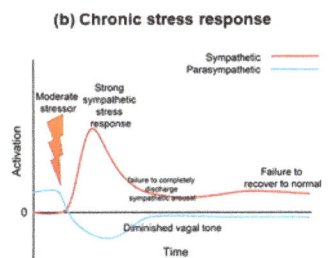

threat or danger has passed, the parasympathetic nervous system takes control again. In contrast, note the failure to recover to normal shown in graph (b), where the sympathetic nervous system remains in control.

[1]Graph modified from Payne, P., Levine, P. A., & Crane-Godreau, M. A. (2015). Somatic experiencing: Using interoception and proprioception as core elements of trauma therapy. *Frontiers in Psychology, 6*(93) https://10.3389/fpsyg.2015.00093 (CC BY 4.0).

Discovery of the Fight-or-Flight Response

The discovery of the fight-or-flight response is credited to Walter B. Cannon (1871–1945), a Harvard Medical School neurologist and physiologist. At the time of his discovery (reported to be around 1897), Cannon was studying the physiology of digestion, including the peristaltic movements of the digestive system. He noticed that, when his research animals became alarmed, they showed a cessation of digestive activity. Having an interest in the physiology of emotion, Cannon conducted further research that ultimately provided evidence of the activation of the sympathetic nervous system as a response to threat or danger. Cannon elucidated the role of epinephrine (adrenaline) in this activation, including the effects of this hormone on blood supply and glucose levels.

Cannon published his initial findings in his 1915 book *Bodily Changes in Pain, Hunger, Fear, and Rage: An Account of Recent Researches Into the Function of Emotional Excitement.* He is regarded as a pioneer of stress research.

Fight, Flight, or Freeze?

Defense Behaviors in Response to Fear

Extensive laboratory and field research in mammals has elucidated characteristic behaviors associated with defense responses to perceived threat or danger. The three most commonly described behavioral responses to fear are fight, flight, and freeze. Fight and flight are active defense responses, supported by physiological changes that enable physical action (if needed). Freeze is a response that temporarily halts the fight-or-flight reaction. By freezing, an animal may avoid detection by a predator. In humans, freezing temporarily suspends the fight-or-flight response, allowing time to assess the situation, including the threat level and the most appropriate defense response.

In addition to fight, flight, and freeze, there are other reactions that contribute to a more complex set of behavioral responses to fear. These include arousal and immobility. Arousal precedes the fight, flight, or freeze response and is characterized by the rapid physiological changes that take place when a threat is first detected. Arousal prepares the body for action. Immobility, by contrast, may occur when fight-or-flight responses have failed. For example, "playing dead" may result in an opportunity to escape or to avoid being killed if it confuses or distracts a predator. In humans, examples of immobility behavior under threat include the temporary inability to move or speak associated with a sense of disconnection or dissociation (tonic immobility) and fainting (collapsed immobility).

Which Defense Behavior When?

In humans, there is evidence of intrinsic bias or individual propensity toward particular defense behaviors in response to fear. For example, two individuals experiencing the same threat may

respond differently, one exhibiting flight behavior and the other choosing to fight, or one individual may exhibit the same fear response (e.g., freeze), irrespective of the nature or level of the threat. Research shows that there are many factors that can play a role in determining which defense response an individual will exhibit. These include whether the perceived threat is environmental or psychological, the perceived threat level, temperament, personality, learned behavior (linked to experiential, vicarious, or verbal learning), aversive associative learning (linking cues to expected negative outcomes), unresolved trauma, fear generalization (generalizing a fear from a past encounter to a future one), sex, cultural conditioning, age, whether there is a direct threat to personal freedom, and social dimensions (e.g., social transmission of fear).

It is helpful to be aware of the different fear responses and to reflect on one's own predisposition to these; however, it does not really matter which fear response is exhibited because all fear can ultimately be managed by cognitive override (except in cases of extreme, real danger when survival depends on allowing the fear response full control).

When working to conquer fear on the journey to becoming **unstoppable**, deep, historic fears related to past trauma may surface. Managing and ultimately moving beyond these deep fears may require professional help. If, as you apply the 7-step process to conquer your fears, you find yourself facing unresolved trauma, please seek help.

Breathe to Manage Stress

The autonomic nervous system operates automatically, outside of voluntary control, but it can be influenced indirectly using breathing techniques. Although breathing is an automated function, it is possible to override the autopilot and intentionally get this body process under voluntary control. Intentional slow, deep breathing can be used to purposefully activate the parasympathetic nervous system and deactivate the sympathetic nervous system.

Breathing and Stress Reduction

Breath control is a powerful way to manage stress because breathing and stress are linked. When stress levels are high and the sympathetic nervous system is in control, rapid, shallow chest breathing dominates because the lungs have to work fast to maximize oxygen supply to the blood and body. But the impact of stress can be countered by enforcing a pattern of slow, deep abdominal breathing. Deep abdominal breathing occurs when the body is in a relaxed and calm state under the control of the parasympathetic nervous system and the metabolic demand for oxygen is low, allowing time for the lungs to fill up on each inhalation.

Voluntary, controlled breathing interventions enable a shift of unhealthy, stress-maintained physiological responses toward more balanced, positive ones. Controlled breathing is especially effective in situations that are stressful but not life threatening, for example, when feeling anxious before a job interview or speaking in public.

A Breathing Technique

This slow, deep abdominal breathing technique is simple, easy to apply, and effective. Note that using it may feel a bit strange at first, but it will come to feel more natural with practice.

Sit or stand in a comfortable position with your shoulders relaxed.

When first learning and practicing this technique, place one hand on your chest and one on your belly. This will help you to be conscious of whether you are executing chest or abdominal breathing.

Inhale though your nose, consciously using your diaphragm to draw air deeply into your lungs. You should feel your belly rise.

Purse your lips and exhale slowly through your mouth, as if blowing air out through a straw. Exhale gently—do not force air out. You should feel your belly fall as you exhale.

Inhalation/Exhalation Ratio and the Vagus Nerve

The vagus nerve is the main component of the parasympathetic nervous system and central to activation of the calming parasympathetic response. Enforcing a pattern of slow, deep abdominal breathing activates the parasympathetic nervous system via the vagus nerve. It is particularly during exhalation that vagus nerve stimulation occurs, so pay attention to the inhalation/exhalation ratio and aim to make the exhale longer than the inhale to maximize activation of the calming parasympathetic response.

Try inhaling for a count of two and exhaling for a count of four. You can also try inhaling for four counts and exhaling for six, or inhaling for six counts and exhaling for eight. Experiment to find a ratio that works for you, but always breathe out for longer than you breathe in to maximize vagal nerve stimulation.

Nose and Mouth Breathing

The nose is designed to warm, moisten, and filter the air that reaches the lungs, so it is important to inhale through the nose. Breathing out through the mouth with pursed lips is important because it helps to control the length of the exhalation.

When Should You Apply This Technique?

Intentionally implement deep abdominal breathing whenever you want to shift the seat of your awareness into your prefrontal cortex. Take three slow and controlled deep belly breaths to help you to pause and step into the calm space of the Office of the CEO.

Be mindful of your breathing as you go about your daily life. Anytime you feel stressed, take control of your breathing to shift your body and brain into a calm state.

Facing Fear: Mindful Cognition

Mindfulness supports the use of cognition to face and manage fear. A mindful state is attained by proactively paying attention to the present moment in a calm and nonjudgmental way. This enables full awareness of thoughts, feelings, and fears with open-minded acceptance. From this nonreactive state of awareness, fears can be identified and faced using cognitive strategies to evaluate them and diminish their negative impact.

The prefrontal cortex plays a key role in mindful cognition because proactively operating from the prefrontal cortex supports both present-moment awareness of thoughts, feelings, and fears and executive control of cognition for top-down emotion regulation. Shifting the seat of awareness into the prefrontal cortex increases the capacity to engage with fears intentionally and constructively.

From a position of mindful awareness, the emotions behind a fear can be calmly and nonjudgmentally explored, and the fear accepted and befriended. Then, cognition can be used to evaluate the fear and diminish its impact. This is accomplished by implementing a systematic disputation process, using questions to assess and challenge the validity of the fear.

When the mind is fully engaged in the disputation process, thoughts dominate. The cognitive brain counters the reptilian brain, and the voice of fear is silenced.

Research shows that mindfulness enhances performance. Mindfulness shifts the focus of attention from rumination on the past or anxiety about the future to present-moment awareness, which supports focus and concentration on the task at hand without the distraction of the reptilian brain's voice of fear. The performance-enhancing efficacy of mindfulness is likely a result of fear reduction and the power of cognitive override.

Facing Fear: Exposure Therapy

Exposure therapy is widely used as a clinical approach to the reduction of reflexive fear responses. It is a form of cognitive behavioral therapy designed to enable an individual to confront or face a fear in a safe way. As the name suggests, exposure therapy involves repeated exposure to a fear combined with a gradual increase in the perceived threat level. For example, exposure therapy to face a fear of spiders may progress from looking at cartoon images of spiders (low perceived threat level) to looking at photographs, to watching videos of spiders, to watching live spiders in a terrarium, to ultimately holding a nonvenomous spider (high perceived threat level). During each of these stages of exposure therapy, the individual uses cognition and relaxation techniques (e.g., deep abdominal breathing) to gain control of their reflexive fear response to the point where the fear no longer activates their sympathetic nervous system. Exposure therapy encourages an individual to approach rather than avoid a fear and to proactively use cognition and relaxation techniques to reduce reflexive fear responses. Ultimately, exposure therapy engenders self-efficacy with respect to facing fear—the individual learns that it is possible to face and reduce the negative impacts of a fear as well as how to do so.

The success of exposure therapy is well documented. While it is more commonly practiced in clinical settings, self-directed exposure therapy can provide an effective approach for individuals to confront fear and reduce its negative impact without the need for professional help. The advancement of technology, enabling fear exposure using augmented and virtual reality, has opened up the possibilities for self-directed exposure therapy. This potential is enhanced by the development of smartphone applications and virtual therapy assistants that guide and support exposure therapy.

Commitment

 **Between this session and the next, I commit to the following:**

☐ Applying the 7-step process to conquer a fear stopping me from moving toward my ideal future.

☐ Helping guide someone through the process for one of their smaller fears or frustrations.

Next up, in Session 7: *Driving Belief*, you'll begin the greatest lesson: intensifying the voice of belief to activate courage and reach your ideal future.

> "Each of us is kept from being our best by our fears. Change is always possible. Understand it, embrace it, be brave about it—and the reward is yours for the taking."
>
> —DR. RODDY CARTER

DRIVING BELIEF

Welcome to Session 7! You've courageously journeyed through your *Brain Operating System* (BOS) to face and conquer your fears. Now, harness the power of your cognitive brain to build unwavering belief and think your way toward success.

Set aside two hours to complete the session content and another hour for your Mastery Missions.

In this session, you will:

- Discover the hidden secret of the world's greatest heroes, influencers, and leaders who have overcome incredible odds, and learn how to invoke this same power in yourself.

- Explore the critical role your thoughts play in enabling belief, and use your cognitive brain to identify, use, and affirm your three most powerful personal assets to quiet the voice of fear and drive success.

- Customize a lasting gratitude practice using your cognitive brain to deliberately flood your mind with positivity and think yourself beyond fear.

How I Overcame Doubt

My health journey hasn't always reflected my best self.

I was dragging through life.

At the start of the coaching, I shared a difficult time in my life. Despite being a well-trained, knowledgeable physician, I was not the best version of myself.

In fact, I was a train wreck waiting to happen: grossly overweight, unable to climb two flights of stairs without gasping, no pride in my appearance, and sleeping poorly. Most of all, I was **unhappy—dragging through life** day to day.

During a grueling transcontinental flight, I felt choked to death in my seat. The discomfort of the restrictive seat belt exaggerated the internal agony I already had over my degenerating state. When I got off the plane, my walk through the airport was one of **desperation**; I couldn't go on the same way.

Something had to change. I needed to *believe*.

I decided that I had to make a change. So, I went back to my scientific roots, drawing on my deep biological insight. With science on my side, I started to reboot my life.

I won't lie; the beginning was hard. I struggled to change my eating and exercise habits. I was fighting an uphill battle—one I'd lost before, over and over again. Then one day, completely by accident, I discovered a power that we all have within us: the power of belief.

In that unexplainable and unexpected moment when I looked into the mirror and saw a reflection of me as a young, fit, healthy athlete, everything changed for me. Instead of seeing the reflection of the sagging, decaying man I'd passed twice a day getting to the shower and back, I saw the eyes of an athlete.

From that moment forward—after years of neglect—I believed in myself again. I *believed* I was an athlete. And when I believed I was an athlete, I acted like one. I exercised like an athlete (starting slowly, of course). I ate like an athlete, skipping the extra donut. I slept like an athlete, which I hadn't done in a long time. I made no excuses—not because I had exceptional willpower, but because a real athlete simply wouldn't.

I *believed* that the future I'd imagined was possible. I became **unstoppable**.

Three years later, I witnessed the transformational force enabled by my belief: I had lost 80 pounds. I could run up a long flight of stairs without pausing. I stopped my rapidly accelerating premature decline.

When you think you can, you can.

In Session 2, I introduced this phrase. We hear it a lot—maybe too much—and its real power can get lost. Take time to appreciate how impactful this statement is to mastering your BOS.

When your **thoughts are unwaveringly positive**...when you **think** you can **so much** that you *know* you can...**it becomes true**!

When you refuse to accept any other alternative, belief becomes your reality.

You *literally* think yourself toward success. The hierarchical structure of your brain explains why this is possible.

> "Whether you think you can or you think you can't—**you're right.**"
>
> —HENRY FORD

The Success Formula

 **When belief is the loudest voice, you move toward success.**

So you can see that there's a very simple balance going on here. When the voice of belief is louder than the voice of fear, we advance toward success—relentlessly. But on the other hand, if the voice of fear overwhelms our belief, we not only move backward and away from success, but truly, we can move toward failure.

Belief unlocks success.

To achieve success, begin to eliminate doubt lurking in the basement of your mind—that's why you've been diligently working to conquer hidden fears. But that's not all you'll need to do. Building belief is crucial.

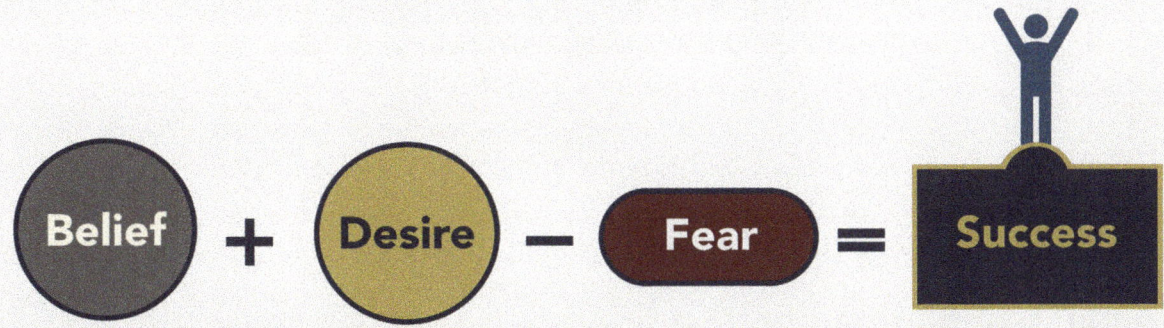

Once you attain unwavering belief, your success and the achievement of your dreams is largely inevitable.

To intensify the voice of belief, take voluntary control of your cognitive brain. The simplest way to achieve this is by focusing your attention on one positive aspect of life.

Big ideas take time to fully develop.

The bigger the idea, the more powerfully you need to evoke belief (using the cognitive brain) to overcome fear or doubt (the voice of the reptilian brain).

Watch the journey of an idea as it ascends the ramp toward success.

Ideas start in the cognitive brain. Your vision of success is a combination of ideas, the thoughts that you imagine for yourself.

Fear pushes back.

Belief (the small gray figure) has advanced the idea, but fear (the small red-brown figure) pushes back. The reptilian brain shouts its messages of fear and doubt, which hold you back from success. Your vision of success is at risk of being crushed before it even gains momentum.

Nourishing belief moves you farther along.

As you nurture your idea, belief grows. But fear also grows. This means that resistance to your idea is growing within.

At this stage, you must work even harder to capitalize on your BOS by nurturing further positive thoughts. As you use your cognitive brain to do this, belief grows even more and continues to drive your idea up the ramp, against the resistance of fear.

Belief plus desire makes you unstoppable.

Using your cognitive brain, you've positioned yourself to overcome fear and doubt and have advanced your idea. Positive emotion (the gold figure) now joins belief to fight against fear.

Remember how the emotional brain flips toward the loudest voice? Together, belief plus positive emotion overcome fear and doubt to move your idea to the top.

Celebrate success!

You've done the hard work. Refusing to contemplate failure, you thoughtfully drove your idea to the top of the ramp. At this moment, under the influence of gravity and with one more nudge, you easily trigger a cascade of meaningful actions. You plan, act, expect, demand, and eventually anticipate success. Hopefully, you'll also pause for the final important action—celebrating your success because you've become **unstoppable**.

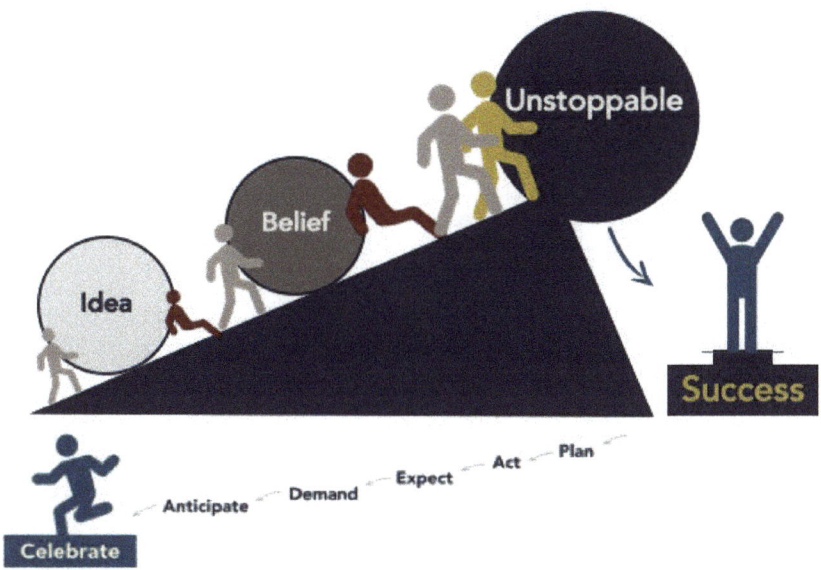

Building belief and activating desire are concomitant processes.

In the next two sessions, you'll learn four methods to invoke belief and think your way to success: owning your assets, expressing gratitude, using mantras, and employing the brain-body connection. In Session 9, you'll go beyond belief by activating your emotional brain to turboboost desire to enhance the powerful effects of belief.

Belief Mindset

If you doubt the power of belief, consider the lives of people who've succeeded despite incredible odds.

Heroes—both public figures and ordinary people—who've accomplished extraordinary achievements aren't immune to the voice of the reptilian brain. They simply never give up. When doubt comes knocking, as it always does, these people believe. ***Truly believe.*** They refuse to accept defeat. They remove all traces of doubt.

Nelson Mandela took on the massive challenge of overthrowing the evil of apartheid and its formal constitutional construct. Through 27 crushing years in prison, he **believed**. He **believed** in his vision. He **believed** in his rights. He **believed** that he would liberate the people of South Africa. He **believed** that he would lead them to freedom. And he did!

Eleanor Roosevelt achieved unprecedented accomplishments in her role as First Lady. She **believed** in the advancement of women's rights. She **believed** in American youth. She insisted on racial equality. She acted as a catalyst for change, circling the globe, visiting scores of countries, and meeting with world leaders. As a result of her unwavering **belief**, her achievements continue to influence national constitutions and serve as the foundation for international laws and treaties.

I'm extremely grateful for the wise words of these two people and many other icons who reflect the power of belief across the wide range of their experiences: Martin Luther King, Jr., Mother Teresa, Steve Jobs, Helen Keller, Rosa Parks, Mahatma Gandhi, Indra Nooyi, Albert Einstein, Oprah Winfrey, Richard Branson, and Arianna Huffington.

There is abundant evidence that regular people have enjoyed extraordinary achievements by believing in success and refusing to contemplate failure. We all know someone who believes they have the power to make a difference. The starting point is unanimously belief.

You may call belief something different, like *confidence*, *determination*, or *intention*. The actual word doesn't really matter.

For me, "belief" describes the deep faith in a current or future state that compels appropriate action and makes success inevitable.

I also chose the word "belief" because it accurately reflects the neuroscience that underpins this power. Thoughts originating in the cognitive brain play a profound role in determining our future. Henry Ford recognized **belief**, too.

Quotes Build Belief

Quotes teach the keys to success.

Quotes about success have one prevailing theme: They reflect the prominent role of belief. I share many of my favorite quotes in this program because I believe they carry genuine scientific weight that substantiates the power of belief.

The value of quotes

Geeky Roddy loves quotes, loves people's ability to capture the essence of powerful things in a few words. But from a scientific perspective, there's a more important reason. And I'll go back to my first book, BodyWHealth.

BodyWHealth I wrote as a scientist, and my objective was to say I've rebooted my life and during the process of this reboot, both from a practical and an academic perspective, I— Roddy the scientist—was determined to figure out the most important things we need to do to live a good life, based on science: exercise, caloric balance, sleeping well. Those were easy to substantiate.

And then I got down to this notion of self-belief. And I went to the literature to find the science of self-belief. And it was dramatically empty. So here I had a completely lopsided book, stacked with science behind the physical directions, and when I got to the psyche, I had very little substantiation. And as a scientist, I felt frail now recommending driving belief as a critical part of overall well-being. And then I started noticing that, over time, I had accumulated these fantastic quotes.

For me, that became the surrogate science. This is what I call "empiric science": Real people who have changed the world, reflecting on what helped them change the world, were telling us in these powerful quotes that belief is one of those things that changed the world. And that became my scientific documentation, which I think is as valid—maybe even more valid—than a thousand randomized, controlled clinical studies. And so that is my deep fascination with these words.

Magnify the impact of inspiring quotes.

Harness the full capacity of your cognitive brain by directing your undivided attention to the positive, belief-building quotes throughout this program. I consider them to be empirical science— perhaps more valid than randomized, controlled studies that hold belief against a placebo.

 **EXERCISE 1**

Reflect on Belief-Building Quotes

ACTION 1 OF 1

Reflect

Reflect on each of the following quotes. To make it more than an inspiring statement, think about each question and write down your reflections in the space provided.

How can you apply this quote to overcome the voice of fear and achieve your dream?

> ## "Believe you can and you're halfway there."
>
> —THEODORE ROOSEVELT

As you read this quote, what are your beliefs when it comes to realizing your dream?

> ## "We are who we believe we are."
>
> —C.S. LEWIS

Do you believe—implicitly and unquestionably—that you will realize your dream?

"When you believe in a thing, believe in it all the way—implicitly and unquestionably."

—WALT DISNEY

How does this quote relate to your dream?

"To be a great champion, you must believe you are the best. If you're not, pretend you are."

—MUHAMMAD ALI

How can you apply this quote to drive belief to achieve your dream?

"Believe in yourself, take on your challenges,
dig deep within yourself to conquer fears."

—CHANTAL SUTHERLAND

How does this quote validate your belief in yourself and your ability to realize your dreams?

"To move ahead, you need to believe in yourself;
have conviction in your beliefs and
the confidence to execute those beliefs."

—ADLIN SINCLAIR

How could you rewrite this quote to personalize it specifically to your dream?

> **"The future belongs to those who believe in the beauty of their dreams."**
>
> —ELEANOR ROOSEVELT

How can you apply this quote to validating the size of your dream—and then achieving it?

> **"Create the highest, grandest vision possible for your life, because you become what you believe."**
>
> —OPRAH WINFREY

I'm sure that you, like me, have noticed that these quotes affirming the power of belief come from world leaders who have attained success across a wide range of fields. Yes, that means that success in your dream and specific life circumstances—whatever they may be—will also be driven by belief.

Own Your Assets

Believe in yourself. Acknowledge your true worth and value.

My client John is a fellow physician. Below, he shares his story—one many of us struggle with.

John had become almost invisible to himself.

Meet my modest client, John, a fellow physician. He walked into my office obviously exhausted. He sat down and told me his story—one many of us struggle with.

From the day he left high school, he'd been on a mission. He cared deeply about people and wanted to help those suffering under the burden of disease. He'd given of himself, unselfishly, throughout his exceptional career. But now he was burned out, with nothing more to give.

Early in our time working together, I gave John an assignment. I asked him to find and celebrate his strengths.

If you'd asked me to do this for John, it would've taken me less than five minutes. I could've come up with a thorough inventory of wonderful assets: intelligence, sensitivity, empathy, compassion, kindness, strength, an analytical mind, foresight…and the list would have continued. But John really struggled with this task.

As John worked through the exercise, the shocking reality dawned on him: He'd become almost invisible to himself.

Can you relate?

During my time as a coach, I've met many invisible people—those who don't reflect back on themselves to see and appreciate their own remarkable gifts, talents, and contributions.

Through a systematic process, he rediscovered his innate value.

As John and I worked together over many months of deep reflection and courageous honesty, we revealed the underlying reasons for his habitual self-sacrifice and rediscovered his appreciation for his innate value. He recognized and embraced his personal assets.

Today, John will share his strengths with you with appropriate modesty—but also with real pride! He still appreciates the benefits of purposeful living, serving a cause bigger than himself. But he now understands that this is only possible when complemented by self-care, which includes his own recognition of his personal strengths, abilities, attributes,

and contributions—all the things that make up his powerful personal assets.

John's bravery has been rewarded. John is now more fully alive and excited about his future. And he's cultivated an invaluable tool that continues to drive his belief in himself and what he's capable of.

Can you relate?

If you're like John—in the habit of putting others first or maybe even thinking negatively about yourself—you'll likely find it challenging to see your own value and self-worth, to identify and embrace your own strengths.

Why do we tend to downplay our achievements?

Often we recognize the value in others yet become blind to our own strengths.

Have you experienced this, too?

You possess unique talents and strengths that make you special. You bring something to society that nobody else offers. However, we sometimes overlook our value because our natural strengths come effortlessly or we prefer to shift attention away from ourselves.

In denying our greatness, we delay success.

Discovering and embracing your personal assets requires deep reflection and courageous honesty. For many, acknowledging strengths can be challenging. To assist you, I'll provide two systematic approaches to reveal your unique value and identify your top three personal assets.

Your personal assets can get lost in the big picture.

A more subtle and surprisingly common problem is that talented people who have many assets are ignorant to their value, precisely because they have so many! How can people who possess numerous great qualities lose sight of their intrinsic value? They lose sight of their specific attributes and get lost in a vague and diffuse sea of strengths.

Here's a good metaphor: Imagine yourself standing in front of a well-stocked refrigerator overflowing with delicious foods.

Too Many Options

There are so many options that you may need to sort through them all before you can make a decision, and when you walk away you forget all of your options.

As you narrow down a wide variety of options, it's unlikely you'll remember the specific details.

On the other hand, what if there are only a few options?

Three Items

Contrast this with the experience of opening the same refrigerator and seeing only a few items: radishes, kale, and bell peppers.

The items in the refrigerator instantly become more memorable because there are just a few of them.

It's not enough to rely on the vague and fuzzy sense of who you are—the "overflowing refrigerator" of assets. The voice of the reptilian brain will focus on specifics, shouting many of the messages of fear we covered in the previous session.

When fear takes over, it's challenging to access your strengths and see yourself in a positive light. You can resolve this by focusing on three key strengths.

When you focus your cognitive brain on three positive personal assets, you successfully access the Office of the CEO and empower yourself with new choices. Like the three items in the near-empty refrigerator, the three assets you choose stand out in your mind. Your assets become visible and memorable.

> "The key driver of my transformation—to becoming **unstoppable**—was my **belief**."
>
> —DR. RODDY CARTER

Identify Your Assets

 **Systematically identify your assets.**

Here are two different approaches you can use to compile a working list of your personal strengths.

Approach 1 is quick and easy but risks being incomplete.

This approach can be done in under 30 minutes. It involves brainstorming a comprehensive inventory of your personal assets. Here, I'll guide you through the instructions.

Approach 2 requires you to spend a few moments twice a day for a week and ensures a more comprehensive view of your personal assets.

This approach involves writing down a few assets each day over a week. I encourage you to take this approach as a Mastery Mission to give your brain time to engage in deep personal reflection throughout the week, enabling you to more surely identify your full set of competencies. The full instructions for this approach are in the *Mastery Missions*.

I urge you to be patient with yourself as you work through these exercises. It's normal for the process of writing your assets to go slowly at first. To help, envision a close friend or family member articulating what they love and appreciate about you.

There are times your assets may quickly come to mind, especially once you've written two or three. After creating a comprehensive list, you'll narrow it down to your top three.

 EXERCISE 2

Identify Your Assets – Approach 1

Approach 1

As you work through this exercise, I encourage you to notice which level of the brain you're operating from. Use your cognitive brain to fully embrace positive traits, attributes, contributions, talents, strengths, skills, successes, and learned abilities. Put aside the voice of caution and self-doubt. Let every trait that's contributed to your success come to mind.

ACTION 1 OF 5

Pause

Before you brainstorm your assets, take a pause. Take a few deeper-than-normal breaths to shift the seat of your awareness into your prefrontal cortex.

ACTION 2 OF 5

Brainstorm

Write down every positive quality and personal asset that comes to mind.

Use your magnificent brain to scan your entire life, recalling every asset you've ever thought, heard, felt, or read about yourself. Reflect on your natural abilities as a child, personal and professional accomplishments, quality relationships, acts of kindness, obstacles overcome, skills mastered, and more!

Consider these prompts:

- What do I love doing?
- When am I happiest?
- In which areas of life do I feel energized?
- What skills come effortlessly to me?
- What do others compliment me on?
- What do others acknowledge me for?
- How have my past successes been enabled by my qualities?
- What activities put me in "the zone"?
- How do my friends, family, and peers recognize me?
- What qualities have driven my past successes?
- What do people remember about me?

Challenge yourself to write your assets as quickly as possible without pausing. Push your cognitive brain to generate 50 or more assets in 15 minutes.

ACTION 3 OF 5

Consolidate

Group similar assets or words together.

You may have written down various words describing similar qualities. For instance, *courageous*, *brave*, *bold*, *intrepid*, and *daring* all convey a willingness to take action, particularly in risky situations. Scan through your brainstormed asset list to identify any overlapping words. Group these words together, select one (your favorite) to represent the group, and write it down.

ACTION 4 OF 5

Select

Select your top three strengths from your consolidated list of assets. I encourage you to trust your first instinct. Then, step away. Come back to this action to revisit and revise your selections, if needed.

ACTION 5 OF 5

Imagine

Verify you've chosen assets that elicit the strongest positive emotions.

The strength of the positive feelings each asset evokes may differ. For instance, the assets you highlight in a job interview may have less emotional temperature than ones your lifelong friend recognizes in you.

As you assess the emotional temperature of each of your three assets, ask yourself if each one is:

- Intrinsically motivating.

- Energizing.

- Compelling.

- Accompanied by positive physical sensations.

- A frequent focus of conversations—either personal or professional.

Now use your full imagination to make this exercise real. Picture you and me seated across from one another at a table. I ask you, "What are your top three assets?"

You lean in and confidently say...

> **YOU**: "I'm...**[INSERT ASSET 1, ASSET 2,** and **ASSET 3]**."
>
> *As an example, let's say you've selected your capacity to be courageous, creative, and tenacious.*
>
> **ME**: "Wow, that's remarkable."
>
> *However, I notice that you don't seem wowed by your powerful assets. So, I continue...*
>
> "Well, I know an incredible person who is courageous, creative, and tenacious! Would you like to meet them?"
>
> *Now I see a shift in you. Your eyes have widened, and a sparkle starts to appear.*
>
> **YOU**: "Yes, I want to meet someone who courageously does what it takes...a person who's a creative, innovative thinker...and a person who's tenacious—who holds bold confidence and unwavering belief."
>
> **ME**: "What beautiful assets!"
>
> *At this point, you're seeing the same undeniable strengths that I see in you.*

If you feel strongly drawn to the assets you've selected, stick with them as your top three. If not, revisit your full inventory of assets and reflect on which ones you're most drawn to in other people. Revise your top three based on your strongest emotional responses.

If your assets evoke strong positive emotions, continue forward.

Express Gratitude for Your Assets

There's a deep glow we feel when we're in a state of gratitude.

You know the feeling of gratitude. Someone may have affirmed you, embraced you, showed you love, given you a special gift, or paid you a compliment—you feel a sense of pride or a warm glow. You feel good.

The good reaches deep into your body, and then something else happens. On a chemical level, gratitude generates a physiological and psychological condition that allows you to thrive both physically and emotionally.

As a physician and a scientist, my work drives me to explore powerful conditions. So, an intense feeling like gratitude intrigues me. Why would nature endow us with these strong feelings? There's more to it than the obvious strengthening of interpersonal connections. Undoubtedly, expressing gratitude toward another enhances the relationship, with mutual benefits. But it's the more personal purpose of gratitude that interests me most.

Scientists and many others have provided various definitions of gratitude, but the essence of these definitions is that gratitude is a state of thankfulness based on the recognition and appreciation of something good.

By now, it shouldn't surprise you that, to enjoy the benefits of gratitude, you need to use your BOS effectively. The better you understand and use your brain, the more powerful gratitude becomes in your life.

Gratitude: Is it a warm feeling or a pervasive state?

Warm Feeling

Gratitude isn't *just* a warm feeling or pleasant consequence of good times.

I call this secondary gratitude—when something good happens and we feel grateful. It's easy to feel grateful when life is good.

Pervasive State

Deep gratitude is a pervasive, enduring state.

Gratitude encompasses our social, psychological, mental, and biological condition. It channels our energy and actions in a positive direction, toward health, happiness, and ultimately unstoppability. This is what I refer to as *primary* or *intrinsic* gratitude. Intrinsic gratitude involves the deliberate, systematic process of generating appreciation and gratitude.

Nature designed you perfectly, with a massive cerebral cortex that is under your complete voluntary control, enabling you to generate intrinsic gratitude. You can intentionally channel your cognitive mental powers to think yourself beyond fear.

Intrinsic gratitude is a powerful condition that surpasses warm feelings. It holds the power to create self-fulfilling effects, accumulating benefits over time.

For instance, expressing appreciation toward others initiates a virtuous loop. Saying "thank you" more often floods your life with positivity, elevates your mood, and uplifts your spirit. Social scientists believe that strengthening any stage in this loop reinforces the overall impact of the cycle. You become increasingly aware of things to be grateful for—and the benefits snowball!

When you practice gratitude, you're not merely accessing a superficial state of happiness or ignoring negative emotions. Rather, you're using a clever approach to override the voice of fear.

Create a daily gratitude practice that empowers you to reframe any situation.

My gratitude exercise has three components to it.

I ask, what is it? What does it do for me, and what does it do for them?

So join me on the beach. I've had a lousy day, and I start a walk on one end of the beach, and I think about my first asset, empathy.

What is empathy? And while you can go to the dictionary, look it up, write it down, and learn it rote, I don't advise that because then you just spout out something somebody else wrote.

What does empathy mean to me or to you?

Empathy means that I am able to reach inside another human being. I'm able to deeply feel what they feel, deeply appreciate how they're seeing the world. I can truly get in their shoes. I have the ability to sometimes see and feel things before they're even aware of it.

That's what empathy is, and it's surrounded with this kindness and goodness and caring. That's what empathy is. I'm just defining it.

What does it do for me?

I'm able to hear a story about being overlooked, unloved, and unworthy, and I feel that woman's pain in, but I feel her joy. I feel her joy as she sees life differently.

I am so enriched by touching you inside, not just seeing your face and the reactions on the outside. I learn not just from the words you say; I learn from who you are deep inside. That's what empathy does for me.

What does it do for them?

Because I see and read who you are, I can touch your life and help you solve your problems in an unimaginable way because there are two of us solving your problem, not one.

I have clients whose lives have been fundamentally transformed.

Wow. Wow, wow, wow. Remember, I started my walk thinking it had been a lousy day. And I focused on empathy. Now I focus on my second asset: my intellect.

Same thing. What is it? What does it do for me? What does it do for them?

Then, I move on to my goal orientation. What is it? What does it do for me? What does it to for them?

That's gratitude. And that gratitude exercise will help you.

Remember those three things that make you undeniably special, undeniably powerful, undeniably you. Those are the standards that you regroup around.

And we have this cognitive brain. Because those are all thoughts, right? All thoughts.

And when I'm doing my gratitude exercise during the day, apart from reinforcing my three standards, I'm getting this part of my brain to talk loudest. And what does this miserable flip flopper do?

It flips to happy, and by the time I'm at the end of the beach, it's a good day.

The 3-question gratitude practice is based on your top three assets and three simple questions.

In my experience, this exercise works ***every time***. As you engage in your own gratitude practice, begin with a pause to shift the seat of your awareness into your prefrontal cortex.

1. What is it?

Identify your first asset, and think about what it means.

Colorfully define and describe your asset without relying on dictionary definitions. Instead, use your own words to express what this asset means to you. Each time you do this, your description may vary, and that's okay. You're actively using your cognitive brain to think about what this asset *really* means to you. To gain deeper insight, consider how you'd define and describe this asset if it belonged to someone else.

> What does empathy (my first asset) mean to me?
>
> *To me, empathy means I'm able to reach inside another human being. I'm able to deeply feel what they feel and deeply appreciate how they're seeing the world. I'm able to stand and walk in their shoes.*

2. What does it do for me?

Ask and answer: *What does this asset do for me?*

Deeply reflect on the value of this asset for you. Consider the benefits you derive from it, exploring how it has enhanced your life in the past, what it does for you today, and its ongoing impact on your future.

> What does empathy do for me?
>
> *Empathy enables me to feel connected to other people. People share their inner pain and struggles with me. I'm enriched by knowing people on a deeper level. If one of my friends feels overlooked or unworthy, I feel her pain. But I also feel a joy that I have this wisdom that allows me to see her future differently. I can be with her, and I get to walk on deep journeys of life because of my empathy.*
>
> *My asset of empathy enables me to see the world through thousands of different eyes. If I had only seen through my own eyes, or heard through my own ears, I would have a very narrow perspective of the world. Instead, this gift allows me to intimately experience the world from a myriad of perspectives. It has truly made me a very fortunate man.*

3. What does it do for them?

Finally, ask and answer: *What does this asset do for others?*

Reflect on how this asset adds value to the lives of others. Consider what your gift enables you to do for—and give to—others and how they are enriched by it.

What does empathy do for others?

Others feel seen and heard. They feel safe knowing they can share freely with me because I understand their feelings and their fears. They benefit from having me walk with them to solve their problems. They don't have to face their challenges alone. We can overcome obstacles in unimaginable ways when there are two of us working to solve problems, not one. They receive the gift of my experience, my wisdom, and my inquiries. These deeper questions elicit insights they may not have had as easily. Their lives are fundamentally changed by these things.

I'm willing to guarantee that, if you truly ask and answer these three questions about any of your top three assets, you will notice that your mood shifts, sometimes dramatically for the positive. In day-to-day life, it can be difficult to shift your mood. This is a powerful tool that you can use any time, any place to do just that!

Commit to a Regular Practice

What makes belief and gratitude especially powerful is their capacity to be systematically nurtured...like a muscle.

A muscle atrophies
when you
forget to use it.

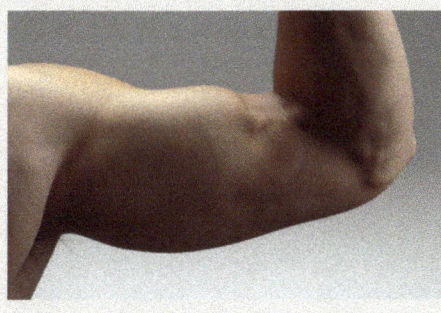

A muscle thrives
when you
deliberately train it.

As you develop your daily gratitude practice, remember that your goal is to graduate to more spontaneous positive thinking, as often as possible. Revisit, acknowledge, own, and celebrate your top three assets frequently enough that you're able to recite these assets on demand, at any time of the day or night.

In the heat of battle on a tough day, it's all too easy to forget your assets and why you deserve what you seek. It's not enough to vaguely think you have what it takes. Consistently and firmly hold a few prime examples of your strengths in the front of your mind to maintain a positive mindset.

You can consciously recruit your cognitive brain and your AFC to help you to do this.

By making an ongoing commitment to practice gratitude, you're actively taking control of the thoughts in your cognitive brain, ensuring they remain positive. As you express gratitude for your top three assets, your AFC is attentively listening, and it quickly starts gathering ample evidence that strengthens your appreciation for these remarkable assets that are undeniably yours to own and celebrate.

> "**Gratitude** is not only the **greatest of virtues**,
> but the parent of all the others."
>
> —CICERO

Mastery Missions

Congratulations!

You've completed Session 7 along with the two session exercises: *Reflect on Belief-Building Quotes* and *Identify Your Assets – Approach 1*. It's very important to systematically build belief. In fact, it's so important that I encourage you to dedicate time each day this week to practicing this fundamental skill.

For five consecutive days, repeat Mastery Mission 3—the practice of owning, reflecting on, and celebrating your top three assets. If possible, do this while taking walks. I also challenge you to take daily actions to identify a more comprehensive view of your personal assets. Once you've completed these missions, you'll be ready to move to the next session.

MASTERY MISSION 1

Drive Belief

ACTION 1 OF 3

Reflect

This mission aims to tap into the power of belief by reflecting on the qualities of people who inspire you—your heroes. Learn more about your heroes and their underlying beliefs. Collect your favorite quotes. Then, use the motivation and inspiration you receive to revise your ideal future statements.

Reflect on the lives and achievements of people you admire:

- What characteristics, strengths, and personal assets have contributed to their success?

- What thoughts, ideas, and actions have empowered their unwavering belief?

- How has their belief motivated them moment by moment and day by day?

- What words or phrases do they use that resonate with you?

ACTION 2 OF 3

Revise

Look at the most recent version of your desired future summary, whether that's what you wrote in Session 1 and have edited by hand along the way or a digital document you've been updating as you've progressed through the sessions. Consider how you could revise it to harness the full power of your heroes. Make any necessary edits, using the space below to rewrite sections of your summary if you'd like.

ACTION 3 OF 3

Share

Share what you've learned and know about your heroes with others, particularly about how belief drove their success. When you share about belief and your heroes' journeys, you reinforce your understanding of your BOS. Teaching and sharing powerfully help you learn and integrate these concepts.

MASTERY MISSION 2

Identify Your Assets – Approach 2

I trust that you completed Approach 1 to identify your top three assets as you worked through the session. This mission, *Identify Your Assets – Approach 2*, involves a challenge for you to take daily actions both in the morning and in the evening for one week. Before you begin, you may find it valuable to revisit the **unstoppable** moments you recorded in Session 1.

ACTION 1 OF 7

Pause

Before you brainstorm your assets at the beginning and end of each day, pause to shift the seat of your awareness into your prefrontal cortex.

Do this by taking a few deeper-than-normal breaths.

ACTION 2 OF 7

Brainstorm

Each morning and night for a week, write down the top three assets that come to your mind. Each time, start with a fresh perspective. It doesn't need to be a new set of three assets each time you write, and it doesn't matter whether you repeat any or all of the assets you've captured on previous occasions. Simply approach the task with a fresh perspective each time, which happens naturally when you're beginning to rest after a long day or waking up in the morning after sleep.

AM

PM

ACTION 3 OF 7

Repeat

Repeat this process every morning and evening for at least seven days, whether each list differs from the last or is the same. Continue to reflect on the question *What are my greatest assets?* and provide your spontaneous, immediate response in the moment.

ACTION 4 OF 7

Analyze

Analyze your cumulative list of assets. Look for trends. Tally how many times each asset appears. These trends and counts may help you in your next action.

ACTION 5 OF 7

Select

Start by reviewing the patterns and trends you found in Action 4. Select your top three strengths from your cumulative list of assets, and record them below. If you are having trouble identifying just three assets, I encourage you to go with your first instinct.

```

```

ACTION 6 OF 7

Verify

To verify that you've chosen assets that elicit the strongest positive emotions, imagine meeting someone with those assets. Do you feel strongly drawn to the assets you've selected? If so, stick with them as your top three. If not, revisit your full inventory of assets and reflect on which ones you're most drawn to in other people.

ACTION 7 OF 7

Calibrate

Seek input from those who know you well. Ask them for their thoughts on your top three assets.

Make use of their feedback to confirm your final choices, and record them below.

```

```

MASTERY MISSION 3

Own Your Assets

Memorize your top three assets—because when we meet in an airport in New York or a restaurant in London, I *am* going to ask you what your top three assets are. And I expect you to remember them automatically, without blinking an eye!

Once you've memorized your assets, use them for a daily gratitude practice. Spend five minutes exploring, reflecting on, owning, and answering three questions for each asset.

ACTION 1 OF 4

Pause

Pause to shift the seat of your awareness into your prefrontal cortex.

ACTION 2 OF 4

Own Asset 1

Spend five minutes exploring, reflecting on, and owning your first asset.

- What is it?
- What does it do for me?
- What does it do for them?

ACTION 3 OF 4

Own Asset 2

Spend five minutes exploring, reflecting on, and owning your second asset.

- What is it?
- What does it do for me?
- What does it do for them?

```
┌─────────────────────────────────────────────────────────┐
│                                                         │
│                                                         │
│                                                         │
│                                                         │
│                                                         │
└─────────────────────────────────────────────────────────┘
```

ACTION 4 OF 4

Own Asset 3

Spend five minutes exploring, reflecting on, and owning your third asset.

- What is it?
- What does it do for me?
- What does it do for them?

```
┌─────────────────────────────────────────────────────────┐
│                                                         │
│                                                         │
│                                                         │
│                                                         │
│                                                         │
└─────────────────────────────────────────────────────────┘
```

Then, pause again. Note how your cognitive brain has overridden the voice of fear and how many positive emotions you experienced during the process.

Supplemental Science

You're invited to delve into the supporting research on the topics covered in this session. Keep in mind that exploring the supplemental science is optional. You can return anytime to read more about the underlying science of the *Brain Operating System* methodology.

Benefits of Gratitude

There are direct physical and emotional benefits of gratitude. Here is a short list of the positive effects of gratitude, taken from scientific research.

- **Healthier behavior:** Grateful people exercise more and are more diligent about going for regular medical checkups and utilizing preventative services.

- **Reduced systemic inflammation:** Gratitude practices reduce chemicals that indicate the presence of systemic inflammation in patients with heart failure. Systemic inflammation plays a role in heart disease, diabetes, neurodegenerative disease, and cancer.

- **Better sleep:** Grateful people sleep better. They fall asleep more easily, get more sleep, and feel more refreshed when they wake.

- **Reduced stress:** Studies have shown that gratitude is related to a reduction in the stress hormone cortisol. Use of gratitude diaries by health care practitioners is linked to a reduction in their perceived stress and symptoms of depression.

- **Improved cardiovascular health:** Studies have shown that gratitude can reduce blood pressure.

- **Greater happiness and enhanced immune strength:** Gratitude increases happiness, enthusiasm, and joy. Independent of its direct impact on health, there are well-researched links between happiness and both immune health and longevity. Gratitude has also been shown to reduce anxiety and depression.

- **Stronger relationships:** Gratitude has been shown to enhance relationships, including romantic relationships. People who are grateful show more kindness and support of others (so-called "pro-social" behavior), even when it comes at a personal cost.

- **Improved recovery from post-traumatic stress disorder (PTSD):** Research on Vietnam War veterans has shown how gratitude practices enhanced their resilience and response to PTSD.

- **Increased community awareness and social contribution:** Grateful people are more inclined to support social causes.

Commitment

 **Between this session and the next, I commit to the following:**

☐ Learning more about my heroes and their underlying beliefs.

☐ Identifying and memorizing my top three assets.

☐ Spending 20 minutes a day practicing the 3-question gratitude exercise by applying the three questions to my top three assets: *What is it? What does it do for me? What does it do for them?*

Next up, in Session 8: *Boosting Belief,* you'll turboboost belief with two powerful techniques to quickly correct course and power up positivity anytime you feel stuck or need a boost.

"Whatever the mind can conceive and **believe**,

the mind can **achieve**."

—NAPOLEON HILL

BOOSTING BELIEF

Welcome to Session 8! Now that you've identified your top three assets and are cultivating a consistent gratitude practice rooted in these strengths, let's power up your positivity with mantras and delve into a simple way you can boost belief using your magnificent body.

Plan to spend two hours on the session content and another hour on your Mastery Missions.

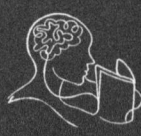

In this session, you will:

- Create empowering and affirming mantras that flood your brain with positivity, whether you're seeking to build strengths or to reinforce change on your journey toward your ideal future.

- Explore a scientifically validated trick to override fear by learning how to enlist your body to boost success.

- Develop a personalized, systematic plan to consistently exercise your belief muscle.

Thoughts Shape Your Life

Your future depends on what you think about.

What you're living with today, you designed and implemented yesterday. Sometimes you've done that intentionally; other times, not. But **you** programmed your BOS—no one else. Not your partner, your boss, your parents, or your kids. **Your predominant thoughts have shaped and continue to shape your actions and your life.**

If you've been practicing gratitude and owning your assets, your cognitive brain is beginning to shout louder than the voice of fear. When you choose to own your assets and consciously focus on the positive instead of the negative, your emotional brain listens and responds to the loud voice of your cognitive brain, flipping to reinforce the positivity. More importantly, your AFC—also listening to the voice of your cognitive brain—responds to your positive thoughts:

- It **focuses your attention** on the data that proves the truth in your positive statements.
- It balances and **contextualizes data** that may appear to dispute these positive statements.
- It **reinforces** your initial **positive thoughts**.
- It **transforms** your life **experiences** for the better.

The statements you think and say about yourself profoundly influence whether you will become **unstoppable** and achieve your dreams. The good news is there are many powerful exercises you can engage in to anchor positivity in your brain. One of these is the regular use of mantras. When you use mantras consistently, you're programming your filter and rewiring your brain for success.

Mantras are powerful belief-builders.

They are short, self-affirming, and empowering thoughts that contain positive words or phrases that concisely express your basic beliefs. A mantra gives you a positive thought to latch onto and, when repeated, can shift your brain from a fear-based focus to positivity.

Mantras invoke unshakable self-belief and confidence.

Mantras can be traced back several thousand years to well-respected spiritual rituals and meditation, and their use is now widely accepted as a motivational practice.

Effective mantras always meet these three key requirements:

- **They are in the first person** ("I am..." or "I have...").
- **They are in the present tense** (as if you are accomplishing or have already accomplished what your mantra states).
- **They contain only positive words and phrases** to focus your attention explicitly on what you want (excluding what you do *not* want).

251

 **Mantras affirm who you are TODAY!**

You know what mantras are? Mantras are short sayings. You take some of your greatest assets, and you put them into a short sentence, and you write them down.

What are the characteristics of a powerful mantra? First person, present tense. "I am!" Not, "I kind of vaguely hope that one day, as a result of some really gnarly work, I may possibly..." No! "I am. TODAY, I am!"

Relate them, if you can, to your greatest assets. It's another way to reinforce them. And often, they relate to an outcome of those assets.

And we write it down, and we own it, because it's true. And people who know you will never argue with that, because it's undeniably who you are.

"Your life today is a result of your thinking yesterday.

Your life tomorrow will be determined

by what you think today."

—JOHN C. MAXWELL

Test Yourself

Before your write your own mantras, test your knowledge of affirming and empowering mantras.

Practice distinguishing affirming and empowering mantras from ones that are not. For each statement, ask yourself: Is it written in the first person? Is it written in the present tense? Does it contain only positive words and phrases?

For each of the 10 statements, circle YES or NO to indicate whether it is affirming and empowering.

STATEMENT	AFFIRMING AND EMPOWERING?
I am no longer stressed and tired.	YES NO
I always see the best in others.	YES NO
I am filled with energy and joy today.	YES NO
I have limitless creative energy that sparks new ideas.	YES NO
I am an accomplished writer.	YES NO
I am wildly successful, with skills to propel my career.	YES NO
I can be wildly successful when I have the right skills.	YES NO
I want to become good at writing.	YES NO
Creative energy sparks new ideas.	YES NO
I am working toward not judging others.	YES NO

Five of the statements are not affirming and empowering because they fail to meet the key requirements of effective mantras.

Read each statement, identify the unmet requirement, and rewrite the mantra. See below the writing space for answers and suggested mantras.

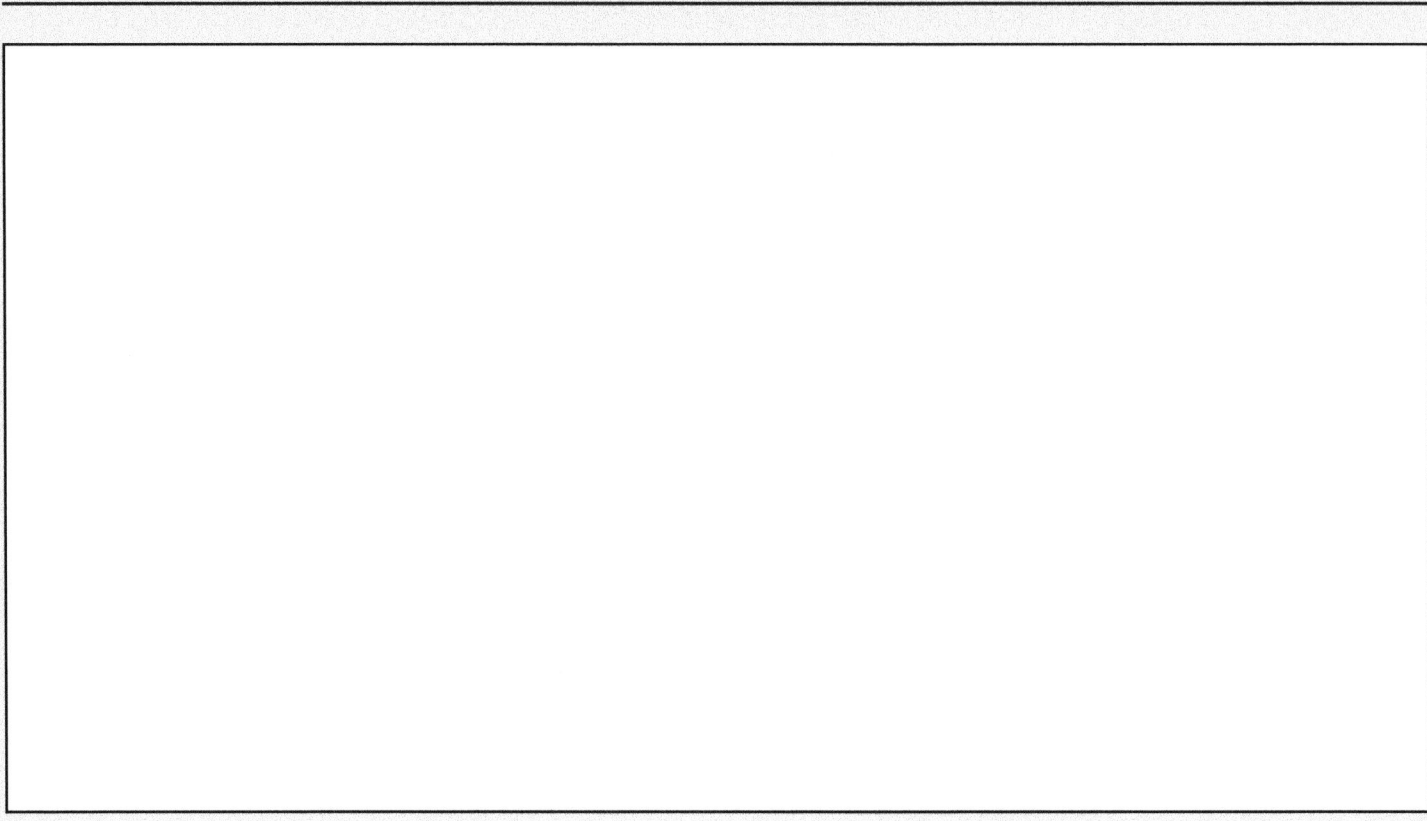

I'm no longer stressed and tired.

- This statement is not positive. Try *I am filled with energy and joy today* instead.

I can be wildly successful when I have the right skills.

- This statement is not in the present tense. Try *I am wildly successful, with skills to propel my career* instead.

I want to become good at writing.

- This statement is not in the present tense. Try *I am an accomplished writer* instead.

Creative energy sparks new ideas.

- This statement is not in the first person. Try *I have limitless creative energy that sparks new ideas* instead.

I am working toward not judging others.

- This statement is not positive and also is not in the present tense. Try *I always see the best in others* instead.

Mantras to Build Strengths

EXERCISE 1

Write Mantras to Build Strengths

Craft personal mantras connected to your top three assets.

It's your moment to write declarative statements filled with enthusiasm that embody the person you already are and want to affirm to reach your dreams.

Let these mantras be born from timeless words—positive statements from your cognitive brain that embrace your full potential.

ACTION 1 OF 5

Pause

Before you begin crafting your mantras, pause for a few moments. Shift the seat of your awareness into your prefrontal cortex.

ACTION 2 OF 5

Encapsulate

Connect each asset to a strong positive emotion. Begin by calling to mind your top three assets. Then, write down one word or phrase that elicits a strong positive emotion for each asset.

As an example, let's explore these three assets: *empathetic*, *introspective*, and *energetic*. You might write:

- **Empathetic:** Deep, meaningful connections
- **Introspective:** Rich insights within
- **Energetic:** Enthusiastic about life

ACTION 3 OF 5

Create

Create statements that align with your ideal future. Use your top three assets, your positive emotions, and the top themes of your ideal future to write three positive statements.

Building on the previous example, if you dream of traveling to other countries, you might use the keyword associated with **energetic**:

- *I'm a vibrant explorer, fueled by boundless energy and **enthusiasm**, venturing to exotic destinations.*

If you're looking for a romantic partner, you might use the keywords associated with **empathetic**:

- *I'm in a **deep, meaningful** romantic relationship overflowing with love and joy.*

If you dream of becoming an influential leader, the keywords associated with **introspective** may inspire you:

- *I'm an influential, effective leader with **rich insights** guiding others to reach their full potential.*

ACTION 4 OF 5

Abbreviate

Abbreviate your statements into mantras—short sentences that capture the essence of what you want to affirm.

For example:

Statement 1: *I'm a vibrant explorer, fueled by boundless energy and **enthusiasm**, venturing to exotic destinations.*

Mantra 1: *My **enthusiasm** fuels my adventures.*

Statement 2: *I'm in a **deep, meaningful** romantic relationship overflowing with love and joy.*

Mantra 2: *I'm in love and **meaningfully connected**.*

Statement 3: *I'm an influential, effective leader with **rich insights** guiding others to reach their full potential.*

Mantra 3: *I inspire others with **rich insights**.*

ACTION 5 OF 5

Check

Be sure you've created affirming and empowering mantras.

Read each mantra, and check that it:

1. Is written in the first person.

2. Is written in the present tense.

3. Contains only positive words and phrases.

If necessary, reword any of your mantras that don't meet these key requirements. Then, ready yourself to harness their power.

Great job!

Once you've created your mantras, continue to speak them, write them, reflect on them, update them, and add new ones as needed. But most importantly, bring them to mind and repeat them daily—because **regular** practice drives belief.

Mantras to Reinforce Change

Mantras help you to make changes.

Mantras can do more than affirm your top strengths and drive confidence in who you are today. They have the potential to assist you in reinforcing change by driving belief in the person you will be tomorrow.

To reach your dream, beyond relying on your top three assets, it's likely that you'll need to make some changes. Perhaps you need to:

- Develop and **grow new strengths**, skills, or habits to move you toward your desired success.

- **Move away from habits**, limiting beliefs, or thought patterns that have kept you stuck in the past.

Harness the power of mantras to help you make the changes you want or need to make.

 EXERCISE 2

Write Mantras to Reinforce Change

Create mantras that will drive you to develop new strengths.

Combine the mantra-writing process you've just completed with these actions to create mantras that will motivate you in developing qualities, skills, and positive habits or in overcoming limiting beliefs that have hindered your progress.

ACTION 1 OF 4

Pause

Before you begin, pause for a moment. Take a deep breath to shift the seat of your awareness into your prefrontal cortex.

ACTION 2 OF 4

Brainstorm

Brainstorm a list of what needs to change to lead you toward success and your ideal future. Include:

- Strengths or skills you lack or want to develop.

- Habits you wish to shift.

- Limiting beliefs holding you back.

- Actions or behaviors negatively impacting you.

Leave nothing on the table. Consider everything you need to cultivate or distance yourself from to achieve success.

ACTION 3 OF 4

Select

Select the top three things you're ready to change right now. Look at your list, and ask yourself:

- What changes or developments will propel me toward my ideal future?

- What are the key areas keeping me stuck and blocking me from reaching my ideal future?

ACTION 4 OF 4

Create

Create statements that communicate the change you desire. Use first person, present tense, and positive words and phrases.

Let's consider some examples:

- If you want to improve your mental focus, your statement might be: *Laser-like focus propels me toward my dreams.*

- If you want to improve your collaboration or communication skills, you could state: *Quality communication strengthens my relationships.*

- If you want to develop or enhance your leadership skills, your statement might read: *I lead with exceptional effectiveness.*

Reinforce who you will be tomorrow.

Mantras drive belief, confidence, and optimism by helping you to think about your desired outcome in the future as if it's real, despite any evident contradictions with your current circumstances.

Because mantras program your AFC to focus on the future, you accelerate your development and create cumulative benefits.

The Brain-Body Connection

If you hit a slump or a temporary state of stoppability, here's a trick to immediately drive belief.

Inevitably, there will be days when your practices slip, belief wanes, or the voice of your reptilian brain shakes your confidence. You might ask yourself: *What now? Does Roddy have any quick fixes or easy tricks to get me through this slump?*

The answer is yes, I do! It's a simple technique to help you **quickly** and **easily correct course** and take the upper hand when you most need to. But more than this, you can also use it to proactively **power up positivity**—anytime you need a boost. And...you can do it in the same amount of time it takes to brush your teeth!

I've purposely waited until now to share this with you, to allow you to first anchor your success in the foundational BOS concepts. Over the past two sessions, you've acquired several immensely powerful belief-building tools. Continue to master these, and they will carry you toward personal mastery and the success you deserve. Now, this last technique has the power to help you **tap into your personal superpowers**—to **drive belief** and **unstoppable** **success**.

Before I share this simple yet powerful tool, I'd like to explore something with you, something we've known about the brain and body for a long time.

Body language often mirrors emotions in the brain.

If you get bad news, feel defeated, or hit any low point in life, your nonverbal cues usually indicate it. Think about how your body responds when this happens—you may feel yourself shrinking back, closing off your body, or hunching over. Your gaze may turn downward, and with lowered head, you may cover your face with your hands.

In contrast, when you're celebrating success, your body language shows it. You may naturally expand, lengthen, and straighten your posture. Your head or chin may lift. You'll put your shoulders back, expand your chest, and perhaps even raise one or both arms.

You see these pronounced postures at competitive sporting events. The winners naturally adopt open, expansive postures with head and arms lifted. The defeated team or athletes often show closed, contractive postures—hunching over or even crouching down. You can spot these postural differences in personal and corporate settings, too.

Consider the body language displayed by the people in each scenario below. Do you notice the difference?

Three people struggle to find answers to why their plan failed.

Colleagues celebrate a record-breaking performance!

So, can you guess the trick? It's all about your magnificent body!

"When you choose to take on a power pose, your posture signals to your brain that you're **powerful**— and your **brain believes it**."

—DR. RODDY CARTER

The Body-Brain Connection

If the brain can influence the body, can the body influence the brain?

Research on the body-brain connection is exciting. Amy Cuddy, an award-winning social psychologist and Harvard lecturer, has contributed significantly to the study of how the body affects the brain. In particular, her research findings show that you're able to change your mindset by changing the way you hold (or move) your body.

(i) References for Amy Cuddy's work:

- Cuddy, A. J. C., Wilmuth, C. A., Yap, A. J., & Carney, D. R. (2015). Preparatory power posing affects nonverbal presence and job interview performance. *Journal of Applied Psychology, 100*(4), 1286–1295. https://doi.org/10.1037/a0038543

- Cuddy, A. J. C. (2019, January 31). *Presence: Bringing your boldest self to your biggest challenges* [Video]. Youtube. https://youtu.be/ATo9sYax-AQ?si=laH3CnfSzyChiupn

Does the body influence the brain?

One influential study answers that question.

There's wonderful research done by Amy Cuddy, in the northeast. And she said, "Let me go into a college, and I'm going to pick a bunch of graduating seniors, and I'm gonna take two groups. And I'm going to give one group state-of-the-art interview training. Let's train them. Really prepare them."

So they were researching who they were going to be speaking to, finding out who the hiring manager was; they were going in, asking more questions, and giving answers—they were sharp.

And then she took the other group, and she did all that...PLUS, she said, "Before you go into your interview, you're gonna go into the bathroom. And you're gonna find a big mirror, and you're going to stand in front of that mirror, and—I don't care if you look stupid—for two minutes, you're gonna stand in a power pose."

And they did it, and they recorded who got the jobs. And when they looked statistically at those two groups, guess who got more jobs than the other?

You know by the way that I've asked the question what the answer is. You go and stand in front of a mirror in a power pose for two minutes, you get a job.

Why?

Because this body was talking to this brain and changed the way I presented myself to my hiring manager, and I impressed from a position of confidence.

Body-brain connections are valuable to drive belief.

The body can reinforce cognitive messages. The message "It's bad. I'm losing," whether resounding in the brain of a struggling student, stressed CFO, or defeated offensive lineman, is often reflected in a closed, hunched-over posture—an unconscious attempt to be small. But when the message is "I've won! I've got this!" individuals sit up straight or stand tall with shoulders back and arms expanded, reinforcing cognitive messages of success.

Signals from expansive body postures reinforce cognitive messages of belief and overcome negative messages of fear from the reptilian brain.

While it's true that communication between the brain and the body often starts with the brain (for example, the brain can instruct the body to sit taller or take an expanded victory pose), it's important to note that **your body is always sending signals to your brain**.

The body affects the brain positively when in expansive postures and negatively when in contractive postures.

Characteristics of expansive postures

Expansive postures and gestures expand the body to take up space. Here are a few common characteristics of expansive postures:

- Head or chin up

- Sitting or standing tall

- Shoulders back

- Hands on hips

- One or both arms raised

Benefits of expansive postures

Expansive postures and gestures can be used as power poses because they build belief through their **positive effect** on the **cognitive brain**. These power poses:

- Elevate **self-confidence**.

- **Reduce fear** and nervousness.

- Drive feelings of **power**.

- Are often associated with **success** and **optimism**.

Characteristics of contractive postures

Contractive or closed postures reduce the amount of space occupied by the body. Here are some common characteristics of contractive postures:

- Sitting, slouching, or hunching over

- Arms held close to the body

- Head or chin down

- Crossed legs

- Hands close to face

Consequences of contractive postures

Contractive postures undermine feelings of success. They may also:

- Drive powerlessness.

- Impede success.

- Cause a person to turn inward and shut down to opportunities.

- Inhibit a person from taking action.

"It's not just about standing like a superhero for two minutes; it's about carrying yourself with power and pride and poise, as you deserve to do."

—AMY CUDDY

Power Poses

EXERCISE 3

Find Your Power Pose

Create your own signature power pose.

Initially, you might feel uncomfortable trying this. Some people do. However, try your best to broaden your perspective and expand your body. Enjoy experimenting with various poses and moving your body in different ways.

ACTION 1 OF 6

Explore

Explore a few power poses. The images below provide some examples. Seek additional inspiration from various aspects of your life. Reflect on:

- Your natural body language when you feel confident and successful.

- The different postures your friends and colleagues adopt in moments of triumph.

- The winning moments of individual athletes or teams.

Arms raised

Hands on hips

Feet on desk

**Arms
behind
head**

**One arm
raised**

ACTION 2 OF 6

Pause

Before you begin the process, pause for a few moments to shift the seat of your awareness into your prefrontal cortex.

Then, notice your current body posture and reflect on the state of your mood and mindset.

Take note of the:

- Angle of your head.

- Position of your shoulders.

- Straightness of your spine.

- Position of your arms in relation to your body—including whether they are crossed.

Gather as many details as possible about your current posture and state.

ACTION 3 OF 6

Express

Choose one power pose, and hold it for two minutes.

ACTION 4 OF 6

Reflect

Reflect on your mood and mindset after holding the pose for two minutes.

You may experience immediate and lasting effects on your productivity, mental state, and stress levels.

I encourage you to measure or score your confidence, energy, enthusiasm, productivity, or presence on a scale of 1 to 5 before and after adopting each power pose. You might try holding the pose every day before starting work or confronting obstacles.

Take note of any changes in your emotions, behaviors, or effectiveness.

ACTION 5 OF 6

Create

Combine different power poses or characteristics of expanded postures to create your own signature pose.

You may naturally look up, reach up, or give a thumbs-up when you feel a boost of confidence. Make use of your expansive movements, and incorporate these into any of the power pose examples.

ACTION 6 OF 6

Imprint

Lock in a mental image of what you look like in your power pose.

This action can feel awkward initially, but it's incredibly useful and your hesitation is likely to be short lived. The objective is to imprint the image of your power pose in your brain to more quickly access it. Consider standing in front of a mirror or taking a selfie of your power pose.

If you're in a situation where you want the benefits of power posing but you don't have the time, space, or freedom to assume the position, visualize yourself taking the pose. In the next session, we'll cover the power of visualization and the science that supports its effectiveness.

Powerfully posed!

Repeat this exercise with many different expansive postures.

Your facial expressions matter, too. Open your eyes wide or lift the corners of your mouth to add lightheartedness into your day. Reflect on every expansive change you make to your posture to help you recognize the impact it has on your brain—and your success.

Swagger

If body *poses* can influence the brain, can body *movements* do the same?

The answer is yes! Amy Cuddy's more recent research provides us with valuable insight into this. She's begun to study whether simple body movements—walking in particular—have an influence on a person's feeling of powerfulness. Here's what she discovered: **If you occupy more space when you walk, you're likely to feel more powerful.**

These three students are walking in to take their physics exam. They've studied. They're prepared. And now, as they walk to the lab for their exam, they take up space. Even though the picture captures a single moment in time, you can see their expansive movements.

Notice that their arms are swinging, their heads are moving, their strides are long, and their postures are tall with shoulders back.

How powerful do you think these students feel right now? How might these movements influence their test-taking abilities?

Contrast that with this student. She, too, is prepared, having studied late into the night. But she looks anxious and fearful, like she might be stuck or moving more slowly as she thinks about making her way to the lab.

Her arms are contracted and folded, held close to her body; her shoulders are slightly slumped over; and her gaze is downward.

How powerful do you think this student feels in comparison to the three students walking with purpose? How might her movements impact her test-taking abilities?

Finding your personal "swagger" is a powerful way to drive belief.

Swagger has everything to do with expressing positive energy. People who swagger radiate confidence. They often appear effortlessly sure of themselves—you can recognize this in their overall behaviors. The totality of their attitude and movements tells their brain, *I am **unstoppable***.

So here are some tips for how to swagger. Let's start with the upper body.

1. Find an upright and elevated seated position.

2. If possible, pull your shoulders back.

3. Expand your heart forward, or puff out your chest.

Just doing these three things automatically causes a lift of your head with a slight upward tilt of your chin. You eyes may naturally gaze up or out in front of you.

4. Consider incorporating gentle shoulder movements, such as small rotations backward or lifts, that can be comfortably performed while seated or in a way that suits your mobility.

5. If possible, position your hands on your hips to shift and expand your shoulders.

Reflect on your feelings as you swagger in your seat. You should feel more powerful, confident, and able to believe in your **unstoppable** success. If you can, stand up and swagger around the room, bringing your lower body into the mix. Imagine swaggering your way into your dream life.

Choose one or more of your favorite moves to use in particular situations or contexts, such as:

- Moves that **motivate** you to get going.

- Moves that **encourage** you to keep going.

- Moves that **help you cope** with bad news or stressful events.

- Moves that **inspire** you when you want to tap into your creativity.

- Moves that you **enjoy** at home.

- Moves that will help you to **celebrate** your success.

Psychic Push-Ups

 **To become unstoppable, you must do your psychic push-ups.**

You have to do psychic push-ups.

You know who gave me that word? A coach, who I coached. And she said to me, "Roddy, I've never had somebody give me so much powerful work, so many psychic push-ups."

And I thought, That's genius. Because in my previous life, I was helping elite athletes become elite physical beings. And they came to me, and they said, "Roddy, I want to weigh 280 pounds and bench-press six times my body weight."

And I said, "Okay, we can do that." And we went into the lab, and we wrote down a training program. And they went away, and they came back six weeks later, and I'd ask, "How are you doing?" And they'd say, "No progress!"

And I'd say, "Let me see your training log." And they'd say, "Nah, we'll talk about it another day" or "No, I left it in the car." And I'd say, "Show me." And it was empty.

No wonder it didn't work.

And the next person came in, and he was bench-pressing what he wanted. And I went to the log...he'd done all the work.

And it's the same with our psyche. It needs constant work.

You need to do the psychic push-ups.

Empower yourself to kick-start your psychic push-ups.

You're here to become **unstoppable**. At this stage of your journey, we've explored essential steps for attaining the clarity, confidence, and success you desire. Now, are you putting in the work?

What are psychic push-ups?

Just as we must regularly do physical exercises in order to effect bodily change, so too we must regularly exercise our psyches in order to make them healthy. "Psychic push-ups" is simply a cool term to help remind us to keep at it regularly, day after day, week after week.

The athletes and clients I work with, who consistently do their psychic push-ups without fail, **take home the gold**—both literally and figuratively.

It's not enough to show up with good intentions. I know from personal experience. I shared my story about carrying 80 pounds of excess weight and being unable to climb the stairs out of the

New York subway without collapsing from exhaustion. When it came time to take action, I always had a reason why I couldn't—too cold...too tired...too jet-lagged...too many work obligations... important family commitments—and I stayed stuck. These may have been valid reasons, but they were not valid *excuses*. As excuses, they were literally killing me.

The day I decided no more excuses and showed up to do the work was the day I took my first steps toward becoming **unstoppable**. I continue to feel younger and healthier, and I plan to continue this trend for the rest of my life. So, I do my psychic push-ups every day.

When should we do our psychic push-ups?

The correct answer is, as often as we can! You may include recurring predictable or calendared times for psychic push-ups (for example, saying your mantras as you wake up), but you may also include unscheduled and more general events as reminders, like saying a mantra at a red light or shifting back to your swagger every time you see yourself in a mirror or walk past the reflective glass in a storefront.

Why should we do our psychic push-ups?

It's easy to see our physical muscles growing as a result of exercise, but it's much harder sometimes to see our psychic muscles growing as a result of our psychic push-ups. So how do we know that they are working?

Think for a moment about this scenario.

Gianna is overcome.

Gianna's had a tough day at work. She comes home to find her kitchen flooded. Immediately, her reptilian brain—having already spent the day chewing on fears related to her stress at work—jumps into action and shouts loudly: *Hey, we've got trouble!*

Her body hears the negatives messages from her brain and doesn't hesitate. Her heart starts beating faster, her breathing becomes shallower and more rapid, and her muscles tense up. Her reptilian brain notices the changes, completely forgets that it initiated this sequence in the first place, and shouts even louder.

Suddenly—before she can even have a conscious thought—Gianna is in a complete panic, unable to think clearly enough to solve the issue of her flooded kitchen.

This is exactly what happens to most of us when we're faced with overwhelming stress. But our psychic push-ups are what make it possible for us to avert this cycle of stoppability. If we practice regularly, we can train our cognitive brain to react faster than our reptilian brain and our body to stay calm in the face of stress—and make ourselves **unstoppable**.

Consider this alternate scenario.

Gianna takes control.

Gianna's had a tough day at work. She comes home to find her kitchen flooded. She notices the voice of fear, but rather than react, she takes a deep breath to access the Office of the CEO.

She overrides the voice of fear and thinks, *I need to close the main water supply to prevent more damage.* Her body hears that her brain has a plan. The stress response is not triggered.

Gianna's brain, in turn, is listening to her body. Her brain can see that her body is calm, that her pulse and heart rate are normal. She's not tense. She is experiencing positive *being*, using her entire brain and body.

She may now even feel her emotional brain responding with a surge of positive emotion. She is in control, and she knows: *I can do this.*

I want to point out that the science we've covered about your BOS is the foundation for driving belief and becoming **unstoppable**. However, to truly live in a state of unstoppability, you must master these skills and build your belief muscle. Consistent practice of these exercises is essential. Without it, you'll be equipped with theoretical knowledge that won't propel you toward your dream. This is a recipe for staying stuck.

Let's revisit the success equation. We've focused on nurturing belief (thoughts from the cognitive brain) and overcoming the voice of fear (originating in the reptilian brain).

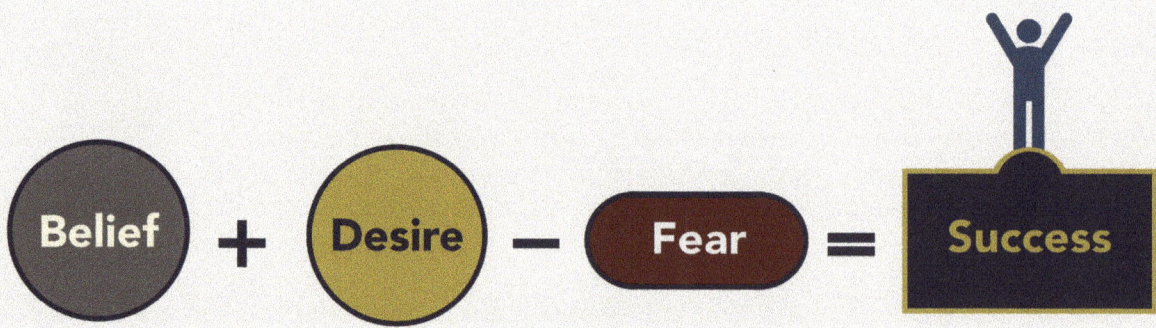

To achieve success, belief must be the bigger variable. Otherwise, you'll end up with an equation where fear dominates and success shrinks.

Remember, each day counts, so don't wait. Procrastination delays the achievement of your success and ideal future. Starting today—and every day—fuel your belief and pave the way to attain **unstoppable** success. Your cognitive brain is capable of this, and more. I believe in you. I know you can do this. You *will* do this.

Develop a Regular Practice

 ### Recite your mantras to keep them alive.

Reciting carefully crafted mantras regularly **floods your brain with positivity** and gives you a structured way of taking control of your thoughts and **consciously focusing on what you want**, especially when the voice of your reptilian brain is strident.

To prevent yourself falling victim to the reptilian brain's repetitive messages of doubt and fear, **recite your mantras every day**.

Employ your power poses to sustain positivity.

Standing in a power pose for two minutes is an easy and effective way to ensure that your cognitive brain is teeming with positive thoughts.

Swagger to counteract doubt.

"Fake it until you make it": Swaggering helps you convince yourself that you're **unstoppable**, despite attempts from the reptilian brain to shout loudly to the contrary.

 EXERCISE 4

Develop a Regular Practice

ACTION 1 OF 3

Reflect

Choose when and where you'll consistently do your psychic push-ups.

Reflect on your daily routine, and write down the options that come to mind. Here are some ideas:

- **Morning and night**: Stand in a power pose for two minutes first thing in the morning and last thing at night.

- **In nature**: Repeat your mantras while walking in nature.

- **Routine activities**: Swagger through daily activities, such as drinking your morning beverage, brushing your teeth, exercising, or completing your daily commute.

- **Mirror gazing**: Stand in front of a mirror and assume a power pose for two minutes.

- **Trying times**: Use your mantras to seed your brain with positivity; for example, if somebody criticizes you or when you find yourself confronting self-doubt.

ACTION 2 OF 3

Decide

Decide how you'll do your psychic push-ups. Will you write out your mantras? Will you go for a daily swagger walk? Will you power pose in front of a mirror or a window?

Brainstorm different approaches, and write down the ideas that you're keen to explore as you develop your daily practice.

ACTION 3 OF 3

Prompt

Prompt yourself with gentle reminders to reinforce consistent practice. For example:

- **Inquire daily**: Just before going to bed, ask yourself, "Did I do my psychic push-ups today?"

- **Set an alarm chime**: Set alerts on your mobile phone to remind you to do your psychic push-ups.

- **Listen to a friend**: Ask a friend, trusted colleague, or family member to remind you to do your psychic push-ups.

Just do it!

The memorable Nike slogan is a mantra in itself that you can use to motivate consistent practice.

Do your psychic push-ups—every day!

Doing your psychic push-ups sustains positivity. Positive thoughts turn into plans...and plans turn into actions that guide you toward realizing your **ideal future**.

Mastery Missions

Congratulations!

You've completed Session 8! Great work on the four exercises: *Write Mantras to Build Strengths*, *Write Mantras to Reinforce Change*, *Find Your Power Pose*, and *Develop a Regular Practice*.

If you felt hesitant while power posing, I understand. I was there, too. If you're willing to join me in assuming a superhero position or practicing your swagger before starting these Mastery Missions and at the start of each day, you'll cultivate belief and success, moving closer to your desired future.

MASTERY MISSION 1

Discover Inspiring Mantras

ACTION 1 OF 2

Seek

Utilize slogans to craft your personal mantras. While I've already suggested the Nike slogan—*Just do it!*—to kick-start your daily practice, you can surely find inspiration in other slogans.

Seek out inspiration. Throughout the day, read billboards, ads, taglines, and headlines—outdoors, in emails, or on social media. Which ones catch your attention and propel you into action?

ACTION 2 OF 2

Craft

Craft new, catchy mantras. Keep them short, compelling, and captivating—these are the building blocks of champion mantras.

Here are a few ideas inspired by slogans and taglines:

- I can do this.

- I am **unstoppable** today!

- I am master of my life.

- I run on awesome.

- **Unstoppable** is my middle name.

- **Unstoppable** starts now.

 **MASTERY MISSION 2**

Commit to Doing Your Push-Ups

ACTION 1 OF 2

Commit

Commit to a week of doing your psychic push-ups using the practice you developed in the *Develop a Regular Practice* exercise. Experiment with power poses, refine your mantras, and adapt your swagger technique to discover your optimal practice.

To keep your practice alive, consistently reflect on the positive benefits of firmly committing to your practice. Are you feeling more positive and empowered about realizing your dream? Are you seeing evidence in your life experiences reflecting your mantras?

Noting, acknowledging, and expressing gratitude for the positive effects of your daily practice will inspire and motivate you to keep going. With this inspiration, make an official commitment to practice daily. Concisely describe the practice you'll implement regularly. Then, sign your name as a symbol of your dedication.

I commit to doing my psychic push-ups every day. I will...

Signature: Date:

ACTION 2 OF 2

Share

Share your practice ideas. Because your mantras, power poses, and swagger are deeply personal and powerful, it can feel vulnerable sharing them with others. However, sharing them is a powerful step to supporting a consistent daily practice.

Please share them with me and the inner circle of people you trust. Here is some sample text that you can copy into an email:

> *Hi! I'm in the process of completing life-changing coaching. During the coaching, I created mantras, power poses, and a swagger to affirm my belief that I can achieve* **unstoppable** *success in all aspects of my life. Part of the exercise is to share those with someone special to me. So I am sharing them with you! Here they are:*
>
> *[INSERT YOUR DESCRIPTIONS]*
>
> *Sharing my psychic push-ups with you is one of the impactful ways I'm transforming my life and achieving my dreams. Thank you for supporting my personal transformation. I'll keep you posted on my progress and would love it if you regularly ask me how my practice is going, so I can keep my psychic push-ups strong. More to come!*

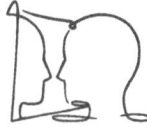 **MASTERY MISSION 3**

Notice Your Body Language

ACTION 1 OF 1

Elevate

Between this session and the next, be mindful of the state of your body and brain to assist you in identifying a power pose or movement that can shift you into a more positive mindset. Elevate positivity, confidence, and belief by heightening your awareness of your brain-body connections.

Consider one or more of these actions to mindfully capture snapshots of your body language in the moment:

- Set your phone alarm to go off at three unexpected times during the day—say, 10:17am, 1:43pm, and 5:26pm—times when you'll "catch" your body language during different situations. Then, take a moment to expand your body. Continue with your daily activities.

- Schedule regular times to turn your awareness to both your posture and your mindset: at home alone or with family, during work in your workspace or in meetings, and while engaging in leisure activities like social gatherings, exercise, or walks in nature.

- Keep a log to track your postures and movements for one week. Plus, take note of your body language in different contexts.

- Observe and reflect on your body language trends. Do you notice any patterns? How might your life be different if you used power poses regularly?

If you naturally find yourself adopting an expansive posture associated with positivity, try adding a power pose or movement to amplify your positivity and sense of empowerment.

If you notice a tendency to assume more contractive postures in specific situations, consider how you could integrate expansive body language in these contexts to elevate your positivity, confidence, and belief.

	Posture/Movements	Mindset
Day 1		
Time 1		
Time 2		
Time 3		
Day 2		
Time 1		
Time 2		
Time 3		
Day 3		
Time 1		
Time 2		
Time 3		
Day 4		
Time 1		
Time 2		
Time 3		
Day 5		
Time 1		
Time 2		
Time 3		

Posture/Movements

Mindset

Day 6

Time 1

Time 2

Time 3

Day 7

Time 1

Time 2

Time 3

Reflections

 **BONUS MASTERY MISSION**

Be Inspired

ACTION 1 OF 1

Revel

In the opening of this session, we explored how the life you're living today is a product of what you designed and implemented yesterday. Your thoughts and your mantras—the little things you tell yourself repeatedly every day—make who you are tomorrow.

Muhammad Ali, still considered by some to be one of the greatest champions of all time, sums up the power of mantras beautifully. Use this quote to inspire you daily. Revel in it.

> "I am the **greatest.** I said that even before I knew I was."
>
> —MUHAMMAD ALI

Supplemental Science

You're invited to delve into the supporting research on the topics covered in this session. Keep in mind that exploring the supplemental science is optional. You can return anytime to read more about the underlying science of the *Brain Operating System* methodology.

Body Language: An Innate Response to Emotions

Science reveals that the physical body language athletes habitually display when winning or losing is not just learned; it is also innate. It seems reasonable to think that the poses Olympic (and other) athletes adopt after they win (or lose) are learned, but the findings of a study conducted by researchers Jessica Tracy and David Matsumoto show that athletes exhibit particular body language as an innate response to winning or losing.[1]

These researchers looked at the body language of Paralympians—blind from birth—competing in the 2004 Paralympics. They observed that these non-sighted winners celebrated their success in the very same way as sighted athletes—with an expansive victory pose, often with their arms raised in the air. What is even more interesting is that these Paralympians, being blind from birth, had never seen anyone else exhibit these victory poses. Thus, the researchers concluded that victory posing is an innate response to the positive emotions experienced when winning, given that these blind athletes had never seen other athletes victory posing, so they could not have learned this behavior.

Similarly, the spontaneous postures displayed by defeated blind-from-birth athletes—head hanging down, shoulders slumped, and chest narrowed—were the same as those exhibited by sighted athletes who did not win. As the non-sighted Paralympians had never seen anyone else hang their head and make themselves small in defeat, this finding further supported the conclusion that the body language displayed by athletes is an innate response to the positive or negative emotions associated with winning or losing.

[1]Tracy, L. J., & Matsumoti, D. (2008). The spontaneous expression of pride and shame: Evidence for biologically innate nonverbal displays. *Psychological and Cognitive Sciences, 105*(33), 11655–11660. https://doi.org/10.1073/pnas.0802686105

More About Amy Cuddy's Research

Amy Cuddy first shared her work on how the body affects the brain in a TED talk[1] (ranked one of the most watched TED talks of all time) and in peer-reviewed publications.[2,3] Many broad circulation publications picked up on the power-posing concept, catapulting it into the public domain. Other social science researchers attempted to replicate Cuddy's study but failed to obtain the same results, leading to scrutiny and questioning of Cuddy's original assertions by members of the scientific community. However, after a meta-analysis and a careful statistical re-analysis performed by Cuddy herself,[4] the original research results were shown to be valid.

Cuddy's body-brain and power-posing research is now generally accepted and supported,[5,6] in part as a result of its solid behavioral logic resonating with any human being who has tried it.

[1]Cuddy, A. J. C. (2012, October 1). *Your body language may shape who you are* [Video]. YouTube. https://www.youtube.com/watch?v=Ks-_Mh1QhMc&t=1s

[2]Carney, D. R., Cuddy, A. J. C., & Yap, A. J. (2015). Review and summary of research on the embodied effects of expansive (vs. contractive) nonverbal displays. *Psychological Science, 26*(5), 657–663. https://doi.org/10.1177/0956797614566855

[3]Cuddy A. J. C., Wilmuth, C. A., Yap, A. J., & Carney, D. R. (2015). Preparatory power posing affects nonverbal presence and job interview performance. *Journal of Applied Psychology, 100*(4), 1286–1295. https://doi.org/10.1037/a0038543

[4]Cuddy, A. J. C., Schultz, S. J., & Fosse, N. E. (2018). P-curving a more comprehensive body of research on postural feedback reveals clear evidential value for power-posing effects: Reply to Simmons and Simonsohn (2017). *Psychological Science, 29*(4), 656–666. https://doi.org/10.1177/0956797617746749

[5]Elsesser, K. (2018, April 3). *Power posing is back: Amy Cuddy successfully refutes criticism.* Forbes. https://www.forbes.com/sites/kimelsesser/2018/04/03/power-posing-is-back-amy-cuddy-successfully-refutes-criticism/?sh=49c8d88c3b8e

[6]Loncar, T. (2021, June 8). *A decade of power posing: Where do we stand?* The British Psychological Society: The Psychologist. https://www.bps.org.uk/psychologist/decade-power-posing-where-do-we-stand

Commitment

 **Between this session and the next, I commit to the following:**

- ☐ Writing personal mantras connected to my top three assets and my envisioned future.
- ☐ Identifying a desired change and writing affirming and empowering cognitive statements.
- ☐ Finding my personal power pose and practicing it daily for two minutes.

Before moving on, send me a photo of you (connect@roddycarter.com)—maybe with your friends, family, or colleagues—in your power pose. With your permission, I'll share this image to encourage others.

Next up, in Session 9: *Activating Desire*, you'll harness the immense power of emotion to boost the skills, tools, and techniques you've mastered in previous sessions. As we revisit your desired future, you'll apply this boost to power you toward **unstoppable** success.

> "Stand up straight, and realize who you are,
> that you tower over your circumstances."
>
> —MAYA ANGELOU

ACTIVATING DESIRE

Welcome to Session 9! You can now see that becoming **unstoppable** depends on unwavering belief. Continue building your belief and confidence daily by doing psychic push-ups. And now, it's time to exponentially harness your powerful emotional brain to activate the great flip flopper to turboboost belief.

Plan to spend a minimum of three hours on this session: one hour for the session content, at least one hour to complete your vision board, and one hour to complete your Mastery Missions. Consider allocating time on two separate days for this session.

In this session, you will:

- Learn how to systematically accentuate the voice of the emotional brain to activate desire to boost belief and achieve success.

- Broaden your emotional vocabulary to fuel the journey into your ideal future.

- Create a vision board to enliven, empower, and bring to fruition your ideal future.

The Emotional Brain and the BOS

Activate desire to unlock unstoppable.

I don't believe there's a magical force or state of mind that unlocks success without any additional effort. Doing the work—your psychic push-ups—is essential. But if we go back to where your ideal future first originated and where all change begins, we find it's with a thought. Your ideas are born in your cognitive brain.

As soon as an idea pops into your head, the first thing you do is create a mental image of it—either consciously or unconsciously. And then, because the human brain has been trained to communicate in language, you add words to the image. But inevitably, you'll encounter situations where positive thinking isn't enough. To achieve **unstoppable** success, you must activate the emotional brain to join in and nurture positive thoughts.

Let's recap the two inherent attributes of the emotional brain. The emotional brain is a:

1. **Diagnostic tool:** Diagnostics help you to assess which level of the brain you—and other people—are operating from. Negative emotion shows the reptilian brain has control. Positive emotion shows the cognitive brain is shouting the loudest.

2. **Turbobooster:** The turbobooster either works for you (boosting positive thoughts in the cognitive brain with positive emotions) or against you (boosting fear and doubt when the voice of the reptilian brain shouts the loudest).

When your emotional brain gets behind a positive thought, you

- **Magnify belief** and

- **Create a reverberating loop that boosts cognition**, moving you toward your dream.

The need to turboboost positive thoughts explains why many people have clarity around what they want to accomplish but fail to actually accomplish it. **An idea alone is not enough.** Too often, we fall short of our goals because of our failure to use our powerful emotional brain.

Here's what you can do to activate desire.

So how do we activate desire? I've already taught you. Say your mantra. Why? What am I doing when I say my mantra? I'm in the present, and I'm having the loudest voice be my cognitive brain. The best way to turn on our emotional brain is to think.

So freaking counterintuitive, right?!

Do you think cold, miserable, negative thoughts? No! Those are fears. Okay. So, just positive thoughts? Yes, just positive thoughts.

> *In the presence of only positive thinking, the emotional brain gets activated. The whole force of love comes to turboboost your efforts.*
>
> *Just by thinking positive.*

If desire is activated by raw, intense emotional power with no cognitive basis, the desire isn't sustained for very long.

Let me give you a real-life example.

Motivational speeches don't sustain long-term change.

Many of us have experienced the power of motivational speakers. These speakers are able to greatly inspire, energize, and recharge our intentions to achieve our big dreams, but our motivation generally declines after a few days.

Why does this happen?

The powerful spike of motivation, inspiration, and confidence that motivational speakers effect in us is temporary because it mainly activates our emotional brain, without engaging our cognitive drive (to support belief). Without cognition leading desire, sustainable, lasting, enduring positivity and change is rare or minimal.

While the positive energy activated by raw emotional power is often strong and compelling initially, it doesn't boost belief, and so any long-term impact on success is unlikely.

Emotion and cognition, combined, are critical for success.

You can use the tools and techniques in this session, plus many others, to activate desire to boost cognitive drive. Whatever you choose to do, it's important to **prioritize cognition as the starting point**. Then, do anything and everything you can to **enhance the power of your emotional brain** to support your positive thoughts.

> ## To achieve something big, you need desire—that deep, nonrational hunger to become **unstoppable**.

Belief Versus Fear

 **The battle is belief versus fear.**

Imagine a seesaw. On one side of the seesaw is a child called Belief. On the other side is another child called Fear, and in the middle, there's a third child called Desire.

When Belief and Fear weigh the same, Desire stays in the middle. But when Belief outweighs Fear, then, just like the emotional brain, Desire slides over to sit with Belief. Boom! The balance tips dramatically, and you achieve success.

When Fear is heavier than Belief, Desire slides down to join Fear in order to reduce risk. When this happens, there's no progress toward the dream.

Now, you'll remember that the position of the emotional brain is determined by whether the voice of the cognitive or the reptilian brain is shouting the loudest. So the emotional brain has no choice in which way it flips, but it does play a huge role in either boosting success or bolstering failure.

You can win the battle!

That's why we've spent the last two sessions building belief (using the cognitive brain) and why, before that, we went deep into the basement of your mind to conquer fear (from the reptilian brain).

Now I'm hoping it all makes sense why there've been times in your life when you (or someone you know) had a big dream and a strong, clear idea of what it looked like but failed to achieve it—because **the idea alone is not enough**.

You can vividly describe your ideal future and all of the things that you truly desire. You can have strong, clear ideas of them—even deep emotional hungers for them. But still, these statistics of life explain why the vast majority of dreams go unrealized: Most dreamers are stoppable.

Ways to Activate Desire

Let's explore four ways to activate desire.

1. Emotional vocabulary

Expanding your emotional vocabulary gives you the ability to activate your emotional brain. You maximize the use of your entire brain and boost your capacity to achieve your dream.

2. Vision boards

Vision boarding brings together your dream with colors and images that evoke positive emotions. The process will help you clarify your dream, illuminate your future vision, and focus your energy on your most important objectives to continuously align your actions with the path that leads toward your dream.

3. The senses

Your senses are a quick and powerful way to drive positivity. As you continue to enliven your dream using your senses, you shift and support your visualizations with a positive mindset and mood.

4. Visualization

Visualization techniques help you consciously, mindfully, and continuously see and anticipate your ideal future. They also help you to program your AFC to keep you focused on tasks that move you toward your dream—even when you're not paying attention to your ideal future.

Emotional Vocabulary

To activate desire, begin with a broad emotional vocabulary.

In a moment, we'll walk through a vision board activity, but first, I'd like you to take inventory of your emotional vocabulary. Here's a scenario.

A trusted colleague says, "Hey! How are you?!" "I'm good," you reply...but "I'm good" is a cop-out.

How are you, actually?

I'm not letting you off the hook. I *really* want to know how you are.

When I work with clients in one-on-one sessions, I make a point of spending the first 10 minutes of each session finding out how they are—and I don't accept "I'm good" for an answer.

I'm always listening to know which part of the brain they're operating from. If their responses have no temperature, I gently guide and support them in describing their current emotional state to me. This helps them get in touch with their emotions and gives me an idea of how they've felt since our previous session.

Common words like *good*, *fine*, and *okay* are hopelessly inadequate to fully express our emotional state. When you work to expand your emotional vocabulary, you have more to draw on to express your emotions and read the cues that indicate other people's feelings. This gives you the ability to activate your emotional brain—and your desire.

> Having a limited emotional vocabulary is like
>
> an orchestra using only a handful of notes
>
> while trying to play a full symphony.

People with limited emotional vocabularies are often in this position because they don't trust—or may even fear—their emotional "voice."

This limited vocabulary may have been taught to them during their childhood years, or they may not have prioritized their emotional literacy as a result of life experiences.

- **Fear of expressing emotion**: Early in life, emotions tend to flow more naturally but often arise in difficult or uncomfortable situations—like getting into trouble at school, being afraid of the dark, or being lost or left alone. Under these circumstances—when a child is not "in control" and they experience strong emotion—they may associate emotion with bad things and proactively avoid connecting with and expressing emotion as they grow into adulthood.

- **Limited experience expressing emotion**: Many professions suit analytical thinkers. Successful execution of work in these professions depends on operating instinctively out of the cognitive brain to get the job done. Because professional success requires demonstration of cognitive excellence, people in these professions may have neglected or ignored building their emotional vocabulary because the realm of emotions doesn't lead to career advancement—and, in some cases, emotions can be perceived as a "danger zone" with respect to their professional (and even personal) functions. People in these professions often demonstrate habitual and strong cognitive override.

Other people may have learned to protect themselves—or believe they're protecting themselves—from the "dangers" of using their emotional brain. However, as you expand your emotional vocabulary, you activate desire and maximize success.

Here are some of the benefits of developing your emotional literacy. You can:

- **Better understand** your emotions and the emotions of others.

- **Improve communication** skills in personal and professional relationships.

- **Express** your **needs** more specifically.

- **Enhance** your **gratitude** practice.

- **Maximize** the use of **your supercomputer**—your brain.

Pause to contemplate these five emotions:

1. Enjoyment
2. Sadness
3. Fear
4. Anger
5. Disgust

Now, how many different, more nuanced emotions can you think of that relate to each one? Start with *enjoyment*. What are the deeper emotions that come to mind?

 **EXERCISE 1**

Expand Your Emotional Vocabulary

ACTION 1 OF 2

Challenge

Look at the five images below, each representing a different emotion. Challenge yourself to call to mind at least three descriptive emotion words for each one.

Enjoyment

Sadness

Fear

Anger

Disgust

ACTION 2 OF 2

Reflect

Take a look at these lists of nuanced emotions for each of the five primary emotions. Reflect on your own experience as you came up with deeper feelings.

Enjoyment

- Pleasure
- Joy
- Happiness
- Amusement
- Pride
- Awe
- Excitement
- Ecstasy

Sadness

- Loneliness
- Unhappiness
- Hopelessness
- Gloominess
- Misery

Fear

- Worry
- Nervousness
- Anxiety
- Panic
- Stress

Anger

- Annoyance
- Frustration
- Bitterness
- Fury
- Insult
- Vengefulness

Disgust

- Dislike
- Revulsion
- Nausea
- Aversion
- Offense
- Horror

What did you experience during this activity? Were you effective in expressing the difference between unhappiness and hopelessness? Or between frustration and vengefulness? Or even between pleasure and pride? If not, there's more work to be done.

Practice using your emotional vocabulary to hone your skills.

You can do this in a variety of ways in different settings. Have fun experimenting with these approaches, or come up with your own.

Watch TV with the sound muted.

As you sit down to binge your favorite show, watch the first five minutes with the volume muted. Try to guess what's being said and felt by using only the nonverbal cues. Then, you can go back to watch the show unmuted and see if you were right.

If you'd like to step up the challenge, tune in to a show that you don't know. See if you can guess emotions without the sound as easily.

Pair sound with the emotion.

Approach this exercise with an innocent and open mind, as if you were helping a child learn the full range of their emotions. For example, when helping a child understand fear, you may use the word "worried." The child may not understand "worried," but they understand a sharp inhale or loud "uh-oh."

Play emotional charades.

While you're on a walk with someone, think of an emotion and act it out for the other person to guess. I recommend using your whole body, but you can do this with facial expressions only. If they're having trouble, try new and different movements—even if you have to expand beyond your comfort zone. Or you can tell them the emotion and ask them to act it out to better understand how they feel it.

Keep a feelings journal.

A feelings journal is a good way to label and keep track of your emotions. In the beginning, you may notice that you use only a few words to describe the range of emotions you feel in a day. With practice, see if you can expand the list of descriptive words you use.

Label different emotions.

Take a look at the different emotions this person is expressing. Study each expression, and use your expanded emotional vocabulary to label it. Try to use a different emotion word to describe each expression.

Vision Boarding

To enliven and empower your dream, create a vision board using your expanded emotional vocabulary.

I'm sure you've heard of a vision board (sometimes called a *dream board*). It's a powerful visualization that brings together a collage of images, text, and graphic elements into an evocative piece of art. Vision boards were traditionally created on poster boards (hence the name), but the format you choose will be as unique or tech savvy as your creativity allows. I have a client who turned the entire back of her office door into a giant vision board!

 **Vision boards activate desire and turboboost dreams.**

What's a vision board do? It takes your view way downstream and captures it on a board, and you can do a vision board exercise with just words. And it can be inspiring and positively motivating.

But when you create a vision board and you actually put colors, romance, love, pathos...I'm now truly evoking my emotional turboboost behind my cognitive brain.

So do a vision board. I'm going to suggest you go way back to the beginning, where you wrote out your dream, and you're going to write it with words, with intellect, and then you're going to color it with emotion. And you're going to ask yourself: When I cast my vision downstream, to that distal future where my dream comes true in the big reveal, what do I see? What do I hear? What do I feel? What do I taste? And even, what do I smell?

And make sure that this vision you're painting has all of those colors in it, because then the words drive you and the emotions around that boost you. They put it into three dimensions for you. That's enduring motivation because it's seated in the cognitive brain.

Prepare yourself to bring deep richness to this exercise.

While the images, elements, artwork, and medium that you choose for your vision board will be unique to you, there are a few supplies many find helpful. If you choose to use a physical, poster-board-style vision board, you may want to have the following on hand:

☐ Vision board background, such as poster board

☐ Clippings of pictures, words, phrases, and inspirational quotes

☐ Scissors

☐ Adhesive or fasteners

☐ Stickers

☐ Colored pens, pencils, or markers

Or, you may prefer to create a digital vision board using a PowerPoint slide deck or an app. You can search online and find endless creative inspiration, including images, illustrations, emojis, fonts, graphics, quotes, and even music.

Creating your vision board on a computer or mobile device will make it easier to update your vision without having to build an entirely new board and to create multiple copies for you to place around your home and workspace, ensuring that these highly evocative stimuli thoroughly infuse your daily awareness.

I encourage you to set aside plenty of time to do this exercise—and to decide how or with whom you want to engage in the process. Some people are private and enjoy exploring their thoughts and feelings on their own in a quiet, secluded space. Others love the social aspect of building vision boards together. If you're socially inclined, feel free to invite people to join you.

After you've decided which medium to use, collected supplies, and selected your space, prioritize creating your vision board by choosing a date and time to do so, ideally within the next seven days.

EXERCISE 2

Create Your Vision Board

Create a vision board based on your ideal future description.

Combining a visual with your written statements is a powerful exercise that will clarify, illuminate, and bring you closer to your future vision.

Some people make the mistake of thinking this is a trivial exercise. Nothing could be further from

the truth. It's a powerful exercise applicable to the most analytical people and serious-minded professionals—in fact, it's *especially* applicable for them.

The format and elements you choose will be unique to you, but following these eight actions will help you to vision board effectively. Work through the process to understand the full instruction set now. Then, between now and the next session, carve out an hour or more to revisit these instructions and create your vision board. Give yourself ample time to create this visual representation.

ACTION 1 OF 8

Pause

Pause for a few moments before you create your vision board. Take a few deep breaths as you shift the seat of your awareness into your prefrontal cortex.

ACTION 2 OF 8

Focus

Focus your full attention on your dream—your desired outcomes. Reread your succinct, consolidated summary statements that highlight the handful of big things that you really want to happen.

ACTION 3 OF 8

Capture

Capture the overarching themes in a few short phrases. For example:

- ☐ Work-life balance or meaning
- ☐ Community or social contribution
- ☐ Relationships
- ☐ Financial metrics
- ☐ Health and wellness
- ☐ Peace, contentment, and clarity of mind
- ☐ Material possessions
- ☐ Personal growth

ACTION 4 OF 8

Find

Find compelling images, phrases, headlines, quotes, graphics, or iconographies that capture your imagination, turboboost emotional appeal, and represent the essence of your overarching themes.

Browse through magazines, stock photo websites, Instagram, creative digital asset sites, or your own photo albums to find a variety of images that catch your attention or specifically evoke the positive feelings you want to enjoy when you realize your dream. Cut or crop the photos that capture the mood and feeling you want to convey.

ACTION 5 OF 8

Select

Select the images that resonate most—you don't have to know exactly why. Choose elements that tap into, express, and evoke powerful positive emotions that will readily activate your desire and boost belief.

For inspiration:

- Go back to your list of emotion words and newly expanded emotional vocabulary to write down feeling words with strong, positive emotion.

- Use one or more of the five senses—hearing, touch, smell, taste, and sight—to add depth and detail.

ACTION 6 OF 8

Assemble

Assemble your favorite images, graphic elements, and words in a creative way on your board.

If you don't know where to start, find one picture that stands out. Place it in the middle of the board. Then, surround that image with other images you've found and words you've chosen.

It's your board, and you can assemble it any way you like. Some people like their vision boards very organized with spaces between the images. Others choose to stack images on top of each other to overlap and fill up all the space.

Listen to your inner voice while you create. Experiment with the layout. Tap into your curiosity. Have fun.

There are no rules. It's your future...your choice...your creation!

ACTION 7 OF 8

Reflect

Once you've completed your vision board, sit back and ask yourself, *What do I notice?*

- What ideas and thoughts do these words and images, together, prompt in you?

- What emotions does your vision board evoke?

- Does your vision board activate your desire to realize your dream?

If you feel surges of positive emotion while looking at your vision board, it indicates you're going in the right direction. If not, consider what changes you could make to align your vision board with your dream. Ask yourself:

- What have I missed? Did I leave something out? Have I overemphasized or underemphasized something?

- Is there anything I would change to help propel myself toward my ideal future?

ACTION 8 OF 8

Exhibit

Exhibit your vision board somewhere you'll look at it often to enable it to turboboost belief.

When you see your future and visualize it frequently, your AFC focuses on tasks that move you toward it.

This means that, during times you're not focused on your dream, your brain is on mental autopilot to navigate you toward your ideal future.

Beautifully created!

There's no right or wrong way to vision board. Find the combination of visual elements, images, emotions, and sensory prompts that works well for you.

Your vision board will keep you on a direct path to achieving your ideal future. If you find yourself stuck or off track, spend extra time with your vision board and do a short visualization to get back on track. The profound impact of conscious visualization will become clear shortly.

The Senses

The senses can be used to quickly and powerfully evoke positive emotion.

Your senses are always hard at work helping you assimilate your environment. Access their untapped potential to drive positivity, and use them mindfully to shift and support a positive mindset and mood.

Hearing

Different sounds affect the body differently. Experiment to find music to boost different emotions at different times. Find music that calms, inspires, energizes, or encourages you. Put together playlists and listen to music to evoke these or other positive emotions.

Touch

Touch is a powerfully therapeutic sense that evokes positive emotions. Think about the healing power of a massage or holding the hand of someone you love. Imagine how refreshing it is to splash cool water on your skin on a hot day or stroke the soft fur of your favorite pet. You might hold a special stone or rub your palms together to add the emotion of touch.

Smell

Smell is a powerful sense that connects you directly with your memories, emotions, and instincts. Think about the scent of ocean air, coffee brewing, or freshly baked bread. Scents have the power to take you back to specific times or events in your life.

Find the scents you love, and choose one (maybe in the form of a candle or aromatherapy oil) to smell each time you look at your vision board. You'll begin to associate your dreams with this scent.

Taste

Words related to taste are often used to describe emotions. Think about a sweet (likable) person or someone who is salty (annoyed) or bitter (unhappy). We understand the emotions these words describe. Bring to mind your favorite tastes or "feel-good" flavors, and think of the emotions you associate with them. Add the enjoyment of taste to the experience of your vision board.

Sight

Think about sights that lift your mood. You might enjoy colorful flowers, dogs at play, lightning streaking across the sky, or your child's latest masterpiece. Your favorite sights trigger positive emotions.

The beautiful images you've assembled on your vision board create a cascade of powerful, positive neurochemicals in your body. So, look at your vision board often.

Visualization

Visualization techniques activate desire and program your AFC (which becomes your GPS) to guide you toward your desired future.

Remember back when you learned about the importance of your AFC—the complex filtering mechanism that protects your brain from data overload and filters in information according to how you programmed it? **Visualization techniques help you consciously, mindfully, and continuously program your AFC in alignment with realizing your ideal future.**

What you see is where you go. When you see your ideal future with great color and detail, you continually reinforce your dream.

Hold a vision of your future that guides your AFC with intention at all times. There's an easy explanation for why looking at your vision board and visualizing your ideal future actually works; it's called **comprehensive sensory anticipation**. Here's what it means: When you see your future displayed in front of your eyes, you anticipate it. If you see it frequently—aka **visualize it regularly**—your AFC focuses on tasks that move you toward it...*even when you're not paying attention*.

Yes, that's right! Even when you're going about your workday, not focused on your dream, you can turn your brain on mental autopilot to navigate you toward it. And you can do it all through visualization exercises. They're that powerful!

Visualization uses the power of the theatre of the mind.

Do you remember engaging in fantasy play as a child?

In reality you may have been in your backyard in suburbia, but in your imagination, you were exploring the Amazon jungle, summiting mountains, playing in waterfalls, or galloping across wide-open plains on a wild mustang.

As a child, you visualized for enjoyment—and now you can tap into the same visualization for **unstoppable** success!

Visualization is the mental road map that takes you to your dream. The more emotion, color, and detail you bring to your visualization, the more expeditiously you move toward your desired future. So, whether you're looking at your vision board, mentally visualizing your dream, or doing both—while enlivening your visualization with the power of the senses—it works because you're **creating your future** and **programming your AFC** at the same time.

And because you create the scene of your future in your mind, you're fully in control of what happens next. You control the outcome. So, when you continually visualize the outcome that you want, you reinforce your desire and boost belief.

Elite athletes use visualization to enhance their performance and success. They seem to know something about visualization that the rest of us haven't fully tapped into yet: **Visualization engages sensory capabilities and unlocks the full brain.**

For example, before they compete or perform, they consciously visualize in their mind the athletic script they need to perform with their body.

Figure skaters may sit in the warm-up area or football players may sit in the locker room, thinking through their pending "performance" on the ice or the field.

They see themselves executing every movement or sequence of play precisely. Their full attention is focused on this very specific, very visual activity.

Using the sense of hearing during visualization drives desired outcomes to win and succeed.

Athletes engaged in preperformance visualization often wear earphones and listen to music to tune out external sounds, so they can focus all their attention on their visualization exercise. In addition to blocking out external noise, the music serves another purpose. The visualization and the music combined co-opt emotions to get behind the cognitive image of their desired outcome: a successful performance.

This is the principle of activating desire: Co-opting positive emotions to get behind the cognitive brain to turboboost belief in achieving **unstoppable** success.

 EXERCISE 3

Visualize Your Ideal Future

Visualize.

Now it's time for you to visualize your ideal future to activate your desire and program your AFC.

Find a quiet place where you won't be disturbed or distracted and where you can sit or lie down comfortably while you do the visualization.

Read through the whole exercise before doing the visualization, so you know the sequence of actions to follow. If you'd like to read and record the instructions yourself, you can play back your personalized recording to guide you.

ACTION 1 OF 6

Pause

Before you begin the visualization, take as many deep breaths as you need to help you relax and establish a calm state of mind.

Shift the seat of your awareness into your prefrontal cortex.

ACTION 2 OF 6

Select

Refer to the most current version of your ideal future summary, and select the outcome you want to focus on in your visualization. Depending on your desired future, you may want to visualize it in its entirety or focus on only one aspect of it.

By selecting the outcome you want to focus on in your visualization, you're thinking positively about what you want and setting the cognitive direction alongside which you're activating desire.

If you focus on one aspect of your dream at a time, repeat this exercise to visualize the successful accomplishment of the other aspects, too.

Use the space below to write down the outcome you want to focus on for this exercise.

ACTION 3 OF 6

Support

Use a sensory prompt that taps into one or more of the five senses to support the outcome you want to visualize.

Here are some examples of sensory prompts you might choose:

- **Hearing**: Play calming or energizing music, or listen to nature sounds.
- **Touch**: Touch items with textures that feel good to you, for example, a soft fabric.

- **Smell**: Burn scented candles or incense.

- **Taste**: Eat or drink something with a taste you really enjoy.

- **Sight**: Look at pictures of things that make you happy, for example, a spectacular sunset, a cute puppy, or a colorful flower bed.

It may be helpful to look at pictures that align with the outcome you're visualizing. Once you've completed your vision board, you could look at it to support your visualization.

ACTION 4 OF 6

Imagine

Imagine your desired outcome as if you've already accomplished it. Begin by getting a clear vision of where you are and what you're doing. You might select a place and time in the future. Use your entire imagination to put yourself in that place and time.

Now, use the following prompts to continue to visualize the scene:

- Notice what you're wearing. What season is it? Are your clothes light or heavy?

- Look around you in every direction. What do you see? Visualize your surroundings in as much detail as possible.

- Notice who you're with. Are you alone? With other people? Who? What are they doing?

- Listen. If you're with other people, what are they saying? What are you saying?

ACTION 5 OF 6

Sense

Go through each of your senses to make your visualization as real and vivid as possible. Use the following questions to guide you through each of the senses:

- **Hearing**: What are you hearing? What are the sounds far off in the distance? Close by?

- **Touch**: What are you feeling? What is the temperature of the air touching your skin?

- **Smell**: What scents are you smelling? Look for the obvious and the subtle scents.

- **Taste**: Is there a taste or texture you sense in your mouth?

- **Sight**: Are there any other visual details you can add to the scene of your desired outcome? Look more carefully at the size, shape, and color of things in the scene.

Is there anything else you can add? Jot down some ideas below.

ACTION 6 OF 6

Feel

Get in touch with the emotions your visualization evokes in you. The purpose of this action is to connect you as strongly as possible with the emotions you'll feel when you actually achieve your desired outcome. The intensity of these emotions serves as a crucial catalyst for driving success.

Begin by naming your emotions. Then, empower your visualization by amplifying what you feel. Use the following questions as a guide:

- How do you feel having achieved your desired outcome?

- What do you feel as you observe your surroundings?

- How are you feeling about what you are doing?

- How do you perceive your actions?

- Which emotions are elicited by the people around you? What emotions are they showing?

Immerse yourself in the emotions that the scene of your desired outcome evokes in you as deeply as you can for as long as possible. Then, slowly and gently end your visualization by bringing your mind back to the present.

Beautifully created!

Take your time resuming your regular activity after this visualization. Let the benefits of the images and emotions sink in.

You can come back to this visualization to practice at night before bed or in the morning after waking.

Repeat your visualization over and over again. In doing so, you'll be activating desire to boost your belief in your **unstoppable** success. And you'll be continuously programming your AFC to navigate you to the life of your dreams.

Mastery Missions

Congratulations!

You've finished Session 9, including the three exercises: *Expand Your Emotional Vocabulary*, *Create Your Vision Board*, and *Visualize Your Ideal Future*. Once you've completed these two Mastery Missions, you can move on to the next session.

MASTERY MISSION 1

Nurture Positivity

ACTION 1 OF 1

Decide

Decide to surround yourself with positivity. Begin by making more time for the things you enjoy. Then, start layering more and more positivity into your life.

- Say yes to something you've been wanting to do but have always said no to.

- Say no to one thing you should do but don't want to.

- Make a list of positive people you want to spend more time with. Embrace them!

- Identify the most positive person you know, and schedule time with them.

- Identify the one person you want to spend less time with right now. Take a break from their company, if possible.

- Assess negative or toxic influences in your life. Reduce as many of these as possible.

Do everything you can to ensure that the positive, beneficial aspects of your life are greater than the negative influences.

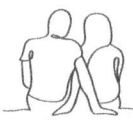 **MASTERY MISSION 2**

Get Curious

ACTION 1 OF 2

Ask

For the next week, be curious about whether your friends, family, and colleagues have a strong emotional connectivity and an expansive vocabulary of emotion words. Ask others often, "How are you?" or "What are you feeling?"

ACTION 2 OF 2

Listen

Listen carefully to their answers, and don't accept "good," "okay," or "fine." If they give you a canned response, ask questions to help guide them to find and express their specific, nuanced emotions or feelings...especially if they are your children.

Helping others expand their emotional vocabulary is a great way to also help you expand yours.

Supplemental Science

 You're invited to delve into the supporting research on the topics covered in this session. Keep in mind that exploring the supplemental science is optional. You can return anytime to read more about the underlying science of the *Brain Operating System* methodology.

The Role of the Amygdala in Emotional Processing

The amygdala in the human brain is a small, almond-shaped cluster of nerve cells located subcortically (below the cognitive brain). It derives its name from the Greek word for "almond." Although commonly referred to as *the amygdala* (singular), it is actually a paired structure with one of the pair located in each brain hemisphere (anatomically, there is a left and a right amygdala).

The amygdala is considered the center of emotion, emotional behavior, and motivation in the human brain. It is also thought to contribute to memory and learning. The role of the amygdala in processing emotional information and how it communicates with other brain regions is a rich area of study, and research on the function of the amygdala has advanced with the use of functional magnetic resonance imaging (fMRI), which provides a noninvasive brain research tool.

When research on the amygdala began, it was thought to be associated only with the experience of fear and the processing of aversive information. Later research has elucidated that the amygdala is also central to the processing of appetitive (pleasant) information and positive emotions.

In the fMRI scans to the right, the yellow and orange highlights within the blue circles mark the approximate location of the amygdala as seen in axial, coronal, and sagittal views of the human brain (L: left side; R: right side).[1] Note its proximity to the emotional and reptilian brain regions.

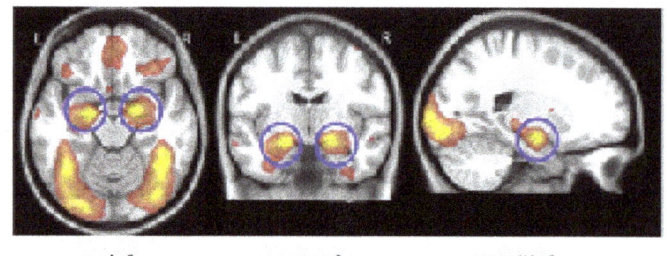

axial   coronal   sagittal

The Amygdala and the Emotional Brain

Neural connections run between the amygdala and the prefrontal cortex as well as the cognitive, emotional, and reptilian brain regions. These connections form brain circuits that support emotional, physiological, and behavioral responses to fear as well as cognitive override and emotion regulation.

Fear influences the emotional brain through the amygdala. When a potential threat or danger is perceived, the amygdala initiates the fear response by signaling for the release of the stress hormones that activate and sustain sympathetic nervous system control to support fight-or-flight behavior. This is associated with feelings of fear, anxiety, and distress.

The impact of positive thoughts on the emotional brain occurs through the amygdala. Research shows a link between cognitive control of emotions, attenuation of amygdala activity, and modulation of physiological and behavioral responses to fear.

The Neurobiology of Emotional Regulation

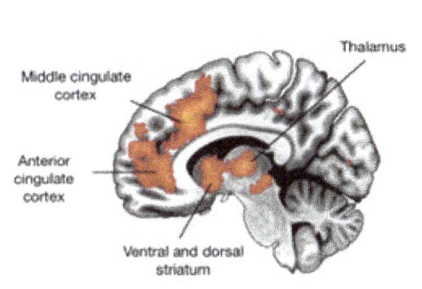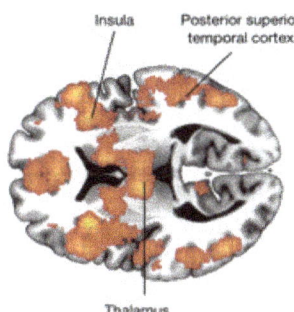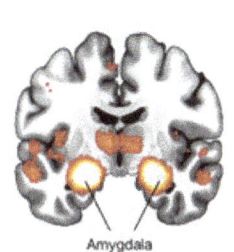

Learning about how the brain regulates emotion through various mechanisms and neural networks can provide insights into how we can better control our emotions. The image to the left is a diagrammatic representation of brain regions thought to be involved in emotional processing.[1] These maps depict a statistical summary of data obtained from neuroimaging research aimed at mapping the neurobiological architecture of emotions. Given the limitations of any visualization technique, the emotion circuits in the brain include, but are probably not limited to, the areas of activity delimited in these maps.

Emotional and Psychological Well-Being

Emotional intelligence, the ability to identify, evaluate, control, and express emotions, has an influence on success and happiness. Mindfulness practices are also known to have positive benefits on emotional and psychological well-being. These include stress management and reduction, improved cognition, and more effective emotion regulation.

Expressive writing as a cognitive practice has been researched for its positive impact on emotional well-being. It facilitates self-reflection and awareness and acknowledgement of emotions, which can lead to emotion regulation.

Visualization, the use of mental imagery, is known to be an effective technique for positively influencing thoughts, emotions, and behaviors. Imagining desired scenarios and outcomes can help with emotion regulation by increasing optimism and positivity. Visualization can also be used to assist with decision-making, problem-solving, planning, and motivation.

Music and Emotion

There is a strong link between music and emotion. This facilitates the use of music in research on emotions and the brain; for example, music can be used to evoke particular emotions and the brain activity associated with these emotions can be recorded using fMRI. This helps with elucidating emotion circuits in the brain. Because music modulates activity in the emotion circuits, it can be used effectively to regulate emotion.

Commitment

 **Between this session and the next, I commit to the following:**

☐ Becoming aware of my thoughts by prioritizing the positive ones and simultaneously enhancing the power of my emotional brain to support them.

☐ Creating a vision board of my ideal future.

Next up, in Session 10: *Making Commitments*, we'll wrap up your journey to becoming **unstoppable**. We'll recap the BOS, and I'll show you how to use everything you've learned in an iterative, dynamic way. Plus, you'll make a commitment to yourself for your long-term success.

The **unstoppable** state doesn't happen overnight. However, with time and the application of the tips in this final session, you'll fully develop and integrate the system to make consistent, incremental progress toward becoming **unstoppable** and realizing your desired future.

> "Create the highest, grandest vision possible for your life because you become what you **believe**."
>
> —OPRAH WINFREY

MAKING COMMITMENTS

Welcome to Session 10! Incredible work on this transformational journey through your magnificent brain. Now, to wrap up, learn to use your *Brain Operating System* (BOS) in a systematic action sequence to support your everyday victories, create an ongoing action plan to ensure your enduring success, and launch the next phase of your **unstoppable** journey.

Set aside two hours to complete the session content and activities. Spend an additional hour on your Mastery Missions.

In this session, you will:

- Crystallize the key takeaways of the BOS and become a brain master by systematically employing your BOS-maximizing tools, techniques, and skills within a 5-action sequence.

- Make a unique, personal, and compelling commitment to realizing your dream life and becoming **unstoppable**.

- Create a weekly, monthly, quarterly, and annual action plan to consistently move toward your dream and reach your full potential.

Become Who You Decide to Be

"The only person you are destined to become is the person you **decide** to be."

—RALPH WALDO EMERSON

I invite you to pause for a moment and reflect on this quote—the same one you reflected on at the start of your journey.

As we wrap up our time together, reflect deeply on these words: "The only person you are destined to become is the person you decide to be."

- What does this quote mean to you, now?

- What emotions does the quote evoke in you, now?

- Do you now believe you can master your BOS, take control of your destiny, and realize the life of your dreams?

While reflecting on this quote today, you probably experienced different thoughts, feelings, and fears than when you started this coaching. And as you continue to master your understanding of your BOS and do your psychic push-ups, you'll realize that the power to transform is in your hands.

Taking charge of your thoughts, feelings, and fears—if you choose to do so—empowers you to decide who you want to be…and to become that person.

Are you becoming the person you decided to be?

Over the last nine sessions, you've gained the skills and knowledge you need to master your greatest resource—your magnificent brain. What now, as you journey on?

Continue your commitment to becoming **unstoppable** by enthusiastically embracing and applying this newfound know-how every day.

Your Pathway to Success

Your dream is achievable!

Some come to this coaching because they have a hunger to become **unstoppable**. More often, people come because of an obstacle or underlying fear—something's holding them back from achieving their full potential. Whatever your reasons, you're now empowered to continue your journey with clarity and confidence.

Your future is in your hands. You can live the life you dream about...because if you *think* you can, you can!

There are many reasons people journey to become **unstoppable**.

Reflect on the reason(s) you started this journey. Do any of these resonate with you?

- **Afraid/fearful**: Your dream may have seemed too big to achieve. You may have felt nervous about whether you could achieve your goals. Or maybe you feared failing or going nowhere because you lacked a big dream to work toward.

- **Stuck**: You may have felt stuck, trapped, or challenged by an obstacle you needed to overcome. Maybe you'd hit a wall and were hoping for a motivational boost.

- **Stressed**: You may have been going too fast in too many directions or needed a reset to prioritize what's most important to you.

- **Frustrated**: Perhaps you'd been trying to reach your dream but weren't getting the desired results. You may have experienced self-doubt or a lack of confidence or enthusiasm.

- **Inspired**: You saw something valuable in this coaching to help you create or enhance your big dream and then to master the tools to realize it.

Regardless of what brought you here, I hope you now appreciate that everything you need to unlock **unstoppable** and realize your dream is in this coaching—and backed by science. There's no magic or mystery about how it's done. Understanding how your BOS is designed to serve you and doing the work to master it gives you control over your life.

Now, you only need to take one action: ***Just do it!***

Mark this as a momentous point in your life, as powerful as your initial decision to begin this coaching. This is it. You decide. Will you do it?

Will you continue to master your BOS to become **unstoppable**?

If your answer is, "Yes! I'm committed to becoming **unstoppable!**" then mastering your BOS is what you need to do. Period.

To master your BOS, do your psychic push-ups. Otherwise, you'll make incremental gains—at best. Or you'll remain hampered by the same or similar challenges that led you here initially.

Handling Lapses in Progress

What can you do if you're not making progress?

Regularly, clients confess they've let their practices slip. I know; I've fallen off track, too.

Even if you are doing your psychic push-ups regularly, at some point along the journey, you may feel frustrated because you're not seeing evidence of your progress. If you don't feel like you're moving toward your dream and success, you might have the thought, *I'm not getting anywhere with this*, and want to shift gears.

Everyone handles lapses in progress differently.

- Some become **more regimented**.
- Others go in the opposite direction and want to **give up**.
- Some may explore new or different transformational teachings to discover a **different way**.

Those who explore other teachings soon realize that every transformational program or strategy, in its own way, taps into the same biology that underlies the BOS. Those programs may or may not explain the neuroscience behind their teachings, but they all lead you toward success through mastery of your magnificent brain.

The truth is that there will be ups and downs along your journey.

If a time comes when you feel like your **unstoppable** state is unattainable or too far off in the future to reach, even though the science assures your inevitable success—before you ease off, abandon your practices, or consider looking elsewhere for another approach...before any other action... use the **power of a pause**. Shift the seat of your awareness into your prefrontal cortex. Then, ask:

- What am I thinking?
- What am I feeling?
- What am I fearing?

The answer that's holding you back is almost always lurking in your reptilian brain. There's likely an underlying fear that hasn't been addressed in a deep, profound, and meaningful way.

This is true for all of us.

Deeply rooted fears can be sneaky. They can hide in the dark crevices of the basement of your mind. It can be frightening to focus your attention on them, so you might look for distractions.

But if you're truly committed to freeing yourself to become **unstoppable** and unlock your dreams, get back on track. Start by exploring your thoughts, your feelings, and especially your fears.

This may not be what you want to hear at the time. And it may feel daunting, but I promise you that unstoppability is always on the other side. Say, "Yes! I will continue to master my BOS to become **unstoppable**," and success will be yours.

Revisit Your Ideal Future

 EXERCISE 1

Revisit Your Ideal Future

By now, you should have a vivid description of your desired future—a dynamic, living document that's your road map to success...one that you'll continue to empower, enliven, build on, and refer to for the rest of your life.

Take out the most recent version of your ideal future summary, and reread it. Soak in every vivid detail. Notice what you are thinking, feeling, and fearing.

ACTION 1 OF 3

Think

What thoughts come to mind regarding realizing your ideal future?

- ☐ It will be hard work, but I think I can do it.

- ☐ Some aspects of my ideal future are out of my reach.

- ☐ It's unlikely that I'll achieve my ideal future.

- ☐ I go back and forth about whether I can achieve my ideal future.

- ☐ I have worried or anxious thoughts.

- ☐ It's elusive. The outcome could go either way.

- ☐ It's exciting, and I have the tools to get there!

- ☐ I have a clear image in my mind. I refuse to accept any other alternative.

Write down your reflections as you think about your ideal future.

[Empty box]

Your thoughts have power.

Your dream is generated in your cognitive brain—and your cognitive brain empowers you with insight. As you read through the possible answers, you allowed your cognitive brain to think about your ideal future from different angles.

These thoughts tell you whether you're winning the battle between belief and fear.

ACTION 2 OF 3

Feel

What are you feeling about your ideal future?

☐ I feel inspired.

☐ I feel calm and clear minded.

☐ I feel empowered and invincible.

☐ I feel confident that I can achieve my ideal future.

☐ I feel apprehensive.

☐ I have some self-doubt.

☐ I'm proud of myself for working toward my ideal future.

Write down the emotions that are coming up for you.

Your emotional brain is the great flip flopper.

Your emotions can boost the positivity of your cognitive brain; however, they can also flip toward negative emotions when the voice of your reptilian brain is loudest.

So, your emotional brain can work for you if you're thinking positive thoughts or against you if you're operating from a place of fear.

Notice your positive and negative feelings. If your emotions are negative, identify and acknowledge the fears behind those emotions—especially the ones hiding away in the basement of your mind.

Once you've identified and acknowledged the fears behind your negative feelings, use one of the belief exercises to help you think positive thoughts. You'll soon notice the positive feelings these thoughts evoke, and you'll begin to activate desire.

ACTION 3 OF 3

Fear

Do you have any of the following residual fears about realizing your ideal future?

☐ Fear of failure: *What if I can't do it?*

☐ Fear of change: *What if I'm not equipped to adapt?*

☐ Fear of unworthiness: *What if I don't really deserve it?*

☐ Fear of loss: *What if I do succeed and people abandon me?*

☐ Fear of being a fraud: *What if I'm just an impostor?*

☐ Fear of introspection: *What if I find there are deeper issues holding me back?*

☐ Other fears, not listed here, are holding me back.

☐ None of these fears apply to me.

Write down any fears lurking in your brain.

There will be times your reptilian brain shouts.

You may be experiencing one or more of the fears on this list. That's normal. And remember: The bigger your desire, the louder your reptilian brain may shout.

Always start with a pause. Then, check your filter to determine whether your fears are based on actual or imagined threats. If they're based on imagined threats, use the skills you've learned to conquer your fears before they grow bigger.

Fears and doubts left lurking in the basement will push back against the positive efforts of your cognitive and emotional brains. But when you use the techniques you've learned to quiet the voice of fear, belief begins to shout louder—driving you toward your ideal future.

Brain Operating System Recap

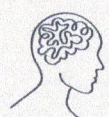 **There are five key regions that make up your Brain Operating System.**

Your reptilian brain helps you survive.

It controls your fight, flight, or freeze response and protects you from danger—it's your default brain in times of crisis.

The language of your reptilian brain is fear. If you notice a negative emotional reaction, you've spotted a fear.

Your emotional brain facilitates nurturing and collaboration.

Your emotional brain serves as a diagnostic tool to help you assess whether you're operating from your cognitive or your reptilian brain, and it also acts as a turbobooster.

The language of your emotional brain is feelings or emotions, both positive and negative. Your emotional brain—the great flip flopper—is always listening to the voices of your cognitive and reptilian brains. When the loudest voice is thought (in your cognitive brain), your emotions are positive and your BOS activates a turbobooster behind the positive thought to drive belief. But as soon as the voice of fear (in your reptilian brain) dominates, your emotional brain responds with a flood of negative emotions. As a result, your BOS turboboosts the voice of fear to drive doubt.

The boosting capacity of your emotional brain magnifies—sometimes enormously—the voice that triggers it.

Your cognitive brain enables you to think your way past fear and increase belief.

The language of your cognitive brain is thought and reason. Thoughts are positive statements with no temperature, but they have power because they evoke your emotional brain to pour out positive feelings. Remember that your thoughts are, in turn, further boosted by adding the energy of emotion.

Your AFC is a complex filtering mechanism that helps you to prioritize crucial information.

Your AFC prevents data overload by filtering out nonrelevant information and focusing your attention on data that's most important to you, thus prioritizing crucial information.

Your AFC filters information depending on how other parts of your brain program it. Your cognitive brain is critical in accurately programming your AFC for **unstoppable** success.

Your prefrontal cortex gives you awareness of your awareness.

Your prefrontal cortex—the Office of the CEO—is the most recently evolved brain region and the center of the executive function of your BOS.

The Office of the CEO is all about calmness and perspective. Operating from your prefrontal cortex, you have awareness of the three levels of your brain and are able to differentiate between thoughts, feelings, and fears. So, it's the first place you want to go when mastering your BOS because, when you're operating from the Office of the CEO, you can make clear, calm decisions.

Use your prefrontal cortex to access an empowered state of mindful awareness. This awareness helps you to stay calm when your world erupts into chaos. And, when you access a calm place and gain perspective on your thoughts, feelings, and fears, you find solutions for life's most difficult challenges. Using your prefrontal cortex in this way, you become the CEO of your life—a key to being **unstoppable**.

Silencing the voice of fear is an active choice.

The voice of the reptilian brain is useful when you're in true danger, but more often, it's a disruptive influence holding you back and keeping you stuck. But now you're empowered to become **unstoppable** because you've learned that you're biologically wired to silence the voice of fear. This gives you the capacity for radical transformation throughout your life.

The three brain levels are wired hierarchically so that, together, the cognitive and emotional brains can override the often compelling, fearful voice of the reptilian brain…when it's safe to do so.

To become unstoppable and achieve your ideal future, just think about it!

It really is that simple. **To become unstoppable and achieve your ideal future, all you have to do is think your way past the fears holding you back.** But, as I mentioned early in the coaching, most people aren't taught this.

And some will say it seems far too simple. But the science explains why it's so simple. You now have the tools to overcome the fears that have held you back in the past. Some of these fears may be the same ones that brought you to this coaching. And, of course, there will likely be new fears you'll face in the future, but you can think your way past those, too.

Learn the *Brain Operating System* 5-action sequence.

I'd like to walk you through how I use the BOS myself—in real-time, everyday life. This is the sequence I advise you to use, too, as you're practicing and learning to master your BOS.

As you navigate through the action sequence, keep in mind the following:

- The prescribed sequence for engaging your brain regions,

- The techniques you've acquired that complement each action, and

- Essential points regarding each action in the sequence.

I'm not going to include much detail for each action here, just provide an overview of the flow. We'll review all the techniques in more detail shortly.

Action 1

Occupy the Office of the CEO

The first action is to pause.

Taking a pause is fundamental to brain mastery. It's the place you should **always** start. Take a few deep breaths. Then, ask and answer:

- What am I thinking?

- What am I feeling?

- What am I fearing?

When you can answer these questions, you know you've stepped into the Office of the CEO—your prefrontal cortex. This gives you the clarity and perspective to solve daily problems, fears, and dilemmas.

Action 2

Program your filter

The next action is to check and program the filter of your AFC.

This allows you to see your actual reality rather than a distorted version of it.

Action 3

Conquer fear

Then ask, *What am I fearing?*

Depending on the nature and intensity of the fear you identify, you might use the 5-step process to gain the clarity and perspective you need to solve the problem you're facing.

However, if you identify a deep fear, use the 7-step fear-conquering process. You may need to repeat the 7-step process multiple times to conquer your most deeply rooted fears.

Action 4

Drive belief

Next, initiate a deliberate cognitive process to flood your brain with positivity.

Think positive thoughts so that the voice of your cognitive brain shouts loudest. To drive belief, own your assets, practice gratitude, recite your mantras, and use your power poses and swagger.

Action 5

Activate desire

The final action is to activate desire to boost your belief.

You can use the following techniques to enhance the power of your emotional brain to support your positive thoughts: develop your emotional literacy, vision board, activate your senses, and visualize.

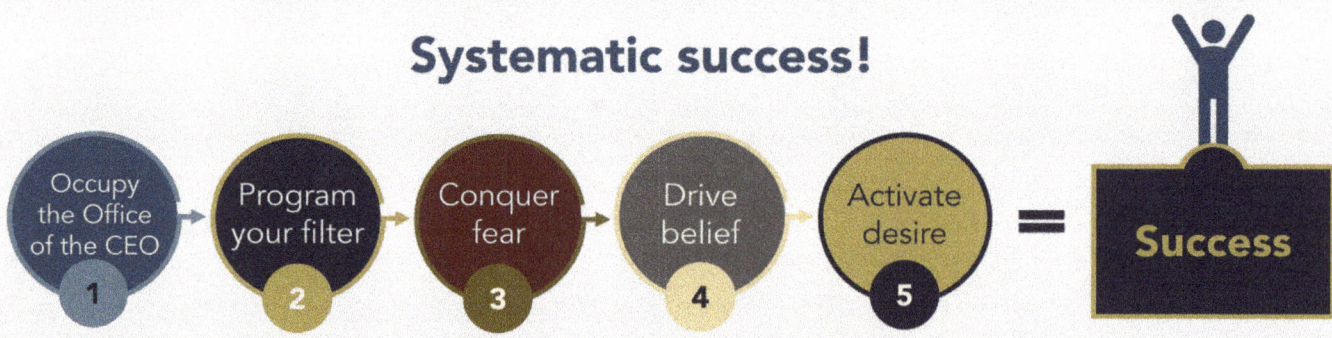

Use this 5-action sequence of BOS techniques to access and sustain your **unstoppable** state.

Let's continue by recapping the essential BOS techniques that we've explored throughout the sessions. Along the way, I'll highlight the most important things you should remember about each action in the sequence.

Nothing can stop you. You can conquer your fears!

The Success Formula Recap

Use the success formula as a quick guide to remember the unstoppable tools and techniques available to you at all times.

1. **Pause**

   Take a brief pause—a mindful moment—to shift the seat of your awareness into your prefrontal cortex.

   To solve problems and overcome obstacles, use the 5-step process to gain clarity and perspective (Session 4).

2. **Build belief**

   The first thing you must do to build belief is to think! Building belief begins with positive thoughts in your cognitive brain.

   To drive belief:

   - Own your assets (Session 7).*
   - Practice gratitude (Session 7).*
   - Recite mantras (Session 8).*
   - Use power poses and swagger (Session 8).

3. **Activate desire**

   Desire originates in the emotional brain and boosts positive thoughts.

   To activate desire (Session 9):

   - Expand your emotional vocabulary.

- Create a vision board.*

- Use your senses.

- Visualize your ideal future.*

4. Conquer fear

Fear originates in the reptilian brain. When fear is greater than belief, the emotion becomes negative (doubt).

To move past fear, use the 7-step process to conquer fear (Session 6).

5. Achieve success

Your reward for following the equation and systematically optimizing your BOS is success!

The probability of achieving success—whatever your definition of it may be—is directly correlated with your investment of time and the precision with which you define it.

To create a clear vision:

- Define your ideal future (Session 1).

- Make commitments (Session 10).

These techniques program your AFC.

Office of the CEO Recap

Stepping into the Office of the CEO is central to brain mastery.

The prefrontal cortex is the first place I start. Always! And it's the first place everybody should start. You want to step into the Office of the CEO, where you gain **clarity** and **perspective**.

Your prefrontal cortex is the executive center that optimizes the operations and resources of your life to achieve success—however you personally define success. So, no matter what's happening—whether you're in the middle of a heated family debate, hustling to make tough deadlines, or doing ordinary activities that require calm and focus...and especially before beginning any of the **unstoppable** exercises and practices—start by taking a mindful pause.

An intentional pause instantly shifts your awareness from the competing voices of your reptilian, emotional, and cognitive brains into your prefrontal cortex. You become aware of your awareness, and this present-moment awareness gives you immense power. You're ready to follow the 5-step process to gain the clarity and perspective you need to solve daily problems and overcome obstacles holding you back.

Session 4: Owning the Office of the CEO

The most important thing you need to do to access the Office of the CEO is always to **pause** and take a few deep breaths. Then:

- Ask and answer: What am I thinking? What am I feeling? What am I fearing?
- Follow the five-step process:

  1. Pause
  2. Feel your negative emotions
  3. Explore your fears
  4. Think
  5. Feel your positive emotions

Programming Your Filter Recap

Program your AFC to make sure you're seeing the world in a way that supports what you want.

Take responsibility to program your AFC to make sure you're seeing your actual reality rather than a distorted version of it. Use the executive and cognitive functions of your brain to **program your filter**, so you can **focus your attention** on what you need to see to become **unstoppable** and step into the life of your dreams.

Use Socratic questioning to challenge the accuracy of what you think about yourself and your life experiences using thoughtful questions to prompt deep reflection and honest inquiry. **Continually question yourself: Is there is something fundamental you haven't seen?**

Every day, you have the opportunity to take voluntary control of your brain to program your AFC to filter in the things you want to see.

When you program your AFC accurately to deliver success, it's like placing your brain into autopilot. Your well-programed AFC allows you to navigate information and tasks subconsciously in a way that automatically leads you to where you want to be.

So, even when you're not working directly on the things you need to do to achieve your dream, your AFC will still be working for you in the background. It's constantly working on your behalf, filtering out what you don't need and helping you to focus your attention on what you do need to become **unstoppable** and successful.

Session 5: Programming Your Filter

There are numerous ways to program your filter—including owning your assets, practicing gratitude, reciting your mantras, creating a vision board, and visualizing your ideal future—but the two fundamental approaches are:

- Pause. Be aware you have a filter—and that it can serve you well or poorly.

- Pause. Ask and answer one key question: Are you seeing your actual reality or a distorted version of it?

Conquering Fear Recap

Fear is what stops you from doing what it takes to realize your ideal future.

If you have residual fears lingering in the basement of your mind, even after doing the five steps to gain clarity and perspective, use the 7-step fear-conquering process.

Even though application of the 7-step process will effectively conquer deeply rooted fears, it's important to practice the process on smaller fears first. Master it, and then keep coming back to the process again and again to conquer all your fears. Multiple iterations of the 7-step process may be required to effectively conquer intense fears.

Session 6: Conquering Fear

To conquer your fears:

- Follow the formula:

  1. Pause

  2. Explore

  3. Thank

  4. Question

  5. Interrogate

  6. Challenge

  7. Disagree

- If you still experience negative emotions because you haven't conquered your fear right away, temporarily ignore the fear and come back to work through the process at another time.

Driving Belief Recap

The first thing you must do to build belief is to think!

Use your mental powers in a **deliberate cognitive process** to literally think yourself beyond fear to success.

In Session 8, I invited you to study the mindset of people who achieved grand success—people who refused to contemplate failure, who did not give in to doubt, and who overcame their fears. I shared with you some of my favorite inspiring, uplifting, motivating, and empowering quotes from my heroes.

I encourage you to continue to look to *your* heroes for inspiration to drive belief. Remember that they, too, had to master how to conquer their fears, build belief, and activate desire to become **unstoppable** and achieve success. Belief is like a muscle—it can be systematically exercised and built.

Session 8: Driving Belief

The most important thing you need to do to drive belief is to think you can. When your **thoughts are unwaveringly positive**...when you **think** you can **so much** that you *know* you can...**it becomes true**!

Identify and own your assets to see yourself in a positive light.

Boost your belief and amplify your self-confidence by focusing on your top three assets. Positive thoughts about your personal assets originate in your cognitive brain. So, when you think about your top assets, you take voluntary control of your cognitive brain—quickly, easily, and automatically.

You can instantly replace negative thoughts with positive ones just by seeing yourself in a positive light.

Memorize your assets, so you always have a positive thought to reach for, especially when you're in the heat of battle—the heat of life. Your assets become your gold standards. You can regroup around your top three assets, which are fundamentally you...where you're safe, grounded, and undeniably strong.

Session 7: Own Your Assets

The most important things you need to do to own your assets are:

- Identify and own your top three assets.
- Commit your assets to memory.

An active gratitude practice builds belief, so you can achieve success.

Your massive cerebral cortex is a gift. Nature placed it under your complete voluntary control, and this allows you to systematically practice gratitude.

Practicing gratitude on a regular basis fills your brain with positivity. By recognizing, acknowledging, and appreciating the good—whether or not it's related to your current situation—you're practicing gratitude. So, it enables you to use the power of choice to transform bad into good, good into best, and best into **unstoppable**.

Session 7: Gratitude

Use your top three assets to practice gratitude daily. Ask and answer the following questions for each of your assets:

- What is it?
- What does it do for me?
- What does it do for them?

Reciting carefully crafted mantras regularly floods your brain with positivity.

Regularly reciting your mantras gives you a structured way of immediately taking control of your thoughts to consciously focus on what you want, especially when the voice of your reptilian brain is strident.

Mantras can do more than affirm your top strengths and drive confidence in who you are today; they can help you to reinforce change by driving your belief in who you will be tomorrow. So, use mantras to own, empower, and build your strengths and help you make desired changes.

Whether you're celebrating and riding an **unstoppable** high or working to quiet the voice of fear in a temporary state of stoppability, use your mantras. They'll carry you forward into the future of your dreams.

Session 8: Mantras

The most important things you need to do to use mantras to drive belief are:

- Write empowering and affirming mantras: Use first person, present tense, and positive language.

- Develop a regular mantra practice—whenever, wherever, and however works best for you.

Expansive postures and movements build belief through their positive effects on the cognitive brain.

The way you move your body powers up positivity and drives belief. Don't underestimate the effectiveness of your power pose. It's both a mood/mindset quick fix and a powerful lifelong technique you'll want to use regularly.

When you take up space in the room, you:

- Elevate **self-confidence**.

- **Reduce fear** and nervousness.

- Drive feelings of **power**.

- Often associate positive emotions, such as **happiness**, **success**, and **optimism**, with these movements.

Session 8: Brain-Body Connection

The most important things you need to do to use the brain-body connection to drive belief are:

- Find and commit to using your power pose.

- Use expansive movements, occupying more space as you move.

Activating Desire Recap

Activate desire to boost cognitive drive.

To achieve something big, you need desire—that deep, nonrational hunger to become **unstoppable**. You need to activate the great flip flopper to turn want into a powerful, irresistible desire. **The emotional brain must nurture positive thoughts to achieve big dreams**.

Emotion and cognition are critical for success, and it's important to prioritize cognition as the starting point. Then, do everything you can to enhance the power of your emotional brain to support positive thoughts. Remember, building belief and activating desire are concomitant processes. The emotional brain supports all your belief-building exercises.

Session 9: Activating Desire

We explored four ways you can systematically accentuate the voice of the emotional brain to enhance its powerful effect and activate desire, and we'll review them in a moment. However, if you only remember one thing, remember this: Nurture positive thoughts.

Expand your emotional vocabulary.

Expanding your emotional vocabulary gives you the ability to activate your emotional brain. As you expand your emotional vocabulary, you activate desire and maximize success.

To expand your emotional vocabulary, pay attention to the emotion words you use most often. Think about other words you can use to describe your emotions—or those of others.

Compile a vision board to create a powerful visual reflection of your ideal future.

Your vision board clarifies and illuminates your future vision. The powerful positive emotions that your vision board evokes readily activate your desire and boost your belief in your **unstoppable** success. When you focus your energy and attention on your enlivened and empowered dream, you continuously align your actions with the path that leads you toward your dream.

When you create your vision board, it's essential to select compelling words and images that evoke positive feelings you want to enjoy. Then, look at your vision board often.

Access the often-untapped potential of the senses to drive positivity.

The senses—hearing, touch, smell, taste, and sight—evoke positive emotions quickly and powerfully. You can use sensory prompts in your day-to-day life or to support your vision board and visualizations.

There are many ways to use the senses to evoke positive emotions. You'll find your own, but here's the easiest and most powerful one to integrate into your daily life: Choose a song, and use your sense of hearing to evoke the emotion you want, when you want it.

Visualization techniques reinforce your dream and program your AFC.

Visualization is the mental road map that takes you to your dream. When you visualize your dream frequently, you program your AFC to focus on tasks that move you toward it—even when you're not paying attention. The more emotion, color, and detail you bring to your visualization, the more expeditiously you reinforce and move toward your desired future.

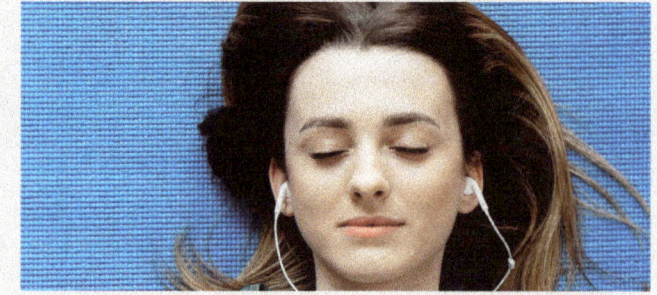

When visualizing your ideal future, use your entire imagination and your senses to put yourself in the place and time of your dream coming true. Imagine your dream—your desired outcome—as if you've already accomplished it.

Commit to Taking Lifelong Action

When you master your BOS, you become unstoppable!

As you continue on your journey to becoming **unstoppable**, remember that your goal is to masterfully use the full power of your brain—all five regions—to maximize your success.

Your reward is growth in resilience, belief, and self-confidence, which can be used to propel your commitment. So, the more you use your BOS, the more success you achieve... And the more **success you achieve**, the more you strengthen your commitment to your practices... And the more you **strengthen your commitment** to your practices, the more you graduate to **spontaneous, positive thinking** and being. You maximize the potential of your magnificent brain to create an **unstoppable** success loop.

So, practice, practice, practice. This is a lifelong journey. Continue to reflect on, digest, experiment with, and apply the tools, techniques, and skills you've learned.

EXERCISE 2

Create Your Action Plan

Create a clear action plan to keep you on track.

Science alone won't deliver your dream. You must take action! Here's a simple way to break down a one-year action plan into specific weekly tasks.

For this exercise, I suggest that you group the components of your dream into a few main categories. For instance, your ideal future may encompass various aspects of health, relationships, finances, or personal projects. Choose a single component of your dream to focus on initially. Then, come back to work through the exercise with each of the other areas of your dream.

ACTION 1 OF 4

12 months

Begin creating your action plan by looking out over the next 12 months.

Brainstorm everything that needs to happen over the next year for you to achieve your desired future.

Here are two examples, one professional and one personal:

Professional goal: Gain three new clients

- Create a list of selling points
- Employ new advertising methods
- Explore networking opportunities
- Submit proposals
- Engage with potential clients
- Bid on projects

Personal goal: Write a book

- Research book ideas
- Find an agent
- Find a publisher
- Write a book proposal
- Write the book
- Find an editor
- Find a graphic designer

Using the space below, create an action plan to achieve over the next 12 months.

ACTION 2 OF 4

Three months

Look at your one-year list of actions. Then, decide what needs to be done over the next three months.

Using the same examples, here's what you might decide you want to accomplish over the next quarter.

Professional goal: Gain three new clients

- Identify key areas of expertise

- Evaluate your current advertising scheme

- Research new advertising methods

- Begin advertising via two new methods

- Research networking opportunities

Personal goal: Write a book

- Choose a book idea

- Outline the book

- Write a book synopsis

- Draft a proposal to submit to potential agents

Using the space below, create an action plan to achieve over the next three months.

ACTION 3 OF 4

One month

Reflect on your three-month action list, and break it down into actions you can accomplish over the next 30 days.

For example:

Professional goal: Gain three new clients

- Brainstorm unique benefits of your business
- Create a complete list of your service/product offerings
- Chart your current advertising scheme
- Identify four potential new advertising methods

Personal goal: Write a book

- Choose a book title
- Draft the first three chapters of the book
- Draw up a list of potential agents
- Complete a first draft of the book proposal

Using the space below, create an action plan to achieve this month.

ACTION 4 OF 4

One week

Reflect on your one-month action list in more detail to decide on your action items for the coming week.

For example, during the next week, you might opt to:

Professional goal: Gain three new clients

- List six advantages of your business over competitors
- Draft a one-paragraph statement highlighting those advantages
- Identify 10 of your service/product offerings
- Add those offerings to your statement

Personal goal: Write a book

- Set up a consistent writing schedule
- Brainstorm a list of book ideas
- Write a one-page summary that outlines the book
- Research examples of book proposals

The one-week plan is your action plan for the week. Write it down below. Create new action plans each week as you progress.

Ready to take action?!

Adapt the process and revise your actions at any stage, but keep your action plan top of mind at all times. Work on your plan consistently, and refresh it weekly, monthly, and quarterly as you progress toward **unstoppable** success.

Do your psychic push-ups and work your action plan, day after day, week after week.

The only thing left to do is to put in the work.

Plan your actions. Then, track your progress. I encourage you to create a log to track your practices. You may even want to recruit a friend or family member to become a brain master, so you can have fun on the journey together, holding each other accountable to practice...and **celebrating each other's wins**!

No matter how you decide to continue your journey, I urge you to prioritize your action plan and your brain mastery practices. There's no other way to achieve success. Do these things, and a positive outcome is certain.

Have Fun

Fill your cognitive brain with fun thoughts.

You can wire your brain for fun, too! As you think positive thoughts about having fun on your **unstoppable** journey, you co-opt your emotional brain to turboboost these thoughts into a strong, passionate desire for fun. And fun is more than an attitude; it's a physical process that starts deep in your brain. It's a contagious positive force.

But what if you're too stressed, too tired, too overwhelmed, too (fill in the blank) for fun? As a brain master, there's only one thing to do: **Think your way to fun**. Because you have voluntary control over your thoughts, you can think your way into fun—even if you're wearing a frown on your face. You can think your way into expanding your facial expressions and your body:

- Open your eyes wide.

- Lift the corners of your mouth.

- Assume your power pose.

As your body moves, your brain responds, because of your body-brain connection. The brain is always listening to the body.

I can't say it enough: **Play** and **have fun**. Use a combination of all the techniques you've learned to infuse your practices with joy and fun. It's simple to influence your brain for lighthearted fun... and through your positive being, you create a ripple effect of positivity that leads you to become outrageously **unstoppable**.

Rewards drive fun—and success.

To celebrate and have more fun, activate a **big**, then **bigger**, and then **huge reward circuit**. I've developed a reward system called the *Rule of Sevens*. It prompts you to choose and deliver three distinct rewards over the next nine months—like the nine magical months of human gestation—while you persistently apply your **unstoppable** tools, techniques, and skills.

You'll give yourself the first reward after seven days, followed by the second reward after an additional seven weeks, marking eight weeks of progress. Finally, anticipate the third reward after seven more months, making it a total of nine months of **unstoppable** progress.

EXERCISE 3

Create a Reward System

ACTION 1 OF 3

Seven days

Decide on the big reward you'll receive after seven days of consistent BOS tool, technique, and skill use. As an example, you might gift yourself a delightful visit, personal service, or entertainment experience—especially with someone whose company you enjoy.

ACTION 2 OF 3

Seven weeks

Decide on the bigger reward you'll receive after seven additional weeks. For example, you might choose to indulge yourself by purchasing something you've wanted for a long time.

ACTION 3 OF 3

Seven months

Decide on the huge reward you'll receive after seven additional months. For example, you might book the vacation of your dreams.

> "When you are **joyful**, when you say yes to life and **have fun** and **project positivity** all around you, you become a sun in the center of every constellation."
>
> —SHANNON L. ALDER

Mastery Missions

Congratulations!

You've completed the final session and three crucial exercises: *Revisit Your Ideal Future*, *Create Your Action Plan*, and *Create a Reward System*. You now have the science as your launchpad for moving forward, and your ideal future summary and action plan are your road map to success. The ultimate step is to wholeheartedly commit yourself to putting in the work.

Make it a habit to regularly revisit these final Mastery Missions. They are ongoing activities that require your continuous attention and dedication. By persistently pursuing these missions, you will achieve an **unstoppable** state and continue steady advancement toward your dreams.

MASTERY MISSION 1

Do Your Psychic Push-Ups

ACTION 1 OF 3

Track

Systematically track your practices and your progress. Use the tracking log below, or use another method—such as a spreadsheet, app, or journal—to track and stay consistent with your practices.

Date	Practice	Mindset

Date	Practice	Mindset

ACTION 2 OF 3

Collaborate

Collaborate with your family, friends, or work colleagues to add fun and accountability. Decide who you want to work with on your journey to becoming a brain master. Jot down ideas you can use to motivate one another to achieve **unstoppable** success.

ACTION 3 OF 3

Celebrate

Celebrate every win—no matter how big or small—always remembering the target dates to deliver on your big, bigger, and huge rewards.

In the space below, jot down ways you'd like to commemorate daily victories, be it through small, moment-by-moment celebrations or daily incentives.

 MASTERY MISSION 2

Schedule Your Action Plan

ACTION 1 OF 1

Merge

Now that you've created action plans spanning one year, three months, one month, and one week, it's time to merge them with your personal calendar. Organize your calendar to ensure your action plan takes center stage and aligns with your priorities.

 MASTERY MISSION 3

Distill Your Vision

Over the last 10 sessions, you've spent time crystallizing your vision of your ideal future. By now, you should have a clear written description of your dream and a vision board depicting what you want your future to look and feel like.

ACTION 1 OF 3

Refine

Refine your ideal future description. Take one more pass to modify, expand, and color your dream with emotion.

ACTION 2 OF 3

Visualize

Visualize attaining your desired future. Begin by using your entire imagination to put yourself in the specific time and place you've chosen. Go through each of your senses to make your visualization as vivid and lifelike as possible while you connect with the flood of positive emotions that your visualization evokes in you.

Write down the key elements of the visualization you want to emphasize. Continue to see your future success over and over again in your mind.

ACTION 3 OF 3

Commit

Commit to your long-term success. Remember that your goal is to masterfully use the full power of your brain—all five regions—to propel your **unstoppable** success.

The more success you achieve, the more you strengthen your commitment to your practices... And the more you strengthen your commitment to your practices, the more you graduate to spontaneous, positive thinking and being. You maximize the potential of your magnificent brain to create an **unstoppable** success loop.

Reflect on your thoughts and emotions as you realize you are truly **unstoppable**. Your ideal future is within your reach. With your ideal future in mind, synthesize and write down the commitment statements you've made to yourself.

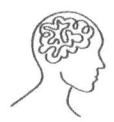 **MASTERY MISSION 4**

Unlock Success

ACTION 1 OF 1

Pause

If now, or at any time in the future, you feel like your dream is unattainable or too far off in the future—despite the science you've learned that supports your inevitable success—before you do anything at all, pause. Shift the seat of your awareness into your prefrontal cortex, and ask yourself: What am I thinking? What am I feeling? What am I fearing?

The answer to what's holding you back is almost always lurking in your reptilian brain. Once you address the underlying fear, success is always on the other side.

In Closing

Congratulations!

Welcome to the finish line—at least for now.

I've enjoyed our time together. I hope you have, too.

And I hope you've learned about this magnificent brain. I hope you've tried. I hope you've failed, actually. I hope some of the exercises were really hard, and I hope you went back and tried over and over again, because the science is absolutely clear: simple, but not easy.

*And when we understand the operating system of our brain, as you do now, there are no excuses. You know those three words I use: "If you choose." If you choose, from this moment on, you truly are **unstoppable**.*

But don't forget two things: You have to do your psychic push-ups; you have to keep the exercise going. And, you must have fun.

*So, until we meet again, thank you. And good luck! You are now **unstoppable**!*

It has been my pleasure and privilege to guide you toward **unstoppable**.

I hope you've begun to embrace the new, expansive opportunities of what's possible for you. I encourage you to dream as big as you possibly can because I know you can achieve your dreams, reach your full potential, and win the "gold medal" of your life.

I celebrate your transformational power and have unwavering belief in your success. I hope you continue to become an accomplished brain master and realize extraordinary achievement through enduring self-belief. As a result, profound joy, lasting prosperity, thriving relationships, and **unstoppable** success will be yours…always!

I encourage you to stay connected!

I hope you will share your continued success with me. Here's how we can keep in touch:

1. **Email** me directly at connect@RoddyCarter.com. Share any part of your journey or continued success, or reach out if you have questions you'd like me to answer.

2. Follow me on **Facebook** and connect with others via the **Unstoppable You** page.

3. See what's happening within our **community**. Learn about online programs, personalized workshop experiences, and my Neurocentric Coaching methodology to help individuals, couples, parents, and entrepreneurial leaders carve a pathway to enduring success.

4. Contact me to experience deeper, personalized, lasting results in a one-on-one **executive coaching** setting or elite mastermind program.

5. Send me a message if you're interested in becoming a **certified *Brain Operating System coach*** to join the mission to help as many people as possible realize their full potential and their dreams through mastery of their magnificent brain.

You can read more in my books and on my blog.

You'll find more in-depth material about me and my work here:

- *The Problem with Anger: And How to Solve It*

  I creatively explore the neural pathways we develop as children, the ways in which they hamper us as adults—and how we can retrain them to enjoy lives filled with peace and joy.

- *BodyWHealth: Journey to Abundance*

  Based on evolutionary principles and scientific evidence, this book provides a proven pathway to health, happiness, and prosperity.

- *Fireside Wisdom: Conversations to Inspire Personal Mastery*

  Integrating cutting-edge neuroscience with deep personal experience, I share colorful and practical insights to help you live your best life.

- *Sunset Lessons: Reflections on Light and Love from the Darkest of Places*

  In this anthology of personal reflections after the death of my wife, Karen, following her courageous battle with cancer, I describe my journey through grief to help others find fresh hope in the promise and power of the sun.

- Keep a look out—more books coming soon!

- The Roddy Carter Blog

  Read featured posts on my blog for more scientific insights, practical applications, and thought-provoking discourse.

If this book resonated with you, I'd be honored if you'd leave a review on the site where you purchased it...your voice helps others find it.

"Watch your **thoughts**, for they become words.

Watch your **words**, for they become actions.

Watch your **actions**, for they become habits.

Watch your **habits**, for they become your character.

And watch your **character**, for it becomes your **destiny**."

—LAO TZU

Congratulations on becoming unstoppable!

It has been a great honor to guide you through this journey. I look forward to meeting you soon, perhaps in an airport terminal or a restaurant, where you'll quickly tell me your top three assets and share the details of the marvelous life you've created for yourself.

Unstoppable success will be yours…always!

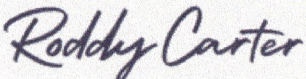

ADDITIONAL RESOURCES

Session 2: Understanding Your *Brain Operating System*

Hierarchical Structure

- Diekhof, E. K., Geier, K., Falkaj, P., & Gruber, O. (2011). Fear is only as deep as the mind allows: A coordinate-based meta-analysis of neuroimaging studies on the regulation of negative affect. *Neuroimage, 58*(1), 275–285. https:/doi.org/10.1016/j.neuroimage.2011.05.0

- Hariri, A. R., Bookheimer, S. Y., & Mazziotta, J. C. (2000). Modulating emotional responses: Effects of a neocortical network on the limbic system. *NeuroReport, 11*(1), 43–48. https://doi.org/10.1097/00001756-200001170-00009

- Javanbakht, A., & Saab, L. (2017). The science of fright: Why we love to be scared. *The Conversation.* https://theconversation.com/the-science-of-fright-why-we-love-to-be-scared-85885

- Ochsner, K. N., & Gross, J. J. (2005). The cognitive control of emotion. *Trends in Cognitive Sciences, 9*(5), 242–249. https://doi.org/10.1016/j.tics.2005.03.010

- Öner, S. (2018). Neural substrates of cognitive emotion regulation: A brief review. *Psychiatry and Clinical Psychopharmacology, 28*(1), 91–96. https://doi.org/10.1080/24750573.2017.1407563

Session 3: Understanding How Your Brain Talks

Chronic Stress

- Carter, R. N. (2015). *BodyWHealth: Journey to abundance*. Aquila Life Science Press.

- Mariotti, A. (2015). The effects of chronic stress on health: New insights into the molecular mechanisms of brain-body communication. *Future Science OA, 1*(3), https://doi.org/10.4155/fso.15.21

Session 4: Owning the Office of the CEO

Controlled Breathing

- De Couck, M., Caers, R., Musch, L., Fliegauf, J., Giangreco, A., & Gidron, Y. (2019). How breathing can help you make better decisions: Two studies on the effects of breathing patterns on heart rate variability and decision-making in business cases. *International Journal of Psychophysiology, 139*, 1–9. https://doi.org/10.1016/j.ijpsycho.2019.02.011

- Gerritsen, R. J. S., & Band, G. P. H. (2018). Breath of life: The respiratory vagal stimulation model of contemplative activity. *Frontiers in Human Neuroscience, 12*, Article 397. https://doi.org/10.3389/fnhum.2018.00397

- Zaccaro, A., Piarulli, A., Laurino, M., Garbella, E., Menicucci, D., Neri, B., & Gemignani, A. (2018). How breath-control can change your life: A systematic review on psychophysiological correlates of slow breathing. *Frontiers in Human Neuroscience, 12,* Article 353. https://doi.org/10.3389/fnhum.2018.00353

Session 5: Programming Your Filter

Survival and Selective Attention

- Frynta, D., Elmi, H. S. A., Rexová, K., Janovcová, M., Rudolfová, V., Štolhoferová, I., Král, D., Sommer, D., Berti, D. A., & Frýdlová, P. Animals evoking fear in the Cradle of Humankind: Snakes, scorpions, and large carnivores. *Science of Nature, 110,* 33. https://doi.org/10.1007/s00114-023-01859-4

- Penkunas, M. J., & Coss, R. G. (2013). A comparison of urban and rural Indian children's visual detection of threatening and non-threatening animals. *Developmental Science, 16*(3), 463–475. https://doi.org/10.1111/desc.12043

- Yorzinski, J. L., Penkunas, M. J., Platt, M. L., & Coss, R. G. (2014). Dangerous animals capture and maintain attention in humans. *Evolutionary Psychology, 12*(3). https://doi.org/10.1177/147470491401200304

Session 6: Conquering Fear

Fight or Flight

- Canon, B. (1994). Walter Bradford Cannon: Reflections on the man and his contributions. *International Journal of Stress Management, 1,* 145–158. https://doi.org/10.1007/BF01857608

- McCarty, R. (2016). The fight-or-flight response: A cornerstone of stress research. In G. Fink (Ed.), *Stress: Concepts, cognition, emotion, and behavior* (pp. 33–37). Academic Press. https://doi.org/10.1016/B978-0-12-800951-2.00004-2

Breathing

- Hopper, S. I., Murray, S. L., Ferrara, L. R., & Singleton, J. K. (2019). Effectiveness of diaphragmatic breathing for reducing physiological and psychological stress in adults: A quantitative systematic review. *JBI Database of Systematic Reviews and Implementation Reports, 17*(9), 1855–1876. https://pubmed.ncbi.nlm.nih.gov/31436595/

- Ma, X., Yue, Z-Q., Gong, Z-Q., Zhang, H., Duan, N-Y., Shi, Y-T., Wei, G-X., & Li, Y-F. (2017). The effects of diaphragmatic breathing on attention, negative affect and stress in healthy adults. *Frontiers in Psychology, 8*(874). https://doi.org/10.3389/fpsyg.2017.00874

Mindful Cognition

- Baer, R. A. (2003). Mindfulness training as a clinical intervention: A conceptual and empirical review. *Clinical Psychology: Science and Practice, 10*(2), 125–143. https://doi.org/10.1093/clipsy.bpg015

- Hjeltnes, A., Binder, P-E., Moltu, C., & Dundas, I. (2015). Facing the fear of failure: An explorative qualitative study of client experiences in a mindfulness-based stress reduction program for university students with academic evaluation anxiety. *International Journal of Qualitative Studies on Health and Well-Being, 10*(1). https://doi.org/10.3402/qhw.v10.27990

- Hofmann, S. G., Sawyer, A. T., Witt, A. A., & Oh, D. (2010). The effect of mindfulness-based therapy on anxiety and depression: A meta-analytic review. *Journal of Consulting and Clinical Psychology, 78*(2), 169–183. https://doi.org/10.1037/a0018555

- Howell, A. J., & Buro, K. (2011). Relations among mindfulness, achievement-related self-regulation, and achievement emotions. *Journal of Happiness Studies, 12,* 1007–1022. https://doi.org/10.1007/s10902-010-9241-7

- Jay, K., Brandt, M., Jakobsen, M.D., Sundstrup, E., Berthelsen, K. G., Schraefel, M., Sjøgaard, G., & Andersen, L. (2016). Ten weeks of physical-cognitive-mindfulness training reduces fear-avoidance beliefs about work-related activity: Randomized controlled trial. *Medicine, 95*(34), e3945. https://doi.org/10.1097/MD.0000000000003945

- Kummar, A. S. (2018). Mindfulness and fear extinction: A brief review of its current neuropsychological literature and possible implications for posttraumatic stress disorder. *Psychological Reports, 121*(5), 792–814. https://doi.org/10.1177/0033294117740137

- Shao, R., & Skarlicki, D.P. (2009). The role of mindfulness in predicting individual performance. *Canadian Journal of Behavioural Science, 41*(4), 195–201. https://doi.org/10.1037/a0015166

- Short, M. M., Mazmanian, D., Oinonen, K., & Mushquash, C. J. (2016). Executive function and self-regulation mediate dispositional mindfulness and well-being. *Personality and Individual Differences, 93,* 97–103. https://doi.org/10.1016/j.paid.2015.08.007

Exposure Therapy

- Arias, M. C., & McNeil, D. W. (2019). Smartphone-based exposure treatment for dental phobia: A pilot randomized clinical trial. *Journal of Public Health Dentistry, 80*(1), 23–30. https://onlinelibrary.wiley.com/doi/abs/10.1111/jphd.12340

- Bentz, D., Wang, N., Ibach, M.K., Schicktanz, N. S., Zimmer, A., Papassotiropoulos, A., & de Quervain, D. J. F. (2021). Effectiveness of a stand-alone, smartphone-based virtual reality exposure app to reduce fear of heights in real-life: A randomized trial. *NPJ Digital Medicine, 4*(16). https://doi.org/10.1038/s41746-021-00387-7

- Kaussner, Y., Kuraszkiewicz, A. M., Schoch, S., Markel, P., Hoffmann, S., Baur-Streubel, R., Kenntner-Mabiala, R., & Pauli, P. (2020). Treating patients with driving phobia by virtual reality exposure therapy – a pilot study. *PLoS ONE 15*(1), e0226937. https://doi.org/10.1371/journal.pone.0226937

- Premkumar, P., Heym, N., Brown, D. J., Battersby, S., Sumich, A., Huntington, B., Daly, R., & Zysk, E. (2021). The effectiveness of self-guided virtual-reality exposure therapy for public speaking anxiety. *Frontiers in Psychiatry, 12,* 694610. https://doi.org/10.3389/fpsyt.2021.694610

Session 7: Driving Belief

Gratitude

- Algoa, S. B. (2012). Find, remind, and bind: The functions of gratitude in everyday relationships. *Social and Personality Psychology Compass, 6*(6), 455–469. https://doi.org/10.1111/j.1751-9004.2012.00439.x

- Alkozei, A., Smith, R., & Killgore, W. (2017). Grateful people are happy and healthy—but why? *Frontiers Young Minds, 5*(55). https://doi.org/10.3389/frym.2017.00055

- Di Fabio, A., Palazzeschi, L., & Bucci, O. (2017). Gratitude in organizations: A contribution for healthy organizational contexts. *Frontiers in Psychology, 8*(2025). https://doi.org/10.3389/fpsyg.2017.02025

- Gabana, N. T., Steinfeldt, J., Wong, Y. J., Chung, Y. B., & Svetina, D. (2019). Attitude of gratitude: Exploring the implementation of a gratitude intervention with college athletes. *Journal of Applied Sport Psychology, 31*(3), 273–284. https://doi.org/10.1080/10413200.2018.1498956

- Giacomo, B., & Jason, T. S. (2018). How gratitude connects humans to the best in themselves and in others. *Research in Human Development, 15*(3-4), 224–237. https://doi.org/10.1080/15427609.2018.1499350

- Gordon, A. M., Impett, E. A., Kogan, A., Oveis, C., & Keltner, D. (2012). To have and to hold: Gratitude promotes relationship maintenance in intimate bonds. *Journal of Personality and Social Psychology, 103*(2), 257–274. https://pubmed.ncbi.nlm.nih.gov/22642482/

- Grant, A. M., & Gino, F. (2010). A little thanks goes a long way: Explaining why gratitude expressions motivate prosocial behavior. *Journal of Personality and Social Psychology, 98*(6), 946–955. https://pubmed.ncbi.nlm.nih.gov/20515249/

- Jans-Beken, L., Jacobs, N., Janssens, M., Peeters, S., Reijnders, J., Lechner, L., & Lataster, J. (2020). Gratitude and health: An updated review. *The Journal of Positive Psychology, 15*(6), 743–782. https://doi.org/10.1080/17439760.2019.1651888

- Krejtz, I., Nezlek, J. B., Michnicka, A., Holas, P., & Rusanowska, M. (2014). Counting one's blessings can reduce the impact of daily stress. *Journal of Happiness Studies, 17*, 25–39. https://doi.org/10.1007/s10902-014-9578-4

- Nelson, C. (2009). Appreciating gratitude: Can gratitude be used as a psychological intervention to improve individual well-being? *Counselling Psychology Review, 24*(3-4), 38–50. https://doi.org/10.53841/bpscpr.2009.24.3-4.38

- Sciara, S., Villani, D., Di Natale, A. F., & Regalia, C. (2021). Gratitude and social media: A pilot experiment on the benefits of exposure to others' grateful interactions on Facebook. *Frontiers in Psychology, 12*, 667052. https://doi.org/10.3389/fpsyg.2021.667052

- Walsh, L. C., Armenta, C. N., Itzchakov, G., Fritz, M. M., & Lyubomirsky, S. (2022). More than merely positive: The immediate affective and motivational consequences of gratitude. *Sustainability, 14*(14), 8679. https://doi.org/10.3390/su14148679

- Wood, A. M., Froh, J. J., & Geraghty, A. W. A. (2010). Gratitude and well-being: A review and theoretical integration. *Clinical Psychology Review, 30*(7), 890–905. https://doi.org/10.1016/j.cpr.2010.03.005

- Yoshimura, S. M., & Berzins, K. (2017). Grateful experiences and expressions: The role of gratitude expressions in the link between gratitude experiences and well-being. *Review of Communications, 17*(2), 106–118. https://doi.org/10.1080/15358593.2017.1293836

Session 8: Boosting Belief

Body Language

- Cuddy, A. J. C. (2019, January 31). *Presence: Bringing your boldest self to your biggest challenges* [Video]. YouTube. https://youtu.be/ATo9sYax-AQ?si=laH3CnfSzyChiupn

- Lanke, P., & Nath, P. (2023). The relationship between dance and well-being: Examining the underlying mechanism and outcomes. *World Leisure Journal, 66*(1), 134–150. https://doi.org/10.1080/16078055.2023.2243249

- Nair, S., Sagar, M., Sollers, J., III, Consedien, N., & Broadbent, E. (2015). Do slumped and upright postures affect stress responses? A randomized trial. *Health Psychology, 34*(6), 632–641. https://doi.org/10.1037/hea0000146

- Shafir, T. (2016). Using movement to regulate emotion: Neurophysiological findings and their application in psychotherapy. *Frontiers in Psychology, 7.* https://doi.org/10.3389/fpsyg.2016.01451

- Shafir, T., Tsachor, R. P., & Welch, K. B. (2016). Emotion regulation through movement: Unique sets of movement characteristics are associated with and enhance basic emotions. *Frontiers in Psychology, 6.* https://doi.org/10.3389/fpsyg.2015.02030

- Takayama, A., & Sekiya, H. (2023). Effects of various sitting and standing postures on arousal and valence. *PLoS ONE, 18*(6). https://doi.org/10.1371/journal.pone.0286720

- Van Geest, J., Samaritter, R., & van Hooren, S. (2021). Move and be moved: The effect of moving specific movement elements on the experience of happiness. *Frontiers in Psychology, 11.* https://doi.org/10.3389/fpsyg.2020.579518

Session 9: Activating Desire

The Amygdala

- Bonnet, L., Comte, A., Tatu, L., Millot, J.-L., Moulin, T., & de Bustos, E. M. (2015). The role of the amygdala in the perception of positive emotions: An "intensity detector." *Frontiers in Behavioral Neuroscience, 9*(178). https://doi.org/10.3389/fnbeh.2015.00178

- Cunningham, W. A., & Kirkland, T. (2014). The joyful, yet balanced, amygdala: Moderated responses to positive but not negative stimuli in trait happiness. *Social Cognitive and Affective Neuroscience, 9*(6), 760–766. https://doi.org/10.1093/scan/nst045

- Garavan, H., Pendergrass, J. C., Ross, Thomas J., Stein, E. A., & Risinger, R. C. (2001). Amygdala response to both positively and negatively valenced stimuli. *Neuroreport, 12*(12), 2779–2783. https://doi.org/10.1097/00001756-200108280-00036

- Garfinkel, S., & Critchley, H. (2014). Neural correlates of fear: Insights from neuroimaging. *Neuroscience and Neuroeconomics, 2014*(3), 111–125. https://doi.org/10.2147/NAN.S35915

- Janak, P., & Tye, K. (2015). From circuits to behavior in the amygdala. *Nature, 517*, 284–292. https://doi.org/10.1038/nature14188

- LeDoux, J. E. (2000). Emotion circuits in the brain. *Annual Review of Neuroscience, 23*, 155–194. https://doi.org/10.1146/annurev.neuro.23.1.155

- Sergerie, K., Chochol, C., & Armony, J. L. (2008). The role of the amygdala in emotional processing: A quantitative meta-analysis of functional neuroimaging studies. *Neuroscience & Biobehavioral Reviews, 32*(4), 811–830. https://doi.org/10.1016/j.neubiorev.2007.12.002

Emotional Regulation

- Diekhof, E. K., Geier, K., Falkai, P., & Gruber, O. (2011). Fear is only as deep as the mind allows: A coordinate-based meta-analysis of neuroimaging studies on the regulation of negative affect. *NeuroImage, 58*(1), 275–285. https://doi.org/10.1016/j.neuroimage.2011.05.073

- Etkin, A., Büchel, C., & Gross, J. J. (2015). The neural bases of emotion regulation. *Nature Reviews Neuroscience, 16*(11), 693–700. https://doi.org/10.1038/nrn4044

- Gao, H., Zhang, H., Wang, L., Zhang, C., Feng, Z., Li, Z., Tong, L., Yan, B., & Hu, G. (2023). Altered amygdala functional connectivity after real-time functional MRI emotion self-regulation training. *NeuroReport, 34*(11), 537–545. https://doi.org/10.1097/WNR.0000000000001921

- Gross, J. J. (1998). The emerging field of emotion regulation: An integrative review. *Review of General Psychology, 2*(3), 271–299. https://doi.org/10.1037/1089-2680.2.3.271

- Hariri, A. R., Bookheimer, S. Y., & Mazziotta, J. C. (2000). Modulating emotional responses: Effects of a neocortical network on the limbic system. *NeuroReport, 11*(1), 43–48. https://doi.org/10.1097/00001756-200001170-00009

- Javanbakht, A., & Saab, L. (2017). The science of fright: Why we love to be scared. *The Conversation.* https://theconversation.com/the-science-of-fright-why-we-love-to-be-scared-85885

- Ochsner, K. N., & Gross, J. J. (2005). The cognitive control of emotion. *Trends in Cognitive Sciences, 9*(5), 242–249. https://doi.org/10.1016/j.tics.2005.03.010

- Ochsner, K. N., Silvers, J. A., & Buhle, J. T. (2012). Functional imaging studies of emotion regulation: A synthetic review and evolving model of the cognitive control of emotion. *Annals of the New York Academy of Sciences, 1251*(1), E1–E24. https://www.ncbi.nlm.nih.gov/pmc/articles/PMC4133790/

- Öner, S. (2018). Neural substrates of cognitive emotion regulation: A brief review. *Psychiatry and Clinical Psychopharmacology, 28*(1), 91–96. https://doi.org/10.1080/24750573.2017.1407563

- Scharnowski, F., Nicholson, A. A., Pichon, S., Rosa, M. J., Rey, G., Eickhoff, S. B., Van De Ville, D., Vuilleumier, P., & Koush, Y. (2020). The role of the subgenual anterior cingulate cortex in dorsomedial prefrontal–amygdala neural circuitry during positive-social emotion regulation. *Human Brain Mapping, 41*(11), 3100–3118. https://doi.org/10.1002/hbm.25001

Emotional Intelligence and Well-Being

- Extremera, N., Sánchez-Álvarez, N., & Rey, L. (2020). Pathways between ability emotional intelligence and subjective well-being: Bridging links through cognitive emotion regulation strategies. *Sustainability, 12*(5), 2111. https://doi.org/10.3390/su12052111

- Megías-Robles, A., Gutiérrez-Cobo, M. J., Gómez-Leal, R., Cabello, R., Gross, J. J., & Fernández-Berrocal, P. (2019). Emotionally intelligent people reappraise rather than suppress their emotions. *PLoS ONE 14*(8), e0220688. https://doi.org/10.1371/journal.pone.0220688

- Salovey, P., & Mayer, J. D. (1990). Emotional intelligence. *Imagination, Cognition and Personality, 9*(3), 185–211. https://doi.org/10.2190/DUGG-P24E-52WK-6CDG

- Schutte, N. S., Malouff, J. M., Simunek, M., McKenley, J., & Hollander, S. (2002). Characteristic emotional intelligence and emotional well-being. *Cognition and Emotion, 16*(6), 769–785. https://doi.org/10.1080/02699930143000482

- Schutte, N. S., Malouff, J. M., Thorsteinsson, E. B., Bhullar, N., & Rooke, S. E. (2007). A meta-analytic investigation of the relationship between emotional intelligence and health. *Personality and Individual Differences, 42*(6), 921–933. https://doi.org/10.1016/j.paid.2006.09.003

Mindfulness Practices and Well-Being

- Compare, A., Zarbo, C., Shonin, E., Van Gordon, W., & Marconi, C. (2014). Emotional regulation and depression: A potential mediator between heart and mind. *Cardiovascular Psychiatry and Neurology, 2014*, 324374. https://doi.org/10.1155/2014/324374

- Garland, E., Gaylord, S., & Park, J. (2009). The role of mindfulness in positive reappraisal. *EXPLORE, 5*(1), 37–44. https://doi.org/10.1016/j.explore.2008.10.001

- Grecucci, A., Pappaianni, E., Siugzdaite, R., Theuninck, A., & Job, R. (2015). Mindful emotion regulation: Exploring the neurocognitive mechanism behind mindfulness. *BioMed Research International, 2015*, 670724. https://doi.org/10.1155/2015/670724

- Herwig, U., Kaffenberger, T., Jäncke, L., & Brühl, A. B. (2010). Self-related awareness and emotion regulation. *NeuroImage, 50*(2), 734–741. https://doi.org/10.1016/j.neuroimage.2009.12.089

- Hölzel, B. K., Carmody, J., Vangel, M., Congleton, C., Yerramsetti, S. M., Gard, T., & Lazar, S. W. (2011). Mindfulness practice leads to increases in regional brain gray matter density. *Psychiatry Research: Neuroimaging, 19*(1), 36–43. https://doi.org/10.1016/j.pscychresns.2010.08.006

- Lutz, J., Herwig, U., Opialla, S., Hittmeyer, A., Jäncke, L., Rufer, M., Holtforth, M. G., & Brühl, A. B. (2014). Mindfulness and emotion regulation—an fMRI study. *Social Cognitive and Affective Neuroscience, 9*(6), 776–785. https://doi.org/10.1093/scan/nst043

- Schuman-Olivier, Z., Trombka, M., Lovas, D. A., Brewer, J. A., Vago, D. R., Gawande, R., Dunne, J. P., Lazar, S. W., Loucks, E. B., & Fulwiler, C. (2020). Mindfulness and behavior change. *Harvard Review of Psychiatry, 28*(6), 371–394. https://doi.org/10.1097/HRP.0000000000000277

- Schutte, N. S., & Malouff, J. M. (2011). Emotional intelligence mediates the relationship between mindfulness and subjective well-being. *Personality and Individual Differences, 50*(7), 1116–1119. https://doi.org/10.1016/j.paid.2011.01.037

Expressive Writing and Well-Being

- Baikie, K., & Wilhelm, K. (2005). Emotional and physical health benefits of expressive writing. *Advances in Psychiatric Treatment, 11*(5), 338–346. https://doi.org/10.1192/apt.11.5.338

- Harrist, S., Carlozzi, B. L., McGovern, A. R., & Harrist, A. W. (2007). Benefits of expressive writing and expressive talking about life goals. *Journal of Research in Personality, 41*(4), 923–930. https://doi.org/10.1016/j.jrp.2006.09.002

- Lepore, S. J., Greenberg, M. A., Bruno, M., & Smyth, J. M. (2002). Expressive writing and health: Self-regulation of emotion-related experience, physiology, and behavior. In S. J. Lepore & J. M. Smyth (Eds.), *The writing cure: How expressive writing promotes health and emotional well-being* (pp. 99–117). American Psychological Association. https://doi.org/10.1037/10451-005

- Pennebaker, J. W., & Chung, C. K. (2011). Expressive writing: Connections to physical and mental health. In H. S. Friedman (Ed.), *The Oxford handbook of health psychology* (pp. 417–437). Oxford University Press. https://psycnet.apa.org/record/2013-01232-018

- Ruini, C., & Mortara, C. C. (2022). Writing technique across psychotherapies—from traditional expressive writing to new positive psychology interventions: A narrative review. *Journal of Contemporary Psychotherapy, 52,* 23–34. https://doi.org/10.1007/s10879-021-09520-9

Visualization (Imagining) and Well-Being

- Huppert, F. A. (2009). Psychological well-being: Evidence regarding its causes and consequences. *Applied Psychology: Health and Well-Being, 1*(2), 137–164. https://doi.org/10.1111/j.1758-0854.2009.01008.x

- Meevissen, Y. M. C., Peters, M. L., & Alberts, H. J. E. M. (2011). Become more optimistic by imagining a best possible self: Effects of a two week intervention. *Journal of Behavior Therapy and Experimental Psychiatry, 42*(3), 371–378. https://doi.org/10.1016/j.jbtep.2011.02.012

- Neck, C. P., & Manz, C. C. (1992). Thought self-leadership: The influence of self-talk and mental imagery on performance. *Journal of Organizational Behavior, 13*(7), 681–699. https://doi.org/10.1002/job.4030130705

- Renner, F., Murphy, F. C., Ji, J. L., Manly, T., & Holmes, E A. (2019). Mental imagery as a "motivational amplifier" to promote activities. *Behaviour Research and Therapy, 114,* 51–59. https://doi.org/10.1016/j.brat.2019.02.002

- Schubert, T., Eloo, R., Scharfen, J., & Morina, N. (2020). How imagining personal future scenarios influences affect: Systematic review and meta-analysis. *Clinical Psychology Review, 75,* 101811. https://doi.org/10.1016/j.cpr.2019.101811

- Spreng, R. N., & Levine, B. (2013). Doing what we imagine: Completion rates and frequency attributes of imagined future events one year after prospection. *Memory, 21*(4), 458–466. https://doi.org/10.1080/09658211.2012.736524

Music and Emotion

- Cook, T., Roy, A. R. K., & Welker, K. M. (2019). Music as an emotion regulation strategy: An examination of genres of music and their roles in emotion regulation. *Psychology of Music, 47*(1), 144–154. https://doi.org/10.1177/0305735617734627

- Koelsch, S. (2014). Brain correlates of music-evoked emotions. *Nature Reviews Neuroscience, 15,* 170–180. https://doi.org/10.1038/nrn3666

- Koelsch, S., & Skouras, S. (2013). Functional centrality of amygdala, striatum and hypothalamus in "small-world" network underlying joy: An fMRI study with music. *Human Brain Mapping, 35*(7), 3485–3498. https://onlinelibrary.wiley.com/doi/ftr/10.1002/hbm.22416

- Lehne, M., Rohrmeier, M., & Koelsch, S. (2014). Tension-related activity in the orbitofrontal cortex and amygdala: An fMRI study with music. *Social Cognitive and Affective Neuroscience, 10*(9), 1515–1523. https://doi.org/10.1093/scan/nst141

- Schaefer, H-E. (2017). Music-evoked emotions—current studies. *Frontiers in Neuroscience, 11,* 600. https://doi.org/10.3389/fnins.2017.00600

- Trost, W., Ethofer, T., Zentner, M., & Vuilleumier, P. (2012). Mapping aesthetic musical emotions in the brain. *Cerebral Cortex, 22*(12), 2769–2783. https://doi.org/10.1093/cercor/bhr353

www.ingramcontent.com/pod-product-compliance
Lightning Source LLC
Chambersburg PA
CBHW051851140626
46547CB00034BA/3001